Literary M

Literary Meaning

From Phenomenology to Deconstruction

WILLIAM RAY

Basil Blackwell

© William E. Ray, Jr., 1984

First published 1984
Basil Blackwell Publisher Limited
108 Cowley Road, Oxford OX4 1JF, England

All rights reserved. Except for the quotation of short passages
for the purposes of criticism and review, no part of this
publication may be reproduced, stored in a retrieval system,
or transmitted, in any form or by any means, electronic,
mechanical, photocopying, recording or otherwise, without
the prior permission of the publisher.

Except in the United States of America, this book is sold
subject to the condition that it shall not, by way of trade or
otherwise, be lent, re-sold, hired out, or otherwise circulated
without the publisher's prior consent in any form of binding
or cover other than that in which it is published and without
a similar condition including this condition being imposed
on the subsequent purchaser.

British Library Cataloguing in Publication Data
Ray, William
Literary meaning.
1. Criticism
I. Title
801'.95   PN81

ISBN 0-631-13457-3
ISBN 0-631-13458-1 Pbk

Typesetting by Oxford Verbatim Limited
Printed in Great Britain by
The Pitman Press, Bath

Contents

Contents

Acknowledgments

Portions of the tenth and twelfth chapters of this study appeared originally in *Diacritics*. I would like to express my gratitude to the National Endowment for the Humanities, the American Council of Learned Societies, and the Mellon Fund at Reed College for their generous financial support.

Introduction

Literary criticism has always exhibited considerable anguish over what it is doing and where it is going. Perhaps because it is the vanity of every generation to think itself on the threshold of a new era, acting either as the capstone or as the overthrower of all that went before, much of the discipline's energy has been devoted to determining the historical significance of new critical developments. During the past decade, a particularly vigorous polemic has developed between those who herald the movements of structuralism and deconstruction as the dawn of a new age of demystified exegesis, and those who decry them as the subversion of everything valuable in the humanistic disciplines.

Yet both of these camps share the same historical assumption: that recent developments in criticism have little in common with the established tradition. Similarly, each new methodological innovation presents itself as drawing on a distinct set of basic assumptions, as if the discipline had lost its common ground. For both reactionary and revolutionary, ours is a period of radical departure from prior beliefs about meaning, reading, and literary criticism – and one must either espouse the revolution or defend the institution against it.

It is the modest goal of this study to challenge the assumption of historical discontinuity underlying both these stances. I intend to demonstrate that the dominant theoretical and critical developments of the last thirty or forty years share a common ground, which is to be found in a pervasive notion of literary meaning underlying theoretical and critical programs from phenomenology to the present. My thesis, simply, is that from roughly the beginning of the period when phenomenologists starting looking closely at literature to the current post-structuralist project, the major theoreticians have all been grappling with the same problem: namely that "meaning," as it pertains to literature, always seems to have at least two meanings, each of which entails a different, and frequently contrary, theory of the literary work, as well as a distinct critical practice. The clearest example of this can be found in the tension between our two common-sense intuitions of meaning, as both historically bound *act*, governed by a particular intention at a particular moment, and permanent textual *fact*, embodied in a word or series of words whose meaning transcends particular volition and can be apprehended in its structure by any individual possessed of the language.

The tension between these two incompatible but curiously coexistent notions — between what "I mean" and what "the word means" — recurs under a variety of guises in the theories I shall discuss, normally manifesting itself in the shape of a binary opposition such as subject *vs.* object, instance *vs.* system, performance *vs.* competence, *parole vs. langue*, figural *vs.* referential, or event *vs.* structure. But I would contend that the very real differences between, say, phenomenological criticism and structuralism, or reader-response criticism and deconstruction, result less from a fundamental disagreement as to the nature of meaning and how it occurs in reading than from divergent strategies of representing this phenomenon within a critical discipline.

The notion of discipline itself incarnates this state of affairs — and my thesis. Literary studies *qua* discipline might best be defined both as an accumulated system of rules and codes within which every instance of interpretation (including those that would set themselves apart from it) must occur, and as an ongoing collective act, each utterance of which is necessarily different and in a sense in opposition to all others. No two readings can be said to be exactly the same, just as no critic can claim to have seized absolutely the author's meaning. It is within this impossibility that the discipline of criticism becomes possible, for if there were such a thing as a perfect reading, all other interpretations, indeed all partial understanding of even the tiniest portion of the text, would be invalidated. That we cannot conceive of such silliness testifies to our belief in the absolute singularity and validity of each new instance of reading. That we are equally intolerant of silly interpretations testifies to precisely the opposite belief: no individual instance of understanding enjoys independent authority.

Much the same tension between instance and system informs all versions of linguistic endeavor, down to the simplest notion of

meaning. A word has a meaning by virtue of its orthographic structure and the lexical spectrum it surveys. We can find *the word's
meaning* in a dictionary or by specifying its surrounding context. At
the same time, however, meaning is vested in its event: what I *mean* is
for me to decide, just as the "author's meaning" is his to determine.
Meaning is from this perspective a function of the intention that casts
it. As E. D. Hirsch reminds us in *Validity in Interpretation*, a sequence
of words can mean nothing in particular until someone means something by it.[1]

It seems self-evident that meaning involves a tension, perhaps an
unresolvable paradox, between system and instance, and that this
paradox must inform literary study. Yet this is a proposition consistently evaded by most of the theoreticians who have focused on
reading and literary meaning during the past half century. For
various reasons, all but a handful of the recent innovations in practical criticism have relied on theories of meaning that deliberately
attempt to simplify the phenomenon in question by repressing one of
its "identities."

As I hope to show in the course of this study, such repression
ultimately vitiates many fine critical programs, but it also provides
the historian with an organizational principle. In fact, the survey I
propose here turns less on chronology than on what I might call
tactical affinities. All of the critics and theoreticians in question are
predominantly interested in literary meaning as generated through
reading: how it comes into being, where it is incarnated, how it
relates to other forms of mental activity, who has authority over it,
and how it can be evaluated. But not everyone approaches the
problem from the same direction, nor do all those who share a
common point of departure belong to the same historical period.

Since my goal is less to draw chronological filiations than to
assemble a clear picture of the many theoretical sides to reading, I
have forsaken a rigorous historical outline in favor of a presentation
that moves from one end of the theoretical spectrum to the other.
The earliest theoreticians of reading used a phenomenological
approach, that is, they attempted an exhaustive description of the
phenomenon of literary meaning as it presents itself to our awareness. In keeping with their conviction that phenomena can be understood through direct intuition, these writers focused primarily on the
activity of the individual subject who constitutes the literary work
and its meaning as an object of consciousness within an intention.

This vision of reading stresses the personal event that weds reader to text or author, and it informs not only most recent reader-response criticism but also some psychoanalytic criticism and, to a lesser degree, subjective criticism.

Because the dichotomy of subjective act and objective structure is familiar to most readers, I not only use it as a point of departure, under the guise of *intentionality*, but maintain it as an organizational framework through many subsequent discussions. I must stress that I am not necessarily construing later literary theory to be a develop- ment of phenomenological thought, but I do think phenomeno- logical categories provide the most powerful ordering principle for sorting through the many models of reading and criticism that have emerged during the period in question. And if I dwell on some early phenomenological models at the outset, it is because their concerns inform a host of problems that will confront criticism subsequently.

For instance, the distinction between subjective and objective meaning, as well as between the author's intention and the reader's, correlates directly with the debates over the role of personal identity in reading and the larger question of referentiality. Both of these issues pertain to post-phenomenological psychoanalytic theories of reading, as well as reader-response criticism and, ultimately, struc- turalism. For it is precisely in response to the preponderance of notions like the "self" and the "subject" that structuralism and its offshoots were founded. Phenomenological concepts of personal ideation are in this sense not just the predecessors or antitheses of later semiotic and deconstructive thought: they are its necessary catalyst.

The relationship between these points of view forms one of the axes of my study, which moves from the consideration of theories that define reading in terms of the *individual's act* (and critical programs concerned with the text's referential value) towards those more preoccupied with collective interpretation and *structural fact*. In line with their own bias, these latter theories associate meaning almost entirely with culturally determined codes and textual mech- anisms rather than with events of personal concretization. Yet because they refuse to acknowledge the idiosyncratic side of meaning – meaning as an act that willfully alters, even subverts, the systems that ground it – "pure" structuralist models of reading prove as vulnerable as the phenomenological notions they demystify. In the history of meaning which I propose here the *post*-structuralists are so called not because they have repudiated structuralism, but because they relocate the "eventual" side of meaning within its structural definition – and vice versa. Rather than suppressing instance in favor of system, or vice versa, the class of writers I call post-structuralist will define and practice reading as the tension between meaning's two meanings.

That the three critics I use to exemplify such an approach are drawn from three different traditions serves to underline my overall thesis: recent developments in criticism are neither isolated nor arcane, they merely put into practice certain theoretical assumptions about literary meaning that have been with us for some time in a variety of guises and national traditions. In this sense, the most radical critical programs of the present day are less a departure than a continuation, less revolution than evolution. Their newness lies not in the ideas they propound, but in their attempt to implement both sides of a paradox at once.

The opposition of theory and practice that pits general category and theoretical system against specific exegetic instance, abstract fact against intentional act, seems particularly suspect in the light of my thesis. In literary studies, this schism predicates an essential difference between the meaning one talks about as an abstract possibility and the meaning one instantiates in the critical act. Because the notion of meaning that interests me implicitly disputes the reliability of such distinctions, because historical surveys necessarily present themselves as personal readings of texts, the theoretical analyses of the present study occur as critical readings.

In other words, this book theorizes under the guise of criticism; it is a book of interpretations, different from other such books only in that the works it interprets are themselves theories of meaning. Accordingly, each of the readings or chapters of this book can to a certain extent stand on its own and be read independently of the others, keeping in mind, naturally, that many of the arguments of any given chapter draw on those of preceding chapters, and that certain key terms are defined early on.

My decision to present theory in the mode of criticism invites at least one confusion: that of voice. Bowing to the exigencies of convention, I have attempted to maintain a reasonably clear line between the ideas of the theoretician in question and my own thoughts about those ideas. Specifically, I have commenced each chapter with a relatively impartial paraphrase of the theory in question, to satisfy the reader who wants untainted information about a given author.

Finally, the immensity of the topic has compelled me to make certain difficult choices. Not all theoreticians of meaning are included in the study, nor do I purport to cover all of the ideas of every theoretician I do treat, much less trace ideas back to their philosophical roots. My topic is meaning as the discipline of literary criticism understands it, meaning as instantiated in reading, and *not* meaning in general, or literary criticism in general, or theories of literature in general.

Similarly, I have focused my study primarily on meaning in prose reading. The theoretical bases for this decision are simple: drama is not designed primarily to be read and contains generic features – such as the presence of stage directions and speaker identifications or the absence of disembodied description, reflection, or action narration – that make its reading atypical; the experience of poetry, while more characteristic of reading in general, is of such a short duration, and interspersed with such frequent periods of reflection and critical musing, that theoreticians have difficulty separating the poetic meaning *per se* from the non-literary cogitations it might provoke. This difficulty has caused several writers to treat poetry as a special case of literary reading. Because prose reading meets all theoreticians' approval as a paradigm for the experience of literary meaning, I have adopted it as my own test case.

Finally, in an attempt to enhance the readability of my own prose, I have renounced all claims of conscience and elected to use the masculine form for all references to the hypothetical reader or critic.

Part One
The Phenomenology of Reading

1

Poulet, Sartre, and Blanchot: Author, Reader, and Work as Intention

The Reader and the Other

On the simplest level of personal intuition, we know reading as the merging of our consciousness with the flow of the text. Historically, this phenomenon has been most frequently phrased in terms of the interaction between an act and a structure. Phenomenological theories of reading are perhaps more elegant than most because they enclose both act and structure within a single concept: that of the *intention*. As I shall be using it throughout this study, this term is not synonymous with a projected desire – or "what the author wanted to say." It defines, rather, the act (and structure) of consciousness, according to the principle of intentionality.

Briefly, intentionality posits that (1) consciousness is always consciousness *of* something, and (2) consciousness is best conceptualized as the act by which a *subject* intends (means, imagines, conceptualizes, is conscious of) an *object*, which thereby comes into givenness in the form of a perception, intuition, or image. Not only is the intentional object contingent on the subject for its givenness, but the intuition of that object constitutes the subject as an awareness. Every instance of consciousness, or intention, therefore presumes both a subject and an object, reciprocally constituting each other as act and structure. Naturally, all manner of object can be intended: imaginary, concrete, abstract, ideal, non-existent, absent, and so forth; and each defines a slightly different intentional act or meaning on the part of the intending subject.

This deceptively simple paradigm of consciousness and its objects has, under a variety of guises, served to justify a wide range of critical theories or programs. Since it authorizes viewing the literary work as an act of consciousness and as a structure, intentionality can be used to underwrite reader-response criticism and "author intention" readings as well as formalistic close reading and structural approaches that objectify the text. And because the same work of literature can exist in the consciousnesses of both author and reader – indeed of many readers – one can postulate a single intentional object for many intentions and use this postulate to ground a theory of objective literary knowledge.

In the coming chapters I shall be treating a number of such theoretical twists and the critical programs to which they give rise. And if I start with the phenomenologists, it is not in order to prove that they somehow govern all later literary theory, but rather because the accessibility of their thought and the wide applicability of intentional theories of meaning make this a convenient point of entry into a rather abstract question.

Of the many paradoxes posed by an intentional theory of meaning, that of the "shared" intentional object is perhaps the most fundamental. Since every intention is to some degree unique, the meaning of any text I happen to be reading is in a very real sense whatever I intend it to be. At the same time, since the work in question stands as the object constituted by the author's original intention, its unique meaning must necessarily be his. This paradox is at the root of the now legendary debates on author intention and textual autonomy which polarized the American academy following the Second World War; but it has received its most fruitful theoretical elaboration at the hands of the French phenomenological critics.

For the writers of the Geneva school, the double identity of the work as reader's meaning and author's meaning functions both as a provocative theoretical paradox and the basis for an interpretive methodology. While the critical work of authors like Georges Poulet and Jean-Pierre Richard overshadows their theoretical writings, a number of shorter pronouncements from these and other phenomenologists do provide a coherent overview of their ideas on reading.

Perhaps the best known shorter piece is Poulet's "Phenomenology of Reading" which appeared in the inaugural issue of *New Literary History*.[1] This short account of the Geneva School's assumptions and activity stresses the alteration one's consciousness undergoes during the reading act. Once absorbed in the work and freed from the bonds of concrete reality, the reading consciousness is, for

Poulet, astonished to discover itself filled with objects that are at once dependent upon it, i.e., clearly the result of its own intention, and yet recognized to be the thoughts of another: "because of the strange invasion of my person by the thoughts of another, I am a self who is granted the experience of thinking thoughts foreign to him. I am the subject of thoughts other than my own" (p. 56). These thoughts include all manner of affective and intuitive consciousness, and they constitute what we normally call the "fictional world." Yet they do not carry with them the sense of separation that perception of the concrete or "real" world normally entails. Instead, the reader feels at one with everything that "surrounds" him: "everything has become part of my mind . . . I am freed from my usual sense of incompatibility between my consciousness and its objects" (p. 55). A strange sort of split identity thus results. Although the reader recognizes the objects filling his mind as those of another subject, he experiences them as his own.

There are two traditional ways of accounting for this "other" subject. One can correlate it with a character in the work according to the time-worn notion of "identification," or one can attribute every thought in the text to the author. But as Poulet points out, whatever connection the work may have with its author's existence, it nevertheless has a life of its own, which is lived in every reading. And since knowledge of the author's biography can only be external to the merging of consciousness that occurs during reading, such knowledge can play no determinative role in the constitution of the work: "to be sure, nothing is unimportant for *understanding the work . . . And yet this knowledge does not coincide* with the *internal* knowledge of the work. . . . at this moment what matters to me is to live, from the inside, in a certain identity with the work and the work alone" (p. 58).

For Poulet, this "work" is nothing less than the activity of the "other" consciousness that the reader activates and shares; moreover, it cannot be identified with any single person, historical or fictional. Similarly, the work-as-consciousness cannot be reduced to a concrete or ideal structure, since its very being depends on the animating intention of the reader: "so long as it is animated by this vital inbreathing . . . a work of literature becomes (at the expense of a reader whose own life it suspends) a sort of human being, . . . a mind conscious of itself and constituting itself in me as the subject of its own objects" (p. 59).

Poulet insists, then, that the literary work is to be rigorously distinguished from the book or text, or any similar concrete or ideal formal entity possessed of an autonomy of its own. Rather, it is an intention constituted within, and indeed subsuming, the reader's animating intention. For the reader thus absorbed, a trance-like state ensues, in which the active intending of a meaning effaces, rather than constitutes, personal identity.

The Work as Reading and Writing

The distinction between book and work articulated in the work of Jean-Paul Sartre and Maurice Blanchot forcefully illustrates the intentional model of reading. In his piece *Qu'est-ce que la littérature?*[2] Sartre portrays the literary work as a strange top (*toupie*) which exists only in motion: "to set it spinning a concrete act called reading is necessary, and the work lasts only as long as the reading can last" (p. 52).

Blanchot's version of the work similarly stresses the primacy of the reading intention, but insists on its capacity to bring into being a complete entity rather than a progressively constituted consciousness. This formulation avoids the implication that the wholeness of the work is in some way contingent upon the temporal duration of the reading. Rather than constituting the work through its progressive apprehension, reading simply and instantaneously reveals it to *be*. "To read, then, would not be to write the book anew but to make the book write itself or be written – this time without the intermediary of the author, without there being anyone who writes it" (*L'Espace littéraire*, p. 256)[3]. Through reading the book becomes a work, is liberated from its author, and constitutes itself as a privileged domain or literary space distinct from empirical reality.

Paradoxically, though, the work also asserts its independence from the reader who allows it to be: open to any consciousness, it must remain separate from each individual subject. For this reason, Blanchot refuses to think of reading as active or productive: "reading makes nothing, adds nothing; it lets be that which is; it is freedom, not freedom that gives being or grasps it, but freedom that assents, says yes" (*Espace*, p. 257).

The metaphor of liberty or freedom is used by both Blanchot and Sartre to characterize reading, but Sartre attaches to it a social function quite alien to Blanchot's thought. For the latter, the free

movement by which reading lets the work *be* is free precisely to the
extent that it is not founded on any prior presence. The literary work,
unlike the scientific proposition, has no origin or referent in the real
world; it is in no way "guaranteed" by empirical reality or substan-
tiated by concrete objects. Because of this, it can only come into
being through an act which lets something *be* which "is not" (cf.
Espace, pp. 258–9). On the other hand, a non-literary or propositional text becomes transparent through reading: it leads its
reader back to a known reality and links our present and future
moments of understanding with our past knowledge. The conceptual meaning (associated with propositional texts) implicitly denies
the intentional model of reading and asserts an objective truth
independent of the subjective act intending it. Scientific language
tries to efface itself as an intention in order to reveal a stable referent,
an origin in empirical reality.

For Blanchot, this is precisely what literature does not do. The
work we read into being has no continuity with the material world
whatsoever:

between the book that is there, and the work that is never there in advance,
between the book that is the dissimulated work and the work that can only
affirm itself in the opacity, brought to the fore, of this dissimulation, there is a
violent break, the shift from a world where everything more or less has
meaning, where there is darkness and light, to a realm where, literally
speaking, nothing yet has meaning, towards which, nevertheless, everything
that has meaning reaches back, as towards its origin. (*Espace*, p. 260)

Reading transports us, then, to a realm of primal meaning that resists
subordination to known reality.

Sartre's version of liberation is quite different. The infinite possibilities reading opens for him are contiguous with reality and result
directly from the reader's productive gesture: "he could always go
further in his reading, create more extensively; and in this way, the
work appears to him inexhaustible and opaque like [real] things"
(*Littérature*, p. 58). The motivation for this limitless creation comes
not from the work, as is the case for Blanchot, but from the author,
who invokes as his accomplice the reader's freedom: "thus the writer
appeals to the freedom of the reader that it might collaborate in the
production of his work" (*Littérature*, p.59). Rather than an intention unto itself, the work becomes the product of human endeavor; it
is an emblem of the reader's and author's free collaboration – and, by

extension, of human freedom in general. As the intention of our reading becomes increasingly complex, we assume a correspondingly intense act on the part of the author: the more elaborate our "reading" of the work, the greater the implied scope of the author's intentions. Thus a greater exercise of our freedom necessitates a greater exercise of his. The end result is an economy of expansive generosity ultimately capable of grounding all possible meaning in human freedom.

But for Sartre this meaning is not the opaque non-referential thing Blanchot envisions. Rather, literary prose consists entirely of significations, which function precisely to the extent that they lead the language user back to a concept or entity predating the language act: "words are not first and foremost objects but designations of objects. The first question is not whether they are pleasing in and of themselves, but whether they indicate correctly a certain thing in the world or a certain notion" (*Littérature*, p. 26).

In a sense, the literary work cannot fail this test of reference: because the reader can only intend a fictional world consonant with his experience of reality, can only bring into being "a world at once *his* world and the external world" (*Littérature*, p. 76), all of the meanings a reader intends will appear to refer to his world. In fact, the ultimate function of literature for Sartre is to designate the world we know while at the same time showing it to be anchored in human freedom. It is the shared, yet absolute, authority of reader and author that makes this possible. Because the world of the literary work imposes its unique meaning on us, it has the aura of essentiality characteristic of empirical reality; but because it also is grounded in our free act of reading, it simultaneously asserts *our* essentiality: "the object is essential because it is rigorously transcendent, because it imposes its own structures, and because one must abide by it and observe it; but the subject is also essential because he is necessary not only to reveal the object (that is, to make the object *be*) but also so that this object might *be* absolutely" (*Littérature*, p. 55). And for Sartre, this experience of the essentiality of free intention *vis-à-vis* the essential world is, finally, the very purpose of art; "the final purpose of art: to recuperate this world by presenting it as it is, but as if it had its source in human freedom" (*Littérature*, p. 73). Thus what Poulet envisions as a very private trance-like fusing of the self with another consciousness, Sartre sees as nothing less than the apotheosis of human freedom within an economy of mutual generosity.

Clearly, the basic paradigm of intentionality can produce both intensely private and deliberately social models of reading. In fact, the doubled subjectivity of the work can easily ground theories of antagonism diametrically opposed to Sartre's happy collaboration or Poulet's comfortable intimacy. Maurice Blanchot is a case in point.

For Blanchot the literary work is torn between its two intentions and can only be thought of as a profound antagonism between two disparate identities and incompatible exigencies: "the intimacy and violence of contrary movements that never reconcile themselves and are never appeased" (*Espace*, p. 304). Rather than a solidarity, the work reveals a permanent struggle "between the measure of the work that becomes a possibility and the excess of the work that tends towards impossibility, between the form in which it is grasped and the limitlessness in which it withholds itself, between the decision that is the being of the beginning and the indecision that is the being of the recommencement" (*Espace*, p. 265). This formulation not only calls Sartre's "collaborative unity" into question, it grounds a model of reading that culminates in a paradox even on the level of private experience. By its refusal to concur with a single intention, the work constitutes an aporia – a logical impasse or double bind – more complex than simple notions of reader/author rivalry would suggest. This idea, particularly as it appears in Blanchot's work, requires some elaboration.

Considered as a writing intention, the work can never be absolutely finished; it is an infinity, an impossibility, a projection of consciousness which, attaining givenness only once it is read, can have for the writing consciousness no shape, no end, no effect. It awaits another time, place, and subject, and can therefore only be present to its author as an absence (*Espace*, p.135). For Blanchot, the obvious analog is death, which seems an imposition of finitude and a closure, but which, for the living, is beyond comprehension (*Espace*, p. 355). Like death, writing seems the absolute power to inscribe and limit; but also like death it undercuts its own closure through the introduction of an endlessness and indeterminacy. In this sense, the work as writing contradicts itself and bears the seed of self-alienation: "the extreme form of my ability (power) not only becomes that which disenfranchises me by depriving me of the ability to begin and even to finish, but becomes that which has no relation to me, has no power over me, that which is divested of any possibility –

the irreality of the indefinite" (*Espace*, p. 130; cf. also pp. 139, 266–7, 331).

On the other hand, the work as *reading* appears a finished whole, a measured form and past decision, with regard to which the intending reader seems almost superfluous: "he does not penetrate it, it is free of him; this freedom is what makes his relationship to it profound, what makes the depth and privacy of his Yes, but, in this very Yes, keeps him at a distance" (*Espace*, p. 269). Our closeness to the work is dependent precisely on our willingness to let it be, to remain at a distance and recognize that it exceeds our control. Like writing, then, reading entails an accession to an aporetic distance from oneself through the intention of an object which is simultaneously ours and not ours, "measure and the immeasurable, form and infinity, decision and indecision"(*Espace*, p. 266). In this light, Sartre's referential theory appears inconceivable.

It is crucial to understand that for Blanchot the separation between reader identity and author identity is only a heuristic device designed to reveal the troubling paradox of literature. In fact the work is at all moments both reading *and* writing, and any attempt to isolate one intention will only reveal the other. For instance, the work as writing necessarily contains an anticipation of the reader – as that possibility of understanding which counters the impossibility of authorship: "to the extent that to write is to wrench oneself free of impossibility, to the extent that writing becomes possible, it then assumes the traits of the exigency of reading, and the writer becomes the nascent intimacy of the still infinitely future reader" (*Espace*, p. 267). Conversely, the emptiness or distance felt by the reader resonates with the impossibility of "completing" the work and thus draws the reader into the authorial intention: "he takes part in the work as in the unfolding of something in the making, as in the intimacy of this nothingness that transforms itself into being" (*Espace*, p. 271). Writing can only occur because it bears within itself the possibility of reading, and vice-versa. The reader can fill with determinate meaning only a work which is resolutely indeterminate.

In *L'Espace littéraire*, then, the work is indeed a unity, but a "torn unity" (*unité déchirée*) possessed of an "exaltant contrariness" (*exaltante contrariété*) which is the animating force of the literary intention (*Espace*, pp. 309–10). For Sartre, the reading and writing consciousnesses mark temporally and socially distant subjectivities moving ever closer through their common enterprise. For Blanchot, those consciousnesses are the obverse faces of the work's single intention; they attain plenitude only within their aporia, "this intimacy where antagonistic forces confront each other, unreconciliable yet having no fulfillment other than in the contestation that opposes them" (*Espace*, p. 304).

Both Blanchot's and Sartre's theories depend, then, on the principle of intentionality, although Sartre stresses the subjective side of the reading intention *qua* act, while Blanchot uses the concept of the work *qua* object as the embodiment of the author's and reader's gestures. Blanchot and Sartre also share a fascination with the intersubjective aspect of reading, the relationship within the literary intention of the two subjects who share a single object (the work).

This emphasis is in accord with the critical programs of Poulet and Richard, which aim not at judging the conceptual value of the texts they treat, but at espousing the perspective of the consciousness inhabiting the work: "criticism must take care not to seek out some sort of *object* . . . what must be reached is a *subject*, that is, a mental activity one can only understand by putting oneself in its place and in its perspectives, in short, by making it re-enact within us its role as subject."[4] But this playing out can only occur as a stream of successive intentions, each of which brings into givenness a further fictional object. This is underlined by Poulet's and Richard's critical writings, which reconstitute the consciousness of the target work as an accumulation of percepts or sensory intentions, each of which must be lived – and its subject inhabited – before the overall intention of the work can be felt from within.

It is the status of these individual intentions and objects which the intersubjective theories of Sartre and Blanchot cannot explain, since they consider the work only as a whole meaning that transcends its constituent intentions. As Sartre puts it, "meaning is no longer contained in words since, on the contrary, it is what allows us to understand the significance of each of them" (*Littérature*, p. 56).

Yet consideration of the intentions making up a work is indispensable to any theory at all attentive to the chronological extension of the act of reading. For it seems self-evident that reading is a *progressive* intending that builds a whole out of successively apprehended parts. And this assumption leads to a whole series of further questions: what exactly is the status of a fictionally intended object? What sort of activity on the part of the reader does it require? How does it differ from other intentions such as perception, imagination, daydreaming, or remembering? It is only in the more philosophical writings of Sartre and others such as Mikel Dufrenne and Roman Ingarden that one can find at least partial answers to these questions.

2

Sartre and Dufrenne:
Reading and Imagination

Watching, Imagining, Perceiving

When phenomenologists examine reading from the perspective of a subject intending a fictional world or object, they assume that such objects are given the reader in the form of an intuition. And since, as the etymology suggests, intuition denotes a gazing upon or contemplation, the theorists frequently rely on analogies with perception or imagination. The most common such analogy is that of the spectator. Merleau-Ponty, for instance, argues that the function of the novel is not to thematize an idea in the manner of traditional philosophy, but to "make it exist in front of us like a thing" (*Sens et non-sens*, p. 51).[1] For him, the only way to express the world in fiction is through "pointing at it" in "stories" (*Sens*, p. 55). Sartre goes even further when he asserts that "in reading, as at the theater, we are in the presence of a world" (*L'Imaginaire*, p. 127).[2] More precisely, "to read a novel is to adopt a general attitude of consciousness: this attitude roughly resembles that of a spectator" (*L'Imaginare*, p. 129).

Above all, such analogies imply that, on the one hand, the mode of givenness of the literary object is a scene or vision, and, on the other, that reading is the passive apprehension of a series of images forming such a vision. This is consonant with Blanchot's remark that great writers are "artists in that they find an equivalent – in form, image, story, or words – to make us participate in a vision similar to theirs."[3] For Poulet, the foreground of this scene or vision is occupied by the consciousness of the work, while the reader, "content to record passively," merely watches the work act itself out: "thus I often have the impression, while reading, of simply witnessing an action" ("Phenomenology of Reading," pp. 49–50).[4]

Blanchot sees this passivity as a withdrawal from one's normal world and the fall into a state of fascination, the object of which seems at once real and yet unrelated to concrete reality: "that which fascinates us . . . abandons the world, withdraws to a place short of the world and draws us with it, no longer reveals itself to us and yet affirms itself in a presence alien to the temporal present and spatial presence" (*Espace*, p. 25). Such a definition suggests a state of consciousness similar to imagination, in which we intend an object fully present to consciousness but alien to our spatio-temporal situation. The conclusions reached by Sartre in his book on images and imagining, *L'Imaginaire*, appear to support this hypothesis.

For one thing, we can explain the paradox of fictionality – the fact that we treat something by definition fictional as though it nevertheless denoted the real world – through an imagination-based model of reading. Sartre defines the mechanism of imaging[5] as "an act that tries to body forth an absent or non-existent object, by means of a physical or psychological content that is not given as such, but as the 'analogical *representative*' of the target object" (*L'Imaginaire*, p. 45). By definition, then, imaging consciousness posits its object as a nothingness: non-existent, absent, existing elsewhere, or suspended (*L'Imaginaire*, pp. 30–3); and this is very close to what fiction does. Yet in both cases, the vividly intended object is considered as a representation within the mind's eye, and can therefore be taken as a designation of something beyond itself: we can read fiction as referring to the real world just as we assume that the image we form of a friend is grounded in that friend's real existence.

One might also suppose that the apparent determinacy of the fictional world and the fact that the work somehow changes in time and yet always remains congruent with our most recent assessment of it can be explained by the way consciousness constitutes images. As Sartre puts it, the representative character of the image is always the result of the imaging intention and can thus never exceed consciousness: "the image object can never exceed the consciousness one has of it" (*L'Imaginaire*, p. 36). Thus all of the "images" intended in reading seem complete and whole at any given moment, yet remain open to revision through further reading.

Yet the notion of reading as image-making does not correlate well with our earlier descriptions. It is difficult to reconcile such an active version of the reader with the original notion of a passive spectator. If, as Sartre argues, it is the self-consciousness of the imaging intention that compensates for the "nothingness" of the imagined object, one can scarcely maintain that the self effaces itself in reading (cf. *L'Imaginaire*, p. 34). And while the active aspect of the imaging consciousness correlates well with Blanchot's insistence that reading must be more than "the gaze from without, behind the window pane, that grasps what is going on in an alien world" (*Espace*, p. 274), it does not accord with Sartre's own metaphor of "a spectator, who, at the theater, sees the curtain rise" (*L'Imaginaire*, p. 129). Similarly, it is difficult to explain the function of the text if one defines reading in terms of images: unlike an image, which is either all there or absent, the object predicated by a text is constituted temporally, by fragments; it is never present in its entirety. Reading is a temporal process; an image is a synchronous structure.

In some ways, then, reading seems to resemble imagination, while in others it appears more of a decoding than a contemplation. As Sartre puts it, "words elicit images when we daydream on them, but when I read, I do not daydream, I decipher".[6] Further, Sartre reports on the basis of experimental data that the work appears as an image only when readers pause to ponder earlier portions of the book: "images appear at the pauses and breakdowns in reading" (*L'Imaginaire*, p. 127). During the remaining time, the reader is engaged in a progressive apprehension, an apprenticeship (*apprentissage*) of sorts. And this apprenticeship finds its closest analog not in imaging, but in perception.

Unlike imaging, perception is relatively passive and predicates contact with a present entity whose existence it presupposes. Further, perception occurs in time: "in perception the object appears only in a series of profiles, projections. . . . one must *learn* objects, which is to say, multiply the possible points of view on them" (*L'Imaginaire*, pp. 21–2). And most important, the perceived object always exceeds the consciousness of the perceiver: no matter how many aspects of that object we perceive in any given instant, we know it to possess an infinite reserve of other possible relations, both to other objects and between its own elements. "It is this infinity of relationships that constitutes the very essence of a thing. . . . there is, at every instant, always infinitely *more* than we can see" (*L'Imaginaire*, p. 24).

Accordingly, a perceptual model of reading neatly explains why a literary work can always elude our attempts to understand it "definitively." At the same time, a model based on perception can account for the apparent opacity of the text – its "essentiality," as Sartre would say: we consider it more like a thing than a transparent signifier.

Unfortunately, the only visible, concrete "thing" reading seems to involve is the book in its materiality, that is, the graphic symbols on the page. And, as Sartre points out, these are not the object one "perceives" when reading: "these marks are no longer important to me, I no longer perceive them: in fact, I have assumed a certain attitude of consciousness which, through them, aims at a further object" (*L'Imaginaire*, p. 47). This "other object" is the fictional object or world, which one cannot truly be said to perceive, lacking any material basis for the perception. Indeed, as we have seen, this "object" in many respects more closely resembles an image.

We are left, then, with a notion of reading that draws both on perception and imagination, but which cannot be entirely likened to either. Accordingly, the objects intended during the literary experience appear to be both things whose determinations, like those of a perceived object, are revealed to us gradually by the narration, and images whose shape one determines completely and uniquely. In other words, the fictional object is, at any given instant, determinate and coincident with our awareness of it, yet subject to change in time and according to the progressive apprehension of the text. Reading appears both an interior gaze and an unending expansion of consciousness in which we progressively apprehend portions of the infinity of relationships contained in the work.

It is not surprising, in this light, that Sartre opts for a new notion to designate the schizophrenic cognitive activity of the reader. This notion is that of imaging knowledge or *savoir imageant.*

Imaging Knowledge

As one might suspect from its name, imaging knowledge is an intermediate form of cognition, combining aspects of perception, memory, and imagination. Knowledge (*savoir*) is for Sartre not an intentional act in itself, but rather a system of rules underlying intentions, the residue of prior experience upon which one draws when constituting new thoughts and images. The image itself can be defined from this perspective as a *full* meaning constituted by an intention grounded in knowledge: "one only represents to oneself in an image that which one somehow knows. . . . An image could not exist without a knowledge that constituted it" (*L'Imaginaire*, p. 116). In the image, in other words, knowledge achieves intuitive fullness in the shape of a specific object.

There is another type of knowledge, however, which in Sartre's view lacks this intuitive fullness and which can exist independently of any specific object. Such a pure "empty" knowledge is an awareness of abstract rules and relationships – a kind of definition lacking any concrete defined object (*L'Imaginaire*, pp. 116–17). An example of such knowledge is the awareness one might have of a color – even if one has no object or specific shade of that color in mind. Although this concept of an "empty consciousness" (ibid.) is suspect within the framework of intentionality, it allows Sartre to postulate the intermediate state of *savoir imageant*, or knowledge inclining towards imaginational fullness yet still functioning as an awareness of an order. And it is this intermediate state of consciousness he ascribes to the reading of fiction: "the sentences of the novel have become permeated with imaging knowledge; that is what I apprehend in the words, not simple meanings" (*L'Imaginaire*, pp. 132–3).

Building on this notion, one could propose the following phenomenological model of reading: it is a process in which a consciousness of empty relationships embodied in the text continually strives to fill itself out into an image. The pure meaning or rules furnished by the text are not the end meaning of the reading, but merely part of the knowledge out of which the fictional world can be synthesized. Still, the fictional world does not attain the intuitive fullness of an image – unless one interrupts the reading in order to gaze back on it. Reading occurs, then, neither entirely in the mode of conceptual meaning nor in that of an intuitively full image. Rather it is the suspension of consciousness between these two poles: no longer pure rule and order, yet not quite full image.

From this perspective the objects and "world" of the novel are less a stable structure than a continual process of synthesis that can never attain completion, because literary synthesis, like perception, can never exhaust the qualities of the object intended. As Sartre puts it, "the relationships will not be arranged as when they compose the denotation of a concept; the rule of their synthesis will be that they must be one to the other as the different qualities of an object" (*L'Imaginaire*, p. 135). In other words, one does not "think" the fictional work as mere meaning, but as a concrete thing. A world constitutes itself beyond the syntactical and semantic rules of the text: "everything that exceeds, envelops, orients, and localizes the bare meaning of the sentence I read is the object of a knowledge. But this knowledge is not a pure meaning. . . . *I think it the way I think things*" (*L'Imaginaire*, p. 130). The system of relationships inscribed in the text persists as the means of generating the fictional object, but it passes to the background, just as does the manifold of relationships or aspects through which a concrete perceived object is given.

Still, Sartre maintains, since it has not yet developed into a full-fledged imaging consciousness, imaging knowledge cannot assume the shape of a specific, fully given thing. Instead, it intends a generalized thing, "some" thing characterized by the qualities hovering in the background: "the thing is still just 'some thing.' Which is to say, a certain positing of opacity and exteriority out of nothingness – opacity and exteriority that are determined precisely by the relationships we have pushed to the background behind their density" (*L'Imaginaire*, p. 131). It is because of this objective density and the pseudo-perceptive attitude of the reader that the fictional world appears autonomous and offers us the continual attraction of determining an "essential" object. Since imaging knowledge is always inclining towards a full image, reading implies "an effort to determine this 'something,' . . . a will to achieve the intuitive" (*L'Imaginare*, p. 132).

Of course, one's striving can easily culminate in an image: if we cease reading and pause to daydream, our consciousness will indeed arrive at a state of full intuition, but it will be that of imagination. Intuition will have been gained at the cost of the object's externality and essentiality. In the absence of such a degeneration into imagination, Sartre's reading remains an intention in suspension – permanently striving towards intuitive determinacy yet never quite attaining it.

A theoretical model of reading based on the notion of imaging knowledge has the virtue of being able to embrace the contradictory notions of reader autonomy and textual authority. At the same time, it explains how the fictional world can appear so solid yet continually shift under our very eyes. What imaging knowledge *cannot* explain, however, is how reading can trigger the conceptual reflection characteristic of literary criticism: Sartre's model allows only for permanent suspension or the fall into fantasy.

For a more satisfactory explanation of reading's place in the ongoing identity of consciousness, one needs a notion of imagination which can address the "fall" into reflective judgement. Such a notion is best formulated by another French phenomenologist, Mikel Dufrenne, in his general study of aesthetic experience, *Phénoménologie de l'expérience esthétique*.[7]

For Dufrenne the complete unity of subject and object suggested by intentionality must continually give way to, and be reborn of, a dichotomy triggered by reflective thought: "it is inevitable that the totality formed by the object and the subject be broken, and that the movement, characteristic of being-for-itself and constitutive of intentionality, by which a consciousness opposes itself to an object, be accomplished" (*Expérience*, p. 433). Dufrenne postulates two distinct forms of intention: that of lived presence, in which subject and object are united, and that of reflection, in which the subject asserts a reflective distance from its object. For Dufrenne the passage from the former to the latter forms the essential dialectic of human consciousness, in which felt presence is continually displaced and brought under control by ideas. And the crucial transitional role in this passage falls, in his system, to imagination. For it is imagination which provides that representation which transforms appearance into the fully perceived world out of which conceptions are built (cf. *Expérience*, pp. 446 ff.).

According to Dufrenne, the role of imagination in the literary work is to fill out the characters and events of the fictional world and, more importantly, to provide distance. By projecting "into" the work of art the spatial and temporal density of reality, imagination converts it into a spectacle for the viewing consciousness, inaugurating the schizoid attitude of participation/contemplation noted by most aestheticians: "the spectator must be interested enough in the show to follow it, not so much as to be duped; . . . enough to be gripped by the action, not so much as to intervene as if it were real" (*Expérience*, p. 448). In other words, it is because he can convert it into an image that the reader can be absorbed yet not deluded by the fictional object. At the same time, Dufrenne assigns imagination the task of providing the "implicit memory" of each narrative, that is, the continually evolving framework of past and present episodes that allows us to "recognize" recurrent characters, themes, etc.

Dufrenne's theory differs most markedly from Sartre's in its insistence that imagination is only a transitional stage leading to reflection, just as brute presence is only a transitional experience leading to representation. For the imagined representation cannot maintain itself in any stable state – it remains subject to the caprices of fantasy. In order to bring it under control and convert its lived unity into a logical unity, one needs reflective understanding:

to reflect is thus to repress at least provisionally the imagination that serves the principle of the lived and to loosen the tie it weaves between the world and me; whereby one discovers a logical, rather than a lived, founding principle. For it is not the same thing to feel within one's imagination the solidarity of two objects and to think with one's reason a necessary link. (*Expérience*, pp. 462–3)

In a sense, Dufrenne's theory adumbrates the dialectic central to literary criticism, that is, the play between reflective understanding and lived meaning. At the same time, it suggests the inevitability of critical reflection: rather than falling into image contemplation, as Sartre's itinerary from *savoir*, to *savoir imageant* to *image* would suggest, reading can lead to conceptual thought. Rather than an immersion in the private worlds of the inner eye, Dufrenne's dialectic of presence, imagination, and idea argues for an inevitable translation of reading intentions into the shared public language of concepts. Before leaping directly into the problem of criticism's relationship to reading, however, we must backtrack to the question of the literary *work* which, in the phenomenological perspective, necessarily correlates with the activity we have outlined.

To this point we have traced a theory of literary meaning based on the activity it entails in the reader and writer. Such structural components as have been mentioned – the underlying order of the reader's knowledge, for instance – have only served to put into relief the primary notion of the meaning subject's intentional act, itself presumed to generate the residue we call "the text's" meaning. Yet it is clear that both Sartre's and Dufrenne's models, by analyzing the activity of reading in terms of three distinct types of consciousness, implicitly problematize the literary work *per se*. In the place of the impressively monadic whole *L'Espace littéraire* or *Qu'est-ce que la littérature* portrayed, we have an object which is at once empty structure of rules, brute felt presence or full image, and conceptual knowledge. The work's identity as collaboration or antagonism does not correlate easily with the proliferation of surrogate constructs (image, percept, idea, rule) which Sartre and Dufrenne associate with the activity of the reading subject. Yet neither Sartre nor Dufrenne pursues this problem, because neither is primarily concerned with literature in the works cited. For the purposes of formulating a coherent phenomenology of reading, nonetheless, it is imperative that we clarify the status of the literary work *in conjunction with* our discussion of the reader's activity. It is this vast double-edged task that Roman Ingarden, a Polish aesthetician and phenomenologist, carries out.

3

Ingarden and Iser:
Reading as Concretization

Ingarden's Schematized Work

As a disciple and friend of Husserl, Roman Ingarden was a fervent advocate of phenomenology as a method of investigation, and in his two monumental tomes, *The Literary Work of Art* and *The Cognition of the Literary Work of Art*,[1] he uses it to establish the ontological status of literary objects and the epistemological status of the cognitive activities to which they give rise. In keeping with the Husserlian tradition, he employs eidetic analysis, or the exhaustive description of the essential qualities of the object of inquiry; and he eschews the psychological approach favored by the French theoreticians treated above. In contrast to the mysterious aporias of Blanchot or the psychological enthusiasm of Sartre, Ingarden's writing is laboriously analytic; and it stands as an extreme case of one approach to reading. Unable to tolerate contradictions or paradox, Ingarden attempts to break down the complexity of reading and the literary work into a constellation of levels, phases, modes, and sub-categories, each of which enjoys a particular ontological status, level of materiality, and function. In keeping with this strategy, he separates his investigation into two distinct parts; the first treats the structure and ontology of the literary work itself, while the second deals with the various modes of cognition involved in reading and criticism. His work thus carries to a logical extreme the tenet of intentionality by approaching reading through its double identity of objective structure and subjective act.

The single most important notion in all of Ingarden's writing is that of the distinction between the work of literature and its concretization. For Ingarden, the work is a purely intentional object, yet it is not entirely dependent on the subject for its existence. Rather it is what he calls an "ontically heteronomous formation." This is to say that the work originates in the intention of the author, but it has the basis of its continued being in the two heterogeneous realms of (1) the *ideal* concepts or "meaning contents" that are actualized in the author's sentences, and (2) the *real* word signs that form the text. In the same way that a melody's existence is not contingent on its current performance, the literary work does not depend for its existence on any particular reading act (cf. *Work*, pp. 118–22, 360–2).

Consequently, Ingarden feels that the work is separable from the reading acts it may occasion, and that if reading produces anything, it is only an actualization of the work's schematized intentionality, its concretization in a determined form similar to that of Sartre's "image". In fact, Ingarden repeatedly uses the same term as Sartre to designate the operations of reading: synthesis. But these syntheses can only give rise to various concretizations, none of which should be confused with the work itself. This latter is a purely schematic skeletal structure close to what Sartre calls empty meaning, but considerably more complex in its makeup.

In *The Literary Work* Ingarden postulates that the literary work is made up of four strata, distinguishable through both their characteristic material and the role they play *vis-à-vis* the other strata and the work as a whole (p. 29). They are (1) the stratum of word sounds and phonetic formations, (2) the stratum of meaning units of various orders, (3) the stratum of schematized aspects, and (4) the stratum of represented objectivities (*Work*, p. 30). Although each plays an essential role in the work and possesses its own characteristic aesthetic values, Ingarden does impose a hierarchy of sorts upon them. He sees the stratum of meaning units as central: "by its very essence it requires all other strata and determines them in such a way that they have their ontic basis in it and are dependent in their content on its qualities" (*Work*, p. 29). On the other hand, the linguistic sound formations of the first stratum serve primarily as the "external, fixed shell . . . in which all the remaining strata find their external point of support or − if one will − their external expression" (*Work*, p. 59). The stratum of represented objectivities appears only as the end product of the other three strata: "all other strata are present in the work primarily for the purpose of appropriately representing objects" (*Work*, p. 288). And this stratum marks the culmination of a multi-phased process of representation.

The first of the several "moments" making up representation is that of the projection, by the meaning units of a sentence, of a developed intentional *state of affairs*, or purely intentional correlate (*Work*, p. 188). This state of affairs is not the intentional object itself, but merely the "medium through which we must cross in order to arrive at the represented objects and have them as a *given*" (*Work*, p. 191). For instance, one state of affairs is that of essence, as in the sentence "Gold is heavy"; while the sentence "In the winter my room is dreary" projects a state of what Ingarden calls thus-appearance; and "My dog is running away" one of occurrence (*Work*, p. 195). One can imagine a great variety of states of affairs and numerous sentences that would project more than one such state at a time. The important thing is that they are only implicitly represented in the work and serve primarily to establish the status of the objects brought into givenness.

The state of affairs alone is not sufficient to lead to an "intuitive givenness of the given object" (*Work*, p. 197), since it only meets what Ingarden calls the objective conditions of intuitive apprehension. The correlate subjective conditions "lie in the execution of quite determinately construed acts of consciousness which bring with them the actualization of the 'aspects' in which every object that can be intuitively apprehended appears" (ibid.). And these "aspects" form the fourth stratum of the literary work.

We remember from the discussion of perception that nothing can be apprehended in all of its aspects: any perception necessarily construes a complete object from a limited but sufficient number of perceived qualities cumulatively apprehended. If I visually perceive a red ball, for instance, only certain aspects of its "sphericality" will be visible at any moment: its outside surface; one side of this surface, appearing as a disc of variable size according to its proximity; a reddish hue whose intensity varies according to the portion of the sphere under observation, and so forth. It is this series of aspects, which Ingarden calls the "manifold" of aspects, that brings the ball into givenness for me. And for Ingarden, this manifold "remains in its existence and essence in continuous reference to 'me,' the perceiving subect, even though it is not dependent solely upon me and is therefore not purely subjective" (*Work*, pp. 256–7).

The aspect, then, is not entirely a function of either the subject or the object. Rather it hovers somewhere in between as perceptive transaction. Ingarden maintains that it is not purely subjective because he sees every object as possessing a skeletal schematization of potential aspects, which governs the range of concrete, lived aspects that can be actualized within an intention. This schematization of proto-aspects correlates with the essential qualities or properties of an object and thereby assures a measure of concordance between different perceptive intentions of that object by different subjects and by the same subject at different times (*Work*, pp. 262–3).

Such schematizations are precisely what the meaning units of the work project, predicating the range of concretizations the reader can intend within the general state of affairs of a given sentence. Here one can locate the bulk of the reader's role in Ingarden's system; for every reader inevitably fleshes out the schemata by the addition of "details which actually do not belong to them and which the reader draws from the contents of other, formerly experienced concrete aspects" (*Work*, p. 265). So, like Sartre's "imaging knowledge," Ingarden's "concretization" postulates that fictional objects are built not merely on the basis of the abstract relationships embodied in the text's linguistic stratum, but also on the basis of the ordered knowledge left by the reader's past experience. And Ingarden's stress on past perception indicates that the field of acquired meanings which goes into the intending of a fictional world far exceeds the limits of conceptual meaning. Acquired meanings include the complete accumulation of past lived percepts, images, sensations, etc., intrinsic to any consciousness.

At this point it may be appropriate to illustrate Ingarden's theory of strata with an example. In *The Magus*, by John Fowles, one reads: "He poured me more tea. It had huge torn leaves and a tarry China fragrance" (p. 77, Dell edition). The stratum of phonetic formations needs little elaboration: a phonetic transcription of the two sentences would render it accessible to anyone familiar with the international phonetic alphabet, whether or not they spoke English. The stratum of meaning units, on the other hand, can only be apprehended by a competent speaker of English. Such a speaker will actualize the states of affairs projected by the semantic contents of the sentences – in this case a state of occurrence and a state of thus-appearance (at least). Within these states one can actualize, in a variety of aspects, the "objects" of the pouring of more tea by an agent (unspecified); the poured tea itself; the contents of the tea; and its fragrance.

But in bringing these "objects" into givenness as lived intentions, one might actualize a number of aspects purely contingent upon one's past experience. Someone who does not drink tea, for example, or even someone familiar only with tea *bags*, might not actualize any particular visual qualities on the basis of the phrase "huge torn leaves," while an ardent loose-tea user might form a particularly powerful intuition not only of the tea leaves, but also of the bizarre "tarry China fragrance." Depending on one's past association with tea, a whole host of further aspects might be actualized in one's concretization, such as the tactile and visual qualities of tarry tea. Nonetheless, certain aspects would *have* to be actualized, according to Ingarden, namely those schematized within the general object of tea: one could not "image" a light-blue, viscous liquid, for instance.

Indeterminacy and the Concretization

Within the limits set by the schematized aspects, then, one concretizes the state of affairs and objectivities projected by the meaning units of a literary work. In Sartrean terms, one fills out the empty conventional definitions by dipping into the stored knowledge of one's private experience and realigning past lived aspects within a present intention both unique and institutional. Yet Ingarden makes clear that this concretization is by no means a fleeting moment of intuition, nor is it purely contingent upon the subject. It may be the reader's intention that makes the work's objects appear "before our mind's eye in living form" (*Work*, p. 297), but this does not make the concretization a mere psychic process. Like the rainbow to which Ingarden compares it, it has the condition of its existence in a subjective experience yet remains rigorously transcendent of the subject (cf. *Work*, pp. 305–13).

By parceling out the foundation of the fictional object between the essential qualities of an ideal entity and the past lived aspects through which concrete embodiments of that entity are intended by a subject, Ingarden's theory of schematized aspects provides a compelling analysis of the "contingent autonomy" of the literary intention. But when he insists that the concretization can continue to exist independently of the act that "originally" intended it, he necessarily reifies the reading process into a stable structure. Indeed, there is a growing tendency in his later arguments to consider the concretization a rival to the work that grounds it. This appears most vividly in Ingarden's lengthy discussions of determinacy.

To the extent that one can speak of objects in a literary work, one must remember they can never be fully determined. No finite set of sentences could ever completely project all schematizations of any object – just as no finite set of perceptions could exhaust the manifold of qualities pertaining to a concrete object. Yet we have noted repeatedly that the objects intended in reading appear as fully constituted at any instant during the reading process. Clearly, the reading act must add a certain amount of determination to the objects the text only skeletally projects. Minimally, this involves the establishment of a spatially and temporally continuous context within which the fictional objects can "appear." This can only occur through the filling in of what Ingarden calls the work's spots of indeterminacy.

Initially, these spots of indeterminacy are defined in Ingarden's work only as gaps between what he calls the "moments" of a represented object. Since no time-filling event can be represented in *all* its phases, the continuum of real time must be represented in literary works by "*isolated* longer or shorter phases, or simply, only momentary occurrences, . . . and what takes place between these phases or occurrences remains indeterminate" (*Work*, p. 237). In reading we normally establish a continuum by filling in these gaps. In the example sentences from *The Magus*, for instance, we assume the existence of teacups and a teapot, even though there is no mention of such objects. Likewise, we link up the states of affairs projected by the two sentences and assume the tea of the first phrase to be that of the second.

Yet a more fundamental sort of indeterminacy concerns not the contextual or temporal continuity of the fictional world, but the identity of the individual represented objects themselves. Since language by definition always provides a merely general designation, aimed at a class of objects, no truly individual determinations can be schematized by a work (Cf. *Work*, p. 250). Only a tiny percentage of an object's innumerable properties can be cointended by the general range of a word meaning. Still, "precisely because this object is simultaneously formally intended as a concrete unit containing an infinite number of fused determinations and, consequently, intentionally created as such, 'spots of indeterminacy' arise within it, indeed an infinitely great number of them" (*Work*, p. 249). Naturally, readers do not perceive these spots of indeterminacy as such (*Work*, p. 251). Instead, as we read, we simply fill in as many as necessary to complete the represented objects to our satisfaction. It is for this reason that the concretized objects can never exceed our intention of them.

It is at this point in our study that the definition of the work and the description of the reader's activity come together. For it is the reader's actualization of previously experienced aspects that fills in the work's spots of indeterminacy and brings the fictional objects into full givenness. As we determine the fictional world, we concretize each intentionally projected object in a number of aspects whose general range is schematized by the work, but whose final choice and concrete form are codetermined by our past experience. And when the aspects held in readiness by the work "attain concreteness in the concretization and are raised to the level of . . . imaginational experience" (*Work*, p. 339), a duration and topography emerge out of the discrete generalized word meanings of the text. A determinate world appears in the place of the indeterminate work.

Because *The Literary Work of Art* is more concerned with the ontological status of the work itself, Ingarden does not elaborate in any detail on how the organic whole of the concretization is formed out of a series of discrete objects. Nor does his later work, *The Cognition of the Literary Work of Art*, which is primarily concerned with reflective evaluation of the work and of the concretization, explain this process any further. However, another continental critic, Wolfgang Iser, picks up Ingarden's ideas some thirty years after they were first formulated and develops them extensively in the attempt to generate a viable critical strategy based on a theory of reading.

Iser's Dialectics of Concretization

Although much of his early work is based on Ingarden's theory, Iser is acutely aware of his predecessor's shortcomings. In particular, he points out the unfortunate vectorization which the theory of concretization promotes, that is, the tendency to see the process of reading as a "one-way incline from text to reader and not . . . a two-way relationship" (*The Act of Reading*, p. 173).[2] In other words, Ingarden's theory reduces reading to a process of "completion" or "filling-in" and does not allow for any exchange between reader and text. This is because Ingarden considers the work ontically heteronomous and not contingent on the reader for the form of its schematizations (see above, p. 28). Iser, on the other hand, is interested in the interaction of reader and text, and he characterizes this relationship in terms of a continual dialectic. This dialectic operates on both the temporal and spatial axes: just as various phases of the reading experience supersede their predecessors, invoke revisions of former textual perceptions, and are in turn displaced, so various thematic structures vie for centrality and push others into the foreground and background.

Like Ingarden, Iser assumes that the text consists of schemata which the reader must manipulate (*Act*, pp. 92, 141), but he seconds the French theoreticians' suggestion that "meaning is no longer an object to be defined, but is an effect to be experienced" (*Act*, p. 10). He further defines this effect as "imagistic in character" (*Act*, p. 8), and aligns it with Dufrenne's middle-term imagination; that is, a state halfway "between the brute presence where the object is experienced and the thought where it becomes idea" (*Act*, p. 136; *Phénoménologie de l'expérience esthétique*,[3] p. 432).

The exact mechanism of literary imagination is, according to Iser, that of a passive synthesis basic to ideation: "it relates to the nongiven or to the absent, endowing it with presence" (*Act*, p. 137). And this synthesis involves schemata similar to those proposed by Ingarden:

for the literary text there can be no . . . "facts"; instead we have a sequence of schemata . . . which have the function of stimulating the reader himself into establishing the "facts." . . . The schemata give rise to aspects of a hidden, nonverbalized "truth," and these aspects must be synthetized [*sic*] by the reader, who through a continual readjustment of focus is made to ideate a totality. (*Act*, p. 141)

Naturally, the role of prior knowledge is central to this process: "it is as if the schema were a hollow form into which the reader is invited to pour his own store of knowledge" (*Act*, p. 143).

Up to this point, Iser's formulation offers nothing new. However, in his further analysis of how each new "fact" is integrated in an organic whole, he refines Ingarden's theory considerably. First of all, he provides a temporal model of dialectical revision:

each individual image . . . emerges against the background of a past image, which is thereby given its position in the overall continuity, and is also opened up to meanings not apparent when it was first built up. Thus the time axis basically conditions and arranges the overall meaning, by making each image recede into the past, thereby subjecting it to inevitable modifications, which in turn bring forth the new image. (*Act*, p. 148)

While Sartre's postulation of *savoir imageant* did not explain how the state of imaging consciousness could maintain itself without degenerating into full image, Iser's model provides an answer. It is not the essential "suspended" nature of the reading consciousness that keeps it from receding into fantasy, but rather the textual extension, that is, the constant barrage of new schema (Sartre would say pure meanings) that need to be integrated.

The formation of an organic whole further requires the development of an ever more inclusive principle of coherence – a pattern that reconciles not only old and new, but also all of the diverse thematic levels of the text. Iser attributes the constitution of such coherence to a process he terms continual gestalt formation. This "grouping activity that is fundamental to the grasping of a text" (*Act*, p. 119) involves the formation of ever higher levels of coherence, that is, ever larger and more comprehensive patterns, in which successive groupings of textual elements find their meaning. According to Iser, "there are two distinct stages in this process: first, the formation of an initial, open gestalt . . . second, the selection of a gestalt to close the first . . . closing can only come about when the significance of the action can be represented by a further gestalt" (*Act*, p. 123). For Iser, then, closure – or the decision as to a text's significance – occurs when we assess its basic meaning configurations from the perspective of a larger framework. This notion draws on the hermeneutic and semiotic notion that significance requires the integration of a lower-level meaning into the next higher level. The essential point in this formulation, however, is that givenness is not the end of reading: each object must be grouped with others of its kind or level, and that group must in turn be grouped with others in a larger group, and so forth. Ultimately, one achieves a single pattern of coherence for the entire text.

This theory of multiple gestalten more thoroughly explains the involvement and detachment of reading that fascinates the French theoreticians. While Blanchot and the Geneva School attribute this suspension to the alien "presence" felt during reading, or to the ontological status of the reading intention, Iser explains it in terms of the continual revision the gestalten undergo. The reader must make constant decisions in order to effect any closure: "a gestalt can only be closed if one possibility is selected and the rest excluded" (*Act*, p. 123). This choice represents a kind of commitment and involvement. But the reader's "entanglement" can never be complete, because it is open to revision when excluded possibilities re-emerge as viable choices. Since "the gestalten remain at least potentially under attack from those possibilities which they have excluded but dragged along in their wake" (*Act*, p. 127), the concretization which Iser's theory describes is less a gradually solidifying structure than a "living event" (*Act*, p. 128).

Predictably, Iser finds a correlate in the structure of the literary text for his postulate of continual gestalt formation. In the text, multiple *perspectives* are orchestrated by *textual strategies*. Four such perspectives are that "of the narrator, that of the characters, that of the plot, and that marked out for the reader" (*Act*, p. 96); it is the role of the textual strategies to regulate the foregrounding of various perspectives against the horizon of the others. (*Act*, p. 96). As the reading progresses, various perspectives will succeed and displace each other, alternately occupying the foreground and the horizon. However, the reader will gradually develop a holistic viewpoint, transcendent of any single perspective. From this privileged state all other points of view projected by the text can be contemplated; and for Iser "this is the ultimate function of the aesthetic object: it establishes itself as a transcendental viewpoint for the positions represented in the text – positions from which it is actually compiled and which it now sets up for observation" (*Act*, p. 98).

The fact that Iser grants the textual strategies a major role in the formation of this transcendental viewpoint suggests that the text is for him rather more determinate and less subject to give and take than his theory initially states. In fact, although he decries the "one-way" incline of Ingarden's theory, his own further ideas on gaps of indeterminacy closely echo those of his predecessor.

To avoid a one-way model of reading, Iser proposes a model of communication, in which the very non-coincidence of reader and textual situation is seen as the origin of their reciprocal interaction. Communication, Iser asserts, "arises out of contingency (behavioral plans do not coincide, and people cannot experience how others experience them), not out of common situation or out of the conventions that join both partners together" (*Act*, p. 166). In more specifically literary terms, he states that "it is the gaps, the fundamental asymmetry between text and reader, that gives rise to communication in the reading process" (*Act*, p. 167). It is difficult to conceptualize such "gaps" in anything but concrete terms, however. Indeed, Iser quickly shifts the burden of his theory to the textual structure, postulating the presence therein of blanks that regulate reader response.

Generally described as "a vacancy in the overall system of the text, the filling of which brings about an interaction of textual patterns" (*Act*, p. 182), the blank differs from Ingarden's gap of indeterminacy in that it is not an unstated portion of the narrative context or a lack of fullness in textual objects, but rather the space or boundary between two textual segments or perspectives. It functions by furnishing a signal to the reader that different segments need to be connected: "by impeding textual coherence, the blanks transform themselves into stimuli for acts of ideation" (*Act*, p. 194; cf. also pp. 182–3). This formulation carefully places the burden of the text's determinacy not on its actual contents, but on the spaces between textual segments. The object which for Ingarden was schematized and projected by the work's meaning units is specifically removed from those meaning units by Iser and relocated in a structuring gesture: "each textual segment does not carry its own determinacy within itself, but will gain this in relation to other segments" (*Act*, p. 195). The object is not simply filled with the reader's past experience, then, but attains meaning by virtue of its juxtaposition to other such objects; and this juxtaposition is controlled by the blanks in the text: "the object itself is a product of interconnections, the structuring of which is to a great extent regulated and controlled by the blanks" (*Act*, p. 197).

The mechanism of such control involves the process of gestalt formation already explained. When a blank appears between two segments in the text, they are placed in an undefined relationship. They are contiguous but not continuous. To resolve this tension, the reader encloses them within a common frame of reference (a higher-level gestalt) which "allows the reader to relate affinities and differences and so to grasp the pattern underlying the connections" (*Act*, pp. 197–8). However, since the frame of reference itself is generated only out of the need to enclose two segments, it does not have any prior content of its own. It needs to be filled out in order to obtain true closure: "this framework is also a blank, which requires an act of ideation in order to be filled" (*Act*, p. 198). There is in fact yet another phase to this process: as the framework is filled out and the segments it integrates gain determinacy, it will take on a specific structure and become associated with a specific reading moment and gestalt. As the reading eye continues on its way, the perspectives which were foregrounded during this process will move to the background again, forming a third type of blank waiting to be filled. Iser calls this last type of blank a vacancy (*Act*, p. 198).

In sum, Iser's "communication" model of reading makes the determination of textual objects a function of the continual dialectical reorganization of the textual segments among themselves and on various levels of coherence. This indeed does away with a one-way version of reading by postulating a continual returning and reorganization of previously read objects: the world of the text is under constant revision, and, thus revised, spurs us on to yet further revisions. In Iser's opinion this is a particularly appropriate model for reading, if only because it parallels the structure of experience in general:

> reading has the same structure as experience, to the extent that entanglement has the effect of pushing our various criteria of orientation back into the past, thus suspending their validity for the new present. . . . our past still remains our experience, but what happens now is that it begins to interact with the as yet unfamiliar presence of the text. . . . in the course of reading, these experiences will also change, for the acquisition of experience is not a matter of adding on – it is a restructuring of what we already possess. (*Act*, p. 132)

The Role of Understanding

However elegantly this dialectical version of concretization elaborates Ingarden's uni-directional model, it nonetheless conceals its own vectorization. By structuring his model according to the paradigm of integration within higher levels of coherence, Iser introduces the notion of significance alongside that of imaging. By convention, significance implies conceptual meaning and reflective cognition. The assumption is that one cannot invoke higher orders of coherence when immersed in an imaginational beholding. Indeed, the constant foray into one's memory, which the dialectic model implies, could scarcely avoid the continual shifting back into the pure rule-based knowledge Sartre outlined.

Yet Iser is not alone in making this shift. All of the phenomenologists agree that imaginational beholding can never sustain itself, nor suffice as any model of literary experience, if only because it is blind to itself. As Sartre says, one cannot know the image as image from within the imaging intention: "in order to determine the proper attributes of the image as image, one must have recourse to a new intention. One must *reflect*" (*L'Imaginaire*, p. 13).[4] In other words, having constituted an image, or a concretization, or a dialectically generated gestalt formation, one must distance oneself from one's creation in order to know it: "thus the image *qua* image is only describable through a second degree act in which our gaze turns away from the object in order to focus on the way that object is given" (*L'Imaginaire*, p. 13).

From one point of view, such reflection appears a natural correlate of the literary-critical gesture. As Poulet points out, the "fascination" of reading can only occur if we are *aware* that the thought we are thinking is that of another: "there would be no cause for astonishment if I were thinking it as the thought of another" ("Phenomenology of Reading," p. 56).[5] Sooner or later, he maintains, this awareness will cause us to ask the crucial question "who is this usurper who occupies the forefront? What is this mind who all alone by himself fills my consciousness?" ("Phenomenology," p. 57). These questions mark the emergence of the critical consciousness alongside that of the reading consciousness. Poulet characterizes this as the ongoing sense of a discrepancy between the moment of the work's "thought" and that of the reader's, "a lag . . . between what I feel and what the other feels; a confused awareness of a delay, so that the work seems first to think by itself and then to inform me what it has thought" ("Phenomenology," p. 60).

Whether or not this critical consciousness is an inevitable correlate of reading, Poulet does not say. But we have already noted Dufrenne's argument that the split from oneself characteristic of reflection states a dialectic intrinsic to *any* consciousness. As Dufrenne sees it, conceptual understanding depends on imaging consciousness for the initial production of meaningful configurations; but reflection is necessary as the ratification of such configurations, the structuring of experience that paves the way for further imaging. In his view, consciousness is necessarily caught up in an unending dialectic: "inferior and superior, nature and mind, never cease merging and separating in us; we never cease being one in the instant we divide to conquer ourselves" (*Expérience*, p. 464).

Whether one views reflective understanding as a necessary phase in an universal dialectic of consciousness, or simply as an adjunct of literary criticism, its emergence in any discussion of reading seems inevitable. Yet the version of reading we have thus far elaborated has little room for conceptual cognition. The different theories of

imagination, imaging knowledge, concretization, and gestalt formation all seem to corroborate each other and confirm the utility of a
composite definition, which might run somewhat as follows:

Reading is a suspended imaging knowledge continually striving to achieve a
representation based on the abstract meaning rules of the text and the past
lived aspects of personal experience. Through imaging, reading attempts to
attain the intuitional fullness requisite for conceptual closure, but this closure is
continually forestalled by the extension of the text, whose string of meaning
units provokes a constant reassessment of the gestalt the reader "perceives."

As noted above, such a definition can account for many of our
intuitions concerning fictional objects, in particular, the pleasant
"alienation" from oneself the absorption in fiction produces. Yet this
definition cannot address the status of the fictional work *following*
reading. Nor can it explain the possibility of a critical consciousness
during reading. Apparently there is another, different, side of reading
that the imaginational model cannot account for. The postulation of
an ever more complex yet coherent latent image assumes the bringing
into play of faculties and operations normally associated with reflective knowledge, just as the organizational process assumed by Iser's
model draws on paradigms of conceptual understanding.

Moreover, the tradition within which Iser works normally associates conceptual understanding with the critical assessment that
follows reading and takes as its object the work of literature globally
conceived, rather than the images making up one's experience of that
work. This suggests that the object of understanding, and by extension of reading dialectically conceived, is multiple. From a phenomenological point of view it is predictable that a "complication"
of consciousness should occasion a more complex object of consciousness. Practically speaking, this reopens the question of what it
is we read when we read. A strictly imaginational model leaves little
room for speculation: we obviously do not try to "perceive" as
object the author's intention or the work's global message when we
read. But we do try to understand such things, and even others, such
as the work as a schematization, when we read. To sort out the
potential complexities of this distinction, we need to return to our
notion of concretization and determine why the objects of reading
are multiple and what those multiple objects are.

4

Ingarden, Iser, and the Geneva School: Three Versions of Phenomenological Criticism

Ingarden's Four Kinds of Cognition

We remember from *The Literary Work of Art*[1] that Ingarden does not believe one produces a work of literature during reading, but only a concretization of that work. Near the end of *The Literary Work of Art* this construct of "represented objectivities," this "immediate correlate" of reading, attains a status apart from the subjective operations that actualize it and the schematized work that grounds it (cf. *Work*, pp. 332–9; also *Cognition*,[2] pp. 44, 48, 57). The separation of work and concretization sets Ingarden off from the French phenomenologists and poses a further theoretical problem: if we do not know the literary work intuitively during reading, how can we know it at all, and how can we distinguish it from the concretization?

These questions first attain pre-eminence in the *Cognition*, where Ingarden breaks down the literary experience into a serial event composed of two distinct types of mental activity. In this sequence, the process of concretization increasingly assumes a character of initial experience, which must be followed – if true knowledge of either the resulting construct or the work is desired – by a reflective investigation.

"Complete" reading is, then, at least a three-phased gesture, involving a concretizing intention, an evaluation of the resultant concretization, and an evaluation of the work in co-operation with which that concretization was generated. Actually, Ingarden describes another mode of reading as well: the slovenly pleasure-oriented consumption of books for diversion or "escape." This kind of reading will not concern us here. At the other end of the spectrum, the reader who carefully actualizes the objects into a faithful concretization may, under certain circumstances, have an aesthetic experience. In Ingarden's opinion this experience does not differ markedly from those called forth by other artistic media. It involves a number of phases in which the reader undergoes successive emotional responses, passes into a "specifically aesthetic attitude," forms a harmonious whole or aesthetic object out of the work's aesthetically valent qualities, and finally beholds and acknowledges the specifically aesthetic value of the work. Since this entire process is presented in vague affective terms, and since it is not specific to literature, I shall not attempt its analysis here. The essential point is that the aesthetic object which the process generates, and upon which it depends for the final revelation of aesthetic value, is, in the case of literature, the concretization.

Hedonistic reading and the aesthetic experience appear to constitute, in Ingarden's scheme, what we normally call reading. They occur as we are parsing the text and cease once we have finished it. It is at that moment that the two further operations of *reflective cognition of the aesthetic object* and *pre-aesthetic cognition* of the literary work become possible. The former of these operations constitutes for Ingarden true cognition of the aesthetic object. As such, it marks the passage from "imaginational beholding" to reflective analysis: "to contemplate the qualitative harmony in intuitive apprehension, is not yet to know (in the narrower sense of the word) what the aesthetic object in question is, how it is constituted, which qualities appear in it, and which immanent value they constitute in it" (*Cognition*, p. 209). To gain this more precise knowledge, we must "capture in concepts what is saturated with emotional elements and . . . determine it predicatively in strictly formulated judgements" (*Cognition*, p. 210).

However, knowledge of the concretization does not necessarily imply knowledge of the corresponding literary work. This requires a fourth kind of "reading," which Ingarden christens the "pre-aesthetic" cognition of the literary work. In this phase of our reading, we are to "look for those elements and factors which intentionally determine the multiplicity of aesthetically valuable 'correct' concretizations and . . . discover those properties of the work upon which are based the kind and the strength of the influence which it exerts on the reader to actualize concretizations of a specific sort in his mind" (*Cognition*, p. 229).

These two goals of reflective cognition, to know our concretization and to understand the structure of the work which co-grounds it, do not differ essentially from those Iser sets himself. And they complicate the systems of both theoreticians by arguing for two incompatible definitions of the concretization. On the one hand, we are to recover a formerly lived intention in all its vividness and make it the object of our critical scrutiny. This suggests that the concretization is both a stable structure and a recuperable presence. On the other hand, we are to use the concretization to lead us back to the schematized work. In this function, the full presence of the concretization is redefined as a transparent referential sign pointing to a structure beyond itself. The tension between these two definitions underscores the weak spot in Ingarden's theory as surely as it puts into question the status of Iser's critical conclusions. The former's attempt to prove in theory the possibility of "faithful" readings is as self-defeating as the latter's project for generating original, yet historically valid, interpretations of the masterpieces.

The Work and its Rival

The first of Ingarden's adjudicative operations, the reflective cognition of the aesthetic object, will not bear the brunt of my analysis, both because it does not directly involve the problems of literary criticism and because sorting out and clarifying Ingarden's vague description would unnecessarily prolong this study. Briefly, it requires maintaining the emotional "value response" of the aesthetic experience while at the same time distancing oneself from one's experience in order to "fix what is thus self-given . . . and . . . conceive it in regard to its qualitative structure" (*Cognition*, p. 305). This fixing occurs in two phases. First, we must find a way "to penetrate the qualitative basis on which [the self-given fullness of the qualitative harmony of qualities of value] is founded and to apprehend it in its qualitative heterogeneity" (ibid.). This will theoretically reveal the "entire interplay of founding component values" and then "the often hierarchical structure of the total value" (*Cognition*, p. 328). Next, we must present the results of this operation in intersubjectively intelligible judgments. These may have any of several goals: the description of the aesthetic object in question, the determination of the particular qualitative values present in the portrayed objects, or merely the praise or blame of the aesthetic object (*Cognition*, pp. 323–5).

In the absence of more specific directives, it is difficult to understand exactly how we can accomplish these goals. The immersion in imaginational beholding that must accompany the aesthetic experience seems to exclude the abstract conceptualization Ingarden calls for. Ingarden admits that purely analytic cognition will destroy aesthetic harmony – which is the object of our scrutiny (*Cognition*, p. 314). Similarly, he asserts that too much excitement hampers true cognition, while too little risks extinguishing the givenness of the value-laden aesthetic qualities (*Cognition*, p. 306).

The timing of the operation is equally problematic. If we wait until we have finished our reading, we will foreshorten our perspective by valorizing the most recent emotional responses. We may even forget previous elements of our aesthetic experience. Ingarden finally suggests that one either pause from time to time in order to reflect, or attempt to experience and reflect on one's experience simultaneously – a procedure he admits may not be possible (*Cognition*, pp. 310–14).

Finally, one wonders what kind of conceptual language would be capable of conveying the qualitative harmony we are charged with describing. If the aesthetic object qualitatively transcends the totality of the components that make it up, how can conceptual language, which derives its value from the relationships it establishes between elements of the same order, possibly be up to the task (cf. *Cognition*, p. 318)? More simply put, how can the language of ideas translate an experience by definition transcendent of conceptual knowledge? If one takes the definition of the concretization rigorously, as an imaginative beholding of aesthetic value that only occurs as a living intention, then it must exceed the grasp of conceptual language.

In short, by separating the aesthetic object from the text that helps ground it, Ingarden isolates it within the problematic notion of presence. And, as contemporary theoreticians have pointed out at some length, language may have certain claims to truth (depending on one's definition of truth), but it cannot recuperate presence. If concretization is a lived event of imagistic ideation, it cannot be rendered adequately by any retrospective account.

It is perhaps for this reason that Ingarden's later arguments in the

Cognition redefine the concretization as a stable structure. This tendency is particularly apparent in his discussions of the reflective analysis of the literary work, where the concretization serves as the template by which one assesses the work's schemata. On the surface of it, the operations involved in this assessment do not seem to differ fundamentally from those of a standard New Critical "close reading." Ingarden urges us to determine how the various elements of the text function with respect to its overall structure, how various readings are generated by these configurations, and how particular stylistic, rhetorical, and symbolic systems cause corresponding concretizations on the part of the reader (cf. *Cognition*, pp. 229 ff.). Throughout all of these phases it is the concretization that serves as the point of departure – the "given" whose shape will guide us back to the schemata out of which it arose. An intense, aesthetic reading is therefore a prerequisite to any understanding of the work: "this first reading provides the reader with just that supposedly 'intuitive' (in the Bergsonian sense) aesthetic concretization of the work . . . and consequently also provides him with the guidelines for what can and should be sought in an analytical investigation of the work" (*Cognition*, p. 283; cf. also pp. 234, 238, 249).

This deceptively simple formulation clashes with Ingarden's global description of reading. If concretization is the reanimation of the reader's formerly experienced concrete aspects, then not only will each concretization be different from all others, but the schemata to which it leads us will be as much those of the reader's memory or knowledge as those of the work. Since the aesthetic experience attains fullness only as it constitutes and arises from the concretization, even a perfect memory of this experience will not necessarily provide access to the work (cf. *Cognition*, p. 225). In fact, there is finally no way to determine the artistic value of the work: Ingarden admits that the realization of an aesthetic object may be as much a tribute to the reader as to the work (*Cognition*, p. 295).

This dilemma can also be expressed in referential terms. Ingarden desires knowledge of the work *per se*. Yet his own theory postulates that the work can be present to us only in the form of a concretization. Consequently, Ingarden tries to coerce the concretization into a referential role. Since it is formed on the basis of the work's structure, he reasons that it ought to bear the trace of that structure. Unfortunately, this use of the concretization clashes with its definition in at least two important ways.

For one thing, Ingarden's theory provides the reader far too much leeway in constituting the concretization: it is as much the trace of the personal schemata of our memory as of the work. This needs no elaboration. More fundamentally, the definition of the concretization as an opaque "thing-like" intentional object, appearing before us as a concrete world, clashes with the notion of transparent reference. The concretization cannot both itself be given and simultaneously bring into givenness the literary work. That which serves as a tool to bring into givenness another object can only be present to consciousness as empty schemata. And in this sense, Ingarden's critical program reverses his earlier model of reading. Rather than a fully given filling-out of the work's schemata, the concretization now appears an empty schematic construct on the basis of which one can actualize the structure of the work.

This reversal would in itself be acceptable, as the critical pendant to the experiential form of reading outlined in *The Literary Work of Art*, were it not for the fact that Ingarden's program requires that the aesthetic object be present in its full, "value-laden" givenness at the same time that one focuses one's analytic understanding on the schematic work. One can only correlate aesthetic value with schematic structure if that value is present as an intuition; and such presence is incompatible with the empty schematic role Ingarden wants the concretization to play. In other words, one can indeed treat the concretization as a vague trace of the work; but so defined, it no longer qualifies as an aesthetic object – the template for our analysis simply disappears.

Ingarden struggles for some time with this contradiction in terms before settling on an alternative strategy. Implicitly acknowledging that the concretization is an obstacle between us and the work, rather than a transparent denotation, he introduces a new notion designed to serve the referential function. Thus, late in the *Cognition*, the concept of the reconstruction is born.

Conceptual Truth vs. Imaginational Pleasure

Ingarden defines the reconstruction as the careful recreation of the schematic organization of the work. This recreation is not based on the aesthetic reading of the work, but on a distanced analytic reading that reinstates those places of indeterminacy we would normally fill out in the course of reading (*Cognition*, pp. 283, 335–49: *Work*,

p. 337). It functions, thus, as an objective, non-aesthetic actualization of the work in its schematized form. In this sense, it is an alternative to concretization, a means of assessing the *work's* value, rather than that of the aesthetic object (cf. *Cognition*, p. 283). If one thinks of the schematized work as an order that has been transformed or obscured by the personal shape of the concretization, then reconstruction appears as the recovery or reconstitution of that "original" order. Although it will necessarily fill out this order to some extent, it will do so only in accordance with the work's structure, excluding all reference to the critic's personal schemata in favor of bringing into givenness those of the work, viewed *per se*.

The phases in this recovery all center on that aspect of the work which distinguishes it from the concretization: its indeterminacy. Ingarden outlines four steps to be taken: (1) determine the places of indeterminacy, (2) decide which should be filled out and which should not, (3) ascertain the range of variability in the filling-out, and (4) determine which fillings-out will generate which aesthetically valuable qualities in their concretizations (*Cognition*, pp. 289–92).

While this program may seem feasible at first glance, it is virtually impossible in the terms of Ingarden's theory; and his own attempts to implement it demonstrate as much. Even the first of his operations directly contradicts the outline presented in *The Literary Work of Art*, by assuming the number of places of indeterminacy in a work to be finite. We could clearly not list a work's places of indeterminacy were they not finite; yet Ingarden himself asserts that there is an infinite number of such spots in any work (cf. *Work*, p. 249).

It is no wonder, then, that Ingarden subtly reformulates his original notion of spots of indeterminacy to exclude all save those specifically emphasized by the text. Ironically, this definition states what all of Ingarden's brief readings unwittingly show: a place of indeterminacy only exists to the extent that it is surrounded by determined objects (*Cognition*, pp. 260–2). As Ingarden finally admits, the gap of indeterminacy is "for the most part determined by certain general nouns and nominal phrases" (*Cognition*, p. 290). These presumably have to be actualized before one can perceive any gap in their description or in the surrounding context. By means of an example, we might recall the Fowles sentence cited above: "It had huge torn leaves and a tarry China fragrance." Any observation about "gaps" in this description – such as the lack of reference to the color of the beverage – presupposes the prior actualization of those qualities that *are* mentioned (the odor and the solid matter floating in the tea) and the decision that something is missing.

In short, before ascertaining gaps in a work's determinacy, one must actualize the work in a determinate form; and it is this determinate concretization that determines the indeterminacy of the work. Ingarden concedes this point implicitly in his description of the second analytic procedure. He suggests that we can decide which places of indeterminacy should be filled out by considering the "context" and the need for "consistency" (*Cognition*, pp. 290–1). Both of these notions imply a greater organic whole, parts of which have been omitted, but whose overall shape shines through to guide the critic in his analysis. Yet the only such transcendent whole Ingarden's theory admits is that of the aesthetic concretization (*Cognition*, pp. 85–7).

Ingarden finally admits that analysis of the work as he outlines it depends on a concretization, and that the reconstruction cannot be thought of as fundamentally different from its aesthetic counterpart (*Cognition*, pp. 335–41). He therefore redefines the reconstruction as a more accurate, correct type of concretization, a "limiting case of the 'concretization' of the work" (*Cognition*, p. 337), in which the personal contribution of previously experienced aspects is held to an absolute minimum. This new formulation hinges on the notion of the reconstruction's "faithfulness" to the work of literature (cf. *Cognition*, pp. 336–58), and it allows Ingarden to associate the concretization with a subjective activity, while the reconstruction is correlated to objective knowledge. Throughout the discussions on faithfulness the rift between these two modes of cognition widens, until two completely opposed and strongly valorized notions emerge. While reconstruction benefits from the prestige of truth, the concretization is increasingly associated with a mode of apprehension "in which the literary consumer is primarily oriented towards amusing himself by means of the work" (*Cognition*, p. 348).

In a faithful reconstruction, on the other hand, the reader's "whole effort is aimed at pressing forward to the characteristic form of the work . . . so that, if a reconstruction is nevertheless involuntarily constituted, it is, so to speak, transparent and allows the scholar to apprehend the work in the original through it, the work itself, and no longer just its reconstruction" (*Cognition*, p. 349). We remember from the discussion of Blanchot (cf. above, p. 12) that such self-effacing designation is characteristic of propositional language –

language which has no value as an object of contemplation *per se*, but which leads us to a referent beyond itself and can therefore be evaluated according to its truth value.

Ingarden's final arguments thus lead him around full circle to the repudiation of imaginational beholding, which is no longer an adequate program for the student of literature. What first appears in his work as a near-mystical communion with pure aesthetic value is demoted in the final pages of the *Cognition* to the status of mere pleasure-taking. It may be an end in itself, but it is not the correct end of literary commerce. Our cognition of objects literary must culminate in truth, not beauty. And for Ingarden this means displacing the spectacle of imaging consciousness with the order of conceptual language.

Such a displacement does more than mark the failure of Ingarden's attempt to overcome the obstacle imaginational models of reading pose for the literary critical project. It also marks the emergence in this study of an alternative to the imagistic model of literary cognition. We are now in a position to see how the theoretically convincing model of reading as imaging knowledge or concretization has definite shortcomings for critical practice. Drawing on the notion of intentionality, one can envision the concretization as an ephemeral moment, a fleeting intention in which we momentarily intuit pure value and harmony. But readings of this sort necessarily elude conceptual understanding. A theory that defines meaning purely in terms of an imaginational event closes the door on any valid critical practice.

Alternatively, one can maintain that the reader produces a construct possessed of a certain structural stability and temporal permanence. This kind of concretization, however, displaces the work that cofounded it: as the template by which all evaluations of the work must be made, the concretization necessarily fills the analytic intuition of the investigator and blocks access to the work.

Even the reconstruction is, finally, just a barer concretization, and its ability to denote the work hinges on a further theoretical move. For it can only reveal the truth of the work to the extent that one can posit a purely referential structure. In other words, one cannot translate an imaginational model of reading into critical practice without opening the question of referentiality and the identity of the "referee," that is, without asking to whose lived experience the concretization correlates.

It goes without saying that perfect reference is difficult to reconcile with an intentional model of meaning. Either the referential device is present merely as the empty rules or latent knowledge underlying imagination, in which case the work is itself directly intuited (and this is the model of Sartre and Blanchot); or, one preserves the ontic heteronomy of the work and makes the referential structure itself the object of the intention, in which case one can claim no direct intuition of the literary work (and this is Ingarden's dilemma).

What one *can* claim, however, is access to one's concretization – or at least its residue. This suggests that the proper object of the critical quest for knowledge should be the reader's response to the text rather than the work itself. This is, in fact, the move Wolfgang Iser elects; and it is only the first of several displacements of the referential question we shall study. As one might expect, each such relocation of the critical task brings its own theoretical refinements – and attendant problems.

The Reader in the Text

Iser, we remember, describes reading as a continual restructuring of our experience, a dialectical process of communication with the text in which components of the concretization are reorganized into further gestalt formations and integrated into ever higher levels of coherence (cf. above, pp. 35–8). Given this model of reading, one would expect a critical program aimed at recovering the interaction between text and reader, rather than understanding the ontically heteronomous work. Charting such a response is no easy task, however.

There are, first of all, pitfalls inherent in the dialectical theory itself: defining the "reading" in terms of an event seems to deprive the critic of any concrete structure open to analysis. Iser sidesteps this problem by insisting that certain elements of response, such as the formation of higher-level gestalten and vacancies, can be correlated with textual structures like the blank. This assertion unabashedly reifies the text and, more importantly, endows it with a definite content. It is this content that restrains the reader in his concretization.

A dialectical model of reading might be expected to grant the reader relative freedom in constituting the fictional world; but Iser sees the subjectivism inherent in such a possibility and goes to great lengths to locate the impetus for specific concretizations in the textual structure. In his view, a reading might seem to exhibit predispositions, but they are "laid down, not by an empirical outside reality, but by the text itself" (*Act*, p. 34). Moreover, Iser assures us that

> it certainly is true that any response to any text is bound to be subjective, but this does not mean that the text disappears into the private world of its individual readers. . . . The process of assembling the meaning of the text is not a private one, for . . . it does not lead to daydreaming, but to the fulfillment of conditions that have already been structured in the text.(*Act*, pp. 49–50)

On the other hand, Iser's dialectical theory of reading cannot underwrite a critical program that merely describes the objects portrayed by the text. What is needed is an interactive locus – an object both "in" the text and "in" the activity of the reader. Ideally, such a locus would only achieve its full meaning within an interaction of text and reader. For Iser, such a notion is that of the convention.

Conventions are just one of the elements in the text's repertoire – defined as the "complete range of contexts which the text absorbs, collects, and stores" (*Act*, p. 55) – but they are by far the most important. Because a convention can only be called a convention to the extent that it is recognized by more than one person, the notion assures that Iser's readings will occur on the general level of what he calls the "implied" reader, rather than on the level of any individual. And because conventions are rules used in various interactions, they can be said to reside neither entirely in the text nor in the reader, but within their relationship.

Of course, one is not normally conscious of the conventions governing one's acts at a given moment: when reading a novel, one is absorbed in ideated images (to use Iser's vocabulary) and not in the conventions of novel reading that make such absorption possible. Iser is therefore careful not to make conventions of novel reading the conventions of the text's repertoire. He concentrates rather on the conventions of everyday life, which he claims are "depragmatized," or taken out of their everyday context so as to strike our attention: "these conventions are taken out of their social contexts, deprived of their regulating function, and so become objects of scrutiny in themselves" (*Act*, p. 61). As a result, we become aware of "precisely what it is that guides us when we do act" in the outside world (ibid.).

This, then, is for Iser the basic function and pattern of novel reading: it is an exercise in self-education that occurs when we objectify the normally unthought conventions governing perception and intellection: "the literary recodification of social and historical norms . . . enables the . . . contemporary readers to see what they cannot normally see in the ordinary process of day to day living" (*Act*, p. 74). Most of the readings in Iser's interpretive collection, *The Implied Reader: Patterns in Communication in Prose Fiction from Bunyan to Beckett*,[3] reiterate the same message. The reader of *Joseph Andrews*, for instance, discovers a series of "divergences" from conventions governing antecedent literary genres (*Reader*, pp. 32– 4). The reader of *Ulysses*, on the other hand, draws on his assumptions about Homer to realize the constitution of individuality initiated by classical allusions (*Reader*, p. 183), while the reader of Bunyan experiences a theological revelation concerning his status as a doubting mortal when he recognizes in the text the "reflection of his own doubts, as well as his own hopes" concerning salvation (*Reader*, p. 13).

The striking thing about these readings and the theoretical elaborations that accompany them is how Iser seems to contradict his own findings. Having assured us that reading is essentially "imagistic in character" (*Act*, p. 8), he proceeds to redefine it in terms of a conceptual revelation. Having stated that "fictional texts constitute their own objects and do not copy something already in existence" (*Act*, p. 24), he blithely declares that "the repertoire reproduces the familiar" (*Act*, p. 74). Having asserted that literature "means nothing but what comes through it into the world . . . [and] cannot possibly be identical to anything already in existence" (*Act*, p. 22), he builds his theory around a repertoire which "incorporates a specific external reality into the text, and so offers the reader a definite frame of reference or invokes a definite range of past experience" (*Act*, p. 212).

We might say that Iser falls into the same trap as his predecessor. He begins with an imagistic version of the phenomenon that interests him, but rapidly abandons it when faced with the difficulty of founding a critical practice. Like Ingarden, he needs access to his object. But since the object in his case is the reader, not the work, and since the text, not the concretization, is available to his scrutiny, he must assign that text all of the referential force Ingarden grants the reconstruction.

What is different about Iser's theory is that it *calls for* transforming imagistic givenness into referential meaning. As I have already pointed out (cf. above, pp. 35–8, 50–1), Iser's central notion of continual gestalt formation implies a constant distancing and reintegration of experience on a higher level of coherence. The "stepping-back" from the reading intention, which fascinates Poulet, does not just occur in relation to the "other" in the work, but also in relation to one's own private experience: "it is impossible for [fictional] meaning to remain indefinitely as an aesthetic effect. The very experience it activates and develops in the reader shows that it brings about something that can no longer be regarded as aesthetic, since it extends its meaningfulness by relating to something outside itself" (*Act*, p. 23).

In this sense, Iser reiterates the gesture of his own theoretical reader: having noted a gap between two objects (the reader and the text), he combines them within a larger frame of reference. However, this frame of reference itself needs to be filled with a content; and it is this content which Iser calls the text's repertoire, that is, "all the familiar territory within the text," which may be in the form of "references to earlier works, or to social and historical norms, or to the whole culture from which the text has emerged – in brief, to what the Prague structuralists have called the 'extra-textual reality' " (*Act*, p. 69).

Unfortunately, by choosing "the familiar" as the organizing principle for his readings, Iser locks himself into a pattern of critical and theoretical redundancy. If one seeks out elements posited as familiar to the reader, one cannot avoid postulating a moment of recognition on the part of that reader. And when the elements are further defined as a "section of [the reader's] person" (*Act*, p. 155), they necessarily prepare a self-assessment. The similarity of Iser's readings to one another is thus as unavoidable as it is striking.

In his interpretation of Bunyan, for example, "members of calvinist sects discovered themselves in Christian" (*Reader*, p. 21), while in *Vanity Fair* "the reader realizes that he is similar to those who are supposed to be the objects of his criticism, and so the self-confrontations that permeate the novel compel him to become aware of his own position" (*Reader*, p. 116). In *Henry Esmond*, the reader discovers "in general the ways in which a man can enter into a relationship with himself" (*Reader*, p. 130); and in *Ulysses*, "the reader is compelled to try and find the frame of reference for himself, and the more intensively he searches, the more inescapably he

becomes entangled in the modern situation, which is not explained
for him but is offered to him as a personal experience" (*Reader*,
p. 183). Finally, Iser generalizes for the entire twentieth century,
whose reader he sees as "forced to discover the hitherto unconscious
expectations that underlie all his perceptions" (*Reader*, p. xiv).

Every work of fiction thus becomes an illustration of what Iser
terms "a dynamic process of self-correction" (*Act*, p. 67). However,
this process is none other than that of dialectical gestalt formation.
And dialectical gestalt formation is in turn only a psychologized
version of the general mechanism of understanding outlined by
hermeneutics: we understand elements by correlating them within a
larger context, which in turn must be reassessed, thereby provoking
a reconsideration of its elements, and so forth. In this sense, Iser's
readings demonstrate a tautology: the understanding of a work of
literature enacts the process of understanding.

This tautology is perhaps the price one must pay for a critical
program that unfalteringly adheres to a theoretical model. To infuse
his interpretations with more variety, Iser would have to venture
beyond the notion of "the familiar" and name themes in his target
texts that could not so easily be parceled out between textual structure and generalized reader. To do so, moreover, would require that
he either attribute the theme to a specific reader, thereby risking the
accusation of subjectivism, or associate it with a concrete textual
form, thereby ignoring his own model of dialectical communication.
One might conclude, then, that although a dialectical theory of
reading is compatible with critical interpretation, the range of that
interpretation is inversely proportionate to its validation of the
theory. Iser could easily explore different themes in his readings, but
to do so he would have to forsake illustrating his theory.

Yet from another perspective, he has already fallen short of his
goal. For his own theory persuasively argues that familiarity is not a
first-level element that can be identified "within" texts, but a second-
level function of gestalt formation pertaining to the concretization.
In other words, familiarity is not something that can be schematized
in a text like an object, but rather a function of personal recognition.
To say something is familiar is not to state its essential qualities, but
to qualify it in relation to a specific subject and a specific intention. In
Ingarden's terms, familiarity is a function of concretization, in which
everything actualized becomes familiar by virtue of being constituted
in previously experienced aspects. In Iser's terms, familiarity is a

function of the second-level integration that makes schematized meaning personally significant: "the significance of the meaning can only be ascertained when the meaning is related to a particular reference, which makes it translatable into *familiar* terms" (*Act*, pp. 150–1), my italics; cf. also pp. 122–3).

Familiarity, in short, is not something that can be found in various elements of a text, but rather a signal that reading, and understanding, have already occurred. In the case of Iser's critical writings, the reading that has occurred, and that allows Iser to "identify" the familiar elements in the text, is, naturally, Iser's. More accurately speaking, the "text" within which Iser locates the familiar is not the text at all, but Iser's *intention* – what Ingarden calls the reconstruction. From this perspective, the "implied reader" is simply one of many objects Iser actualizes in his complex concretization of the works he reads. It is different from other such objects only insofar as it is compiled out of lower-level actualizations – the conventions, contexts, etc. – that form the repertoire. In the terms of his own theory and that of Ingarden, Iser differs from other critics only in that he attributes his concretizations to a reader implied by the text, while they attribute theirs to its form, historical period, rhetorical strategy, or authorial intention. In all cases, what we call the work, or text, is always already our own concretization.

The point I am making, then, is not that Iser fails to demonstrate his theory of reading, but that he demonstrates it in spite of himself. Intent on avoiding subjectivism, he attributes familiar patterns to the text. He claims these patterns serve as catalysts for complex gestalt formations, but they are really the product of his own such formations. By confusing his understanding and the textual structure, he persuasively, if inadvertently, corroborates his model of dialectical understanding: the familiarity of the familiar elements he sees in the "text" is the proof of their enclosure within his personal gestalt formation. In other words, Iser can locate familiar conventions only because he has already concretized them according to the synthetic dialectic his theory describes. The "text" cannot help but confirm and thematize his theory, precisely because it has already been read, and made sense of, within the gestalt furnished by that theory. Similarly, Iser's theory undergoes a constant revision as it incorporates and responds to new texts; for each reading "recognizes" this method based on familiarity and provokes its reassessment. In this sense, his whole critical practice is emblematic of his theoretical model: it is an ongoing process of self-correction that, having concretized texts into familiar shapes, is confronted with the image of its own theoretical energy and forced continually to reassess it. This perhaps explains why Iser's theory, while retaining its basic shape, has continually expanded over the past fifteen years to incorporate everything from hermeneutics and speech-act theory to gestalt psychology, while his critical work, intent on recovering original reader responses to fictional texts, can only reiterate a response to the text of his theory.

Phenomenology and Referentiality

The inability of Ingarden and Iser to attain their critical goals does not mean that they are poor phenomenologists. Rather, it points to a problem intentional models of meaning pose for criticism. If one defines literary meaning as an imaging intention, one reduces it to an ephemeral event, a uniquely self-present intuition. Such a model may explain the euphoria associated with aesthetic experience, but it also closes the door on intersubjective communication about a work's meaning. If each intuition is an event unique unto itself, no conceptual account can hope to preserve it for examination.

A dialectical model of reading seems to solve this dilemma by positing a continual transformation of image into idea. In reality, such a model carries its own double bind. The fullness of the image can metamorphose into conceptual truth only to the extent that a single construct can be granted two divergent identities and functions: Iser's "text" must exist both as a positional force and a referential field. It must both found a new world unique at every instant and efface itself in the designation of familiar pre-existent reality. This double identity does not lend itself to a simple critical program. Any attempt to seize the gestalt "in formation" displaces it with the already known: the virtually new world is lost in the language of the known. Conversely, Iser's attempt to start with the known, by identifying familiar references, obscures its object under the personal concretization of the reading intention.

Ingarden tries to avoid this dilemma by deliberately separating the work from the concretization. This allows him to assign the positional force to the schematizations of the work and confine the referential function to the concretization. Unfortunately, this move also separates reading into two opposed operations, each of which serves as an obstacle to the other. The work of "experiential" reading that synthesizes new "objects" out of previously experienced aspects and the conventional pure meanings of the text finds itself undone by a "reflective" reading that recasts the private construct into a transparent, shared conceptual structure. And because the concretization (act) of the first reading serves as the referential (structure) for the second, Ingarden's serialization raises the suspicion that criticism is inevitably self-referential. Yet this is a conclusion he adamantly rejects.

Paradoxically, the same conclusion forms the basis for a different approach to phenomenological criticism: that of the Geneva School critics, at least two of which, Georges Poulet and Jean-Pierre Richard, renounce any claim to a "former" experience or stable textual schema. Instead of focusing on their own, or any implied reader's, concretizations, Poulet and Richard animate their reader with a consciousness unique to the critical text and the event of its reading. In other words, their works perform the very event of concretizing consciousness rather than recounting its evaluation.

Each movement in this performance reasserts the assumptions of the intentional model of meaning as the French theoreticians apply it to the "work" of literature. Because they prefer an intersubjective model to Ingarden's or Iser's "object-centered" approach, Poulet and Richard focus almost entirely on the writing consciousness. However, they do not attempt to find this consciousness in a single text. Rather, they build their works out of citations gleaned from every conceivable source – letters, confessions, journals, newspaper articles, literary criticism, poetry, drama, and fiction. Their criticism, then, quite literally forms its own text: the phrases (or schemata) it examines belong to an "other", but they cannot be found, *in such a configuration*, in any of that "other's" works. In this way, the critical piece is assured of "representing" the consciousness of the author in question; but it cannot interfere or compete with any previous concretizations of his work by the reader.

Further, to ensure that their readers will indeed be able to "live" the consciousness in question, Poulet and Richard focus on passages that schematize aspects likely to resonate in the reader's own past experience. Specifically, they articulate their critical performance around the most primal "meanings": those of the body, its sensations, perceptions, and spatio-temporal matrices. Out of such meanings, the critic – and his reader – gradually extract a consciousness; in so doing they convert the lived percepts and sensations into conceptual certainty. From his experience of a consciousness, the reader derives his ideas of the author.

In Poulet's work this identity constitutes itself temporally. Starting from the moment of Cartesian reflection, consciousness develops certainty through duration and reason, ultimately defining its world. For Richard, the same self-definition occurs spatially: the subject gains definition by enclosing itself in an ever more complex series of relationships with the objects of its world. The dialectic we live in Poulet's texts is that of perception and reflection: each successive perception triggers a reflection that advances "me" on the road to self-certainty and prepares further perceptions. In Richard's work, the same dialectic takes place between act and object: an obsessive property is located within an object; that object correlated to the act it implies; that act correlated to a further object it intends, and so forth.

In both of these types of criticism, the question of the original schematic text, or of its concretization by a reader, has been displaced by a *present* intention that continually transforms itself from image to idea. The process of this transformation no doubt parallels that described by Iser's theory, but while Iser tries to examine the residues left by prior intentions, Poulet and Richard are content to animate in their reader a gestalt formation that can never be correlated to any specific work or even a specific moment of their target subject. In other words, rather than choosing a referent and then seeking a means of reference, they turn their writing intention back on itself, so that the search for conceptual truth becomes its own explicit referent.

This critical strategy produces interpretations which are intensely self-reflective; but it also elegantly solves the problem of referentiality. Poulet and Richard reconcile the conceptual exigencies of traditional criticism with the lived meaning that interests them by making the positional event of reading the referent of its own referential thrust: the imaging consciousness develops into an idea of itself as an image developing into an idea. In this way, imagination and reflection are welded into a single gesture; understanding no longer obliterates the aesthetic experience because it is itself the concretization occasioning that experience.

There are, of course, other ways of coping with the issue of referentiality that phenomenological theories of meaning raise. As the coming chapters will show, there has been a tendency during the past twenty years to defuse the problem either by redefining the *object of critical knowledge* or by redefining the *nature of objective truth*. In the next chapter, I shall consider the first of these strategies, taking as my point of departure a critic whose preoccupation with individual meaning exceeds that of the phenomenologists: Norman Holland.

Part Two
Subjective and Objective Criticism: Psychoanalytic and Hermeneutic Theories of Meaning

5

Norman Holland:
Reading as Self Re-Creation

The Self in the Text

If I place Holland immediately after the phenomenologists in this study, it is because his work carries to its logical extreme one implication of their theories, namely that individual readings refer above all to the subject who intends them. Like the phenomenologists, Holland sees reading as an interaction between textual object and individual consciousness. This is particularly the case in his first work of theory, *The Dynamics of Literary Response*,[1] where the object of scrutiny – a "work" generated by the reader's simultaneous introjection and conceptualization of the text's fantasy material, as modulated by the text's "form" – very closely approximates concretization as described in the preceding chapter.

A distilled version of the same notion persists in Holland's more recent work, *5 Readers Reading*,[2] where reading emerges as one manifestation of our ongoing project of self-replication. By redefining identity in holistic terms, this more resolutely subjective model grounds itself in a form of dialectical logic quite akin to that used by Iser in his theory of gestalt formation.

And like both Iser and Ingarden, Holland puts himself in a double bind when he attempts to reconcile theory and practice. His theoretical model persuasively argues that literary meaning is a personal experience unique to each reading subject; but his allegiance to the discipline of criticism forces him to argue the feasibility of translating such radically private experience into shared knowledge. Consequently, Holland's averred goal, "to understand the subjective reactions of others" (*Dynamics*, p. 108), carries within it a contradiction in terms: truly subjective reactions are by definition those which fall outside of the conventional, shared categories into which understanding must translate its public objects.

This belief in institutional knowledge can also be seen in Holland's insistence that theories of reading must describe literary response in terms of more general systems and principles. Critics like Poulet, who correctly point out the merger of self and other in reading, leave the job half done, according to Holland: they merely "describe the phenomenon without explaining it" (*Dynamics*, p. 67). A complete theory of literary response should "explain why we respond to literary works as we do," and "to explain a phenomenon is to relate it to principles more general than itself" (*Dynamics*, p. 309). For Holland, such principles can be found in the overall study of personality and behaviour we call psychology.

Holland's earliest theory of reading, articulated in the *Dynamics*, makes the transition to psychology by recasting the traditional formalist description of the literary artifact in psychoanalytic categories. In other words, he retains the notion of a semi-autonomous literary structure but assigns each component in that structure a psychological function. Meaning, for instance, is not merely the conceptual judgment of literary criticism, but a more fundamental, multi-leveled process of transformation by which fantasy material *in* the text, yet *shared* by the reader, is elaborated or repressed in such a way as to produce gratification. For Holland, literary criticism which "understands" a text by reducing it to a limited number of known systems or terms is only a secondary operation that follows the primal affective experience of the reader (*Dynamics*, pp. 4–7). This primary experience takes place when the work suddenly "grabs us by the lapels" and absorbs us completely within its texture (*Dynamics*, pp. 5, 27).

To explain such absorption, Holland postulates a deeper type of meaning operating at the unconscious as well as the conscious level in the reader. He theorizes that the literary work embodies a "core" fantasy, which is recognized by the reader and embellished so as to form the apparent meaning of the story. At the same time, this apparent meaning is modulated by the form of the work, which thus functions like the defense processes used by the ego to manage its fantasies. The result is a complex interaction of reader and text through which "primitive wishes and fears" are transformed into "significance and coherence," thereby providing the reader with "pleasure" (*Dynamics*, p. 30). For Holland, this basic paradigm informs virtually all narrative. "All stories –and all literature – have this basic way of meaning: they transform the unconscious fantasy discoverable through psychoanalysis into the conscious meanings discovered by conventional interpretation" (*Dynamics*, p. 28).

The two sources and two phases of this transformation can be roughly organized according to the dichotomies of conscious or unconscious and text or psyche. On the level of the unconscious, Holland postulates, we "introject the text and feel its nuclear fantasy as though it were our own unconscious fantasy"; consciously, we produce conceptual meaning "by a process of successive abstraction and classification from the words and events of the text" (*Dynamics*, p. 180). In the first of these two interactions, the reader, upon unconsciously recognizing a particular core fantasy, "introjects the literary work so that what happens 'in' it feels as though it were happening 'in' him, more properly, in some undifferentiated 'either'" (*Dynamics*, p. 179). This introjection allows one to feel a text's fantasy as though it were one's own, and it has been described elsewhere by Simon O. Lesser as "analogizing."[3] Roughly speaking, analogizing is the psychoanalytic theoretician's answer to Ingarden's theory of previously experienced aspects: it attributes the personal shape of literary objects to a stock of past experience. However, in Holland's theory this experience takes the form of our entire psychic makeup: "when we perceive things in life, we bring to them our pre-existing psychic structure and experience; we do the same when we perceive literature" (*Dynamics*, p. 180).

Thus, while Ingarden limits his theory to the aspects of perceptions, and Sartre focuses on the abstract rules that underlie imagination, Holland's theory includes under a single notion all manner of fantasies, defensive structures, "intellectual ideas of meaning" (*Dynamics*, pp. 179–80), "memories of similar pleasures we have had" (*Dynamics*, p. 75), and "feelings [the work] did not stimulate" (*Dynamics*, p. 102). Still, the reader can only bring into play such a vast store of experience if the text somehow elicits it. For Holland, then, the work "brings . . . its potentialities for fantasy, for defensive transformations, and for meaning" (*Dynamics*, pp. 179–80); while "the reader unconsciously elaborates the fantasy content of the literary work with his own versions of these fantasies" (*Dynamics*, p. 52).

At the same time as we elaborate a fantasy in conjunction with the text, we nonetheless maintain those higher ego functions that permit both the perception and processing of words on the page *and* the anticipation and appraisal of successive episodes of the story. In other words, while reading, "our minds are split in two" (*Dynamics*, p. 81), much as they are during psychoanalysis and other such phenomena: "if in psychoanalysis, hypnosis, and dreaming, we have a kind of 'core' in ourselves which is regressed to the most primitive level of our being and, surrounding that core, a sort of 'rind' of higher ego-functions, then we might well be in the same schizoid state when we are engrossed in a literary 'entertainment'" (*Dynamics*, p. 89).

This explanation dovetails neatly with Sartre's theory of a reading consciousness at once empty knowledge and imaging knowledge: on the one hand, our mind maintains a vestige of reflective awareness necessary to synthesize a whole out of discrete rules; on the other, it inclines toward a state of undifferentiated plenitude where the subject/object distinction no longer obtains.

In sum, *The Dynamics of Literary Response* casts reading as a form of self-actualization and self-analysis through which the inner-most text of the self surfaces in the guise of the literary narrative. Thus disguised, it is available as an object of reflection for the higher ego-functions. So when a reader introjects a work, he does not just feel what is going on "within" it as though it were going on "in" him; he also sees his unconscious fantasies and fears in the innocuous form of "another's" experiences. In this sense, the inner/outer exchange of introjection is only a preliminary version of a more important exchange between our primitive unconscious core and our higher ego-functions. Knowing the literary work is not the end of reading. Instead, by opening a path of communication between the conscious and the unconscious, reading serves a profound thera-peutic function.

Obviously, this model shifts the center of attention away from the work of literature as an independent or "ontically heteronomous" entity. In Holland's "self-centered" model, a work is just that: *work* performed by a reader, an extended process of self-actualization undertaken by an individual subject. Accordingly, the task of the critic needs to be redefined. Neither the text nor its subjective correlate, the author, can be considered the central object of inquiry; for the "other" we encounter in reading, which Blanchot makes into a principle of absolute antagonism, which Sartre uses as the founda-tion for an economy of expansive freedom, and which Poulet visualizes as an alien yet interior consciousness, is in Holland's theory none other than the reader himself. In this light, critical programs such as Poulet's or Richard's, intent on animating an authorial consciousness within the reader, seem as off track as the more traditional attempts to recover the author's "intention" or the "autonomous" work's form.

Even Ingarden's goal of matching the concretization to the work becomes less interesting in light of Holland's theory: the central transaction does not, after all, take place between personal text and objective text, but between the reader's core identity and his conscious identity. In this sense, the *Dynamics* carries to its extreme the conclusion implicit in Ingarden's theory of aspects: the readings we produce are not "about" the literary work, they are "about" us, or, more rigorously speaking, about their own genesis.

Identity Themes: The Text of the Self

It is only with Holland's more recent theoretical works, and in particular *5 Readers Reading*, that the implications of his theory for criticism become apparent. Abandoning the notion of an objective text as pendent to the reading activity, Holland proposes what he calls a transactive model of reading, in which the literary work is divested of any autonomous content or independent identity: "the inanimate literary work is not that, not a work in itself, but the occasion for some person's work" (*Readers*, p. 17). And the "work" which texts occasion is that of the reader's re-creation of his own identity: "we use the literary work to symbolize and finally to replicate ourselves. We take the work into ourselves and make it part of our own psychic economy – identity re-creates itself" ("Transactive Criticism: Re-Creation Through Identity," p. 342).[4]

In this new perspective, the work's loss is the individual reader's gain. Holland attributes to the reader the enduring sameness he denies the literary artifact; and he locates the principle of that sameness in what he calls the *identity theme*. This functions as a unique personal paradigm, a sort of deep structure of the personality that is expressed in every thought, act, or perception of the individual. It is not a static construct, but a continually evolving gestalt that takes in external reality and reorders it according to the unique psychic makeup of the individual. The identity theme thus shapes experience in its own image at the same time it is undergoing modifications in response to that experience. Holland conceptualizes this process as a constant self re-creation through which identity is maintained: "the individual (considered as the continuing creator of variations on an identity theme) relates to the world as he does to a poem or a story; he uses its physical reality as grist with which to re-create himself, that is, to make yet another variation of his single, enduring identity" (*Readers*, pp. 128–9).

Because individual identity is the only enduring order in Holland's system, it necessarily takes the place of the text and the work as the object of literary study. The critical program in *5 Readers Reading* therefore concentrates primarily on the identity themes of five individuals as they relate to texts. The procedures Holland prescribes are as follows. One chooses a certain individual, determines his identity theme, and then seeks correlations between that theme and the particular responses a text provokes. In principle, the response should bear the mark of its identity theme, in the form of the associations, emphases, suppressions, and assumptions that distinguish the subject's idiosyncratic interpretation.

The crucial step in this program is the uncovering of the identity theme. For Holland, this involves examining a selection of the subject's oral and written expressions, such as verbal responses to literary texts, personality tests, and literary interpretation, in view of extracting a coherent theme or pattern. In other words, one determines the subject's identity theme in much the same way one locates thematic or formal patterns in any text.

The difficulty with this procedure is that it renders the identity theme of the subject in question inseparable from that of the critic who describes it. As Holland outlines them, both the identity theme the critic formulates and the reading responses he then correlates with that theme are grounded in articulated texts – interviews, test results, conversations, writing samples, etc. Yet these texts themselves must be interpreted by the transactive investigator in order to yield their information; and that investigator can only perceive according to the patterns of *his* identity theme. Holland himself argues that "objective analysis of a text . . . reveals only the story as it was re-created in the mind of the analyser" (*Readers*, p. 130).

What transactive criticism reveals, then, is not objective truth, but just one more instance of self-replication – a re-creation of the analyst's identity theme, under the guise of objective analysis. And the subject whose self re-creation fills *5 Readers Reading* is none of the five students described, but Holland himself, whose hundreds of pages of interpretation have predigested and reformulated the raw data of the readers' responses and therefore represent the only sustained reader transaction to which we could possibly respond.

This conclusion is not something I am imposing on Holland's program from the outside, but the extension of his own principles. Indeed, if we take the transactive model seriously, there is no way criticism could represent anything but the critic's self-replication, nor any reason why it should claim to. Holland himself periodically stresses the fact that from the transactive perspective there is no difference between literature traditionally conceived and literary criticism: "if we absorb literature like the rest of the outer world, through adaptations that protect gratification in terms of one particular identity theme, then we respond to statements about literature in the same way" (*Readers*, p. 210). By dissolving the distinction between literary reading and the reading of literary criticism, this formulation does away with the distinction between literary texts and critical texts. And it suggests that propositional knowledge as traditionally defined is beyond the critic's grasp: there are simply no such things as objective facts about literary texts or meanings.

Still, even as it repudiates traditional objectivity Holland's theory adumbrates a way to re-establish the epistemology of criticism on intersubjective grounds. True, texts can no longer be thought to carry a "message" from author to reader, nor to have any autonomous identity, since they are always already each reader's self-replication and have no function other than to reinforce and prolong reader (and author) identity. From this point of view, critical and literary works alike are little more than the loci for isolated and multiple projects of self-perpetuation. Yet the very fact that multiple projects of self-reenactment can share a single textual locus suggests that Holland's ideas could be extended to found a theory of purely *intersubjective* identity capable of grounding a notion of shared understanding.

5 Readers Reading, for instance, simultaneously incarnates Holland's self re-creation (through a transaction with the subject reader's texts, which it partially incorporates), my re-creation (through transaction with its texts, parts of which subsist here as citations), and my reader's re-creation. Thus, while it may have no autonomous "objective" identity, *5 Readers Reading* nonetheless does mark a common ground for our different self-replications; and to that extent we could doubtless negotiate some definition of it or statement about it which, by common consent of the interested parties, we could declare to be "true."[5]

Short of taking this step and regrounding "objective facts" in intersubjectivity, one cannot justify any notion of critical truth within Holland's theory. Only by relinquishing the claim to objective authority can the transactive critic bring his practice into line with his theory. Yet this is precisely the step Holland refuses to take. By steadfastly maintaining for himself the privilege of objectivity he denies other readers, Holland invalidates his own theory and inadvertently reinforces the very notions of reading and meaning he claims to be subverting. This paradoxical behaviour is exemplified in his treatment of the identity theme.

Holistic Logic vs. Causal Logic

Given Holland's holistic view of identity – his assumption that it perpetuates itself by absorbing and reforming reality at the same time that it expands and realigns itself in response to that reality – one might expect him to define the identity theme in functional rather than historical terms. After all, as the very condition of identity, in the absence of which no event or perception could be registered, the identity theme could scarcely be attributed to any specific event in an individual's existence. Sum of all the moments on one's life, the identity theme is also the principle which founds those moments as discrete, meaningful instances.

Indeed, Holland's general definitions of the identity theme stress how it works rather than where it comes from: "a human being experiences by adding a variation to his identity theme. In this way he re-creates his identity theme" (*Readers*, p. 231). Rather than a simple structure, identity is a means, "a way of grasping the mixture of sameness and difference which makes up a human life."[6]

Such functional definitions refuse to qualify identity as either the cause or the effect of particular acts, insisting rather that identity and experience are inextricably bound. This is particularly striking in the more aphoristic definitions Holland offers, most of which could be inverted without affecting their validity. For instance, "identity re-creates itself" or "interpretation is a function of identity" ("Criticism," pp. 342 and 340) can, in the framework of a transactive theory, just as correctly be stated: the self recreates its identity and identity is a function of interpretation. Neither term is the origin of the other because neither can exist without the other. In the terms of Holland's theory, each "is" only through its transactions with the other, and it is the ongoing dialectic of such transactions that we normally call "identity."

Of course, the same could be said of identity *vis-à-vis any* "other" term: the self recreates itself by making everything into itself. Thus, Holland's breakdown of the operations of self-replication involved in reading: defenses must be matched, style seeks itself, fantasy projects fantasies, and character transforms characteristically (*Readers*, pp. 113–23). From a purely functional perspective, identity involves the ongoing determination of sameness or similarity. This applies as well to Holland's critical work.

It is by ascertaining sameness between two elements that the critical patterns can be developed by the transactive critic. That is, the discovery of patterns such as the reader's identity theme and the themes of his idiosyncratic interpretations necessarily draws on a figural logic based on resemblance. Holland describes such activity as "grouping the particular details of a work together under certain themes, then grouping those particular themes together until I arrive at a few basic terms which constitute a central theme."[7] Within this operation, it is the similarity of the components, their fit within a single overall pattern, that validates the critic's work, just as it is the fit of this pattern to other verbalizations of the subject that validates those verbalizations – and the critic's pattern – as portions of his identity. So both the formulation of specific identity themes and their subsequent validation draw on figural or holistic logic rather than on causal filiation.

This redefinition of critical truth succeeds in defusing the referential question, but it almost succeeds too well. The transactive interpretation can only be judged on the basis of its thematic consistency, and given the postulates of Holland's theory, it can hardly fail. Since both the pattern of the identity theme and that of the reader's reading are generated by the same *critical* identity, they cannot help but resemble each other. Their apparent separateness, which Holland is at great pains to maintain, dissembles their reproduction of a single pattern – that of the critic's identity theme. If Holland's theory is at all on the mark, the diverse interpretations of any given critic can always be aligned within a figure of similarity regardless of their source – and that should hold true whether the nominal object of interpretation is a "literary" text, a critical text, or a text of free associations elicited by psychoanalysis. In this sense, Holland's practical program is most notable in its amazement at a tautology it clearly does not perceive as such: one's interpretations resemble one's interpretations.

If Holland does not perceive this tautology, it is because he does not consider the derivation of the identity theme and its correlation to the reader's interpretations to be operations of the same status. This is because he supplements the holistic operations of the first phase with psychological "evidence" he clearly considers to be factual – which is to say propositional and referential. This factual supplement takes the form of a "clinical" analysis of psychological data such as writing samples, test results, and personal history; and its apparent objective rigor obscures for Holland the figural under-pinnings of the identity theme. It thus conceals from him the tautology of his critical work at the same time it assures him the authority of objective knowledge.

In fact, the intrusion of objective knowledge occurs at every level of Holland's work. We have seen that a functional or holistic defini-tion is all that a theory of self re-creation needs or can validate. Yet early in his theoretical description, Holland turns to the causal paradigms of scientific discourse in order to "prove" the presence of identity themes. His recourse to psychological "data" redefines identity in terms of its origin:

a newborn child is born with a great (but not unlimited) range of potentialities. In all the various transactions of maternal care, particularly feeding, but also giving, touching, bathing, changing, and the rest, its mother-person actuates a specific way of being. She imprints on the infant a "primary identity," ... an unchanging core of continuity which the individual brings to all later trans-actions and all later changes in himself. ("Criticism," pp. 337–8)

This "historical" account of the identity theme finds its pendant in Holland's critical practice, where the initial "clinical" phase collects various pieces of "data" as evidence for an objective determination of the identity theme. The process differs from the matching of patterns Holland undertakes in the second phase of his criticism, in that it locates the identity theme referentially, through certain proven indicators. And the theme that emerges does so bit by bit, as the effect of a constellation of causes, rather than holistically, as a pattern always present in its totality. Finally, the validity of this identity theme is assured by its filiation to the discipline of psychology:

the plain fact of the matter, however, is: no one, until quite recently, knew what went on in the mind of the reader because no one had a psychology adequate to the problem. Today, however, we do have such a psychology. We can know more about the writer and about the way he set down a fragment of his personal myth. By the same token, we can also know more about the reader's personal myth and we can discover from his associations with a text how he is responding to the writer's original creation. (*Poems in Persons*, p. 60)[8]

Of course, a "plain fact" is something that Holland's theory cannot accommodate. Propositional language that claims to make true statements about an objective reality is in direct contradiction to the kind of personal meaning his notion of transaction underwrites. Yet Holland frequently speaks in "facts" in *5 Readers* (see p. 355, for instance) and refers to the kind of understanding they provide as a "richer kind of knowledge" (*Readers*, p. 67). Indeed, this privileging of a type of meaning alien to his own system occurs in virtually all of his work. His dependence on Freudian models of psychological development in the *Dynamics* scarcely needs to be cited. In the later works, the ideas of Lichtenstein supplant those of Freud, but the supremacy of factual discourse is maintained. In *Poems in Persons*, for instance, Holland bastions his interpretation, and justifies his choice of a relatively minor poet, H.D., with a text he grants the status of unique document (p. 45). As he ingenuously puts it, "the singular importance of H.D. lies not in her poems (or her fiction and essays) but in one unique source of insight she has left us, her account of her analysis with Freud" (*Poems*, p. 9). Because H.D. recorded her experiences with the master in the enlightened language of psychoanalysis, Holland feels her journal can give us "an absolutely unparalleled picture of the infantile forces that engendered a poet's life pattern, including the fact of her writing, and, indeed, the very style of her writing" (*Poems*, p. 45).

Contrary to what he would have us believe, then, identity has two different identities in Holland's work. On the one hand, it is a clinical fact, having its origins in the early stages of infancy and discernible through the analysis of experimental data. On the other hand, it is a continually evolving pattern, figurally derived through grouping according to similarity, and functioning holistically in a way that defies linear causality. Similarly, Holland himself maintains two disparate identities – in defiance of the unity of self his theory predicates. During the first phase of his work he is Holland the lay psychoanalyst, versed in the intricacies of referential proof and drawing his authority from the objectivity of scientific fact. During the second phase, he is Holland the literary critic, generating thematic patterns on the basis of metaphoric recombinations whose proof lies in their consonance with the patterns he attributes to various identities.

It is obvious to what degree this schizoid posture undermines Holland's own thesis: a theory postulating universal self-replication cannot draw on an assumption of self-less objectivity. What is not so obvious is the reason for Holland's "self-denial." While his own theory of identity could explain it in terms of a recurrent ambivalence unique to Holland – who ceaselessly pits fact against figure, outside against inside, in his attempts to unite them – there are also less obvious theoretical reasons for this schizophrenia.

Identity, Tautology, and Collective Effort

If Holland consciously or unconsciously grounds his identity themes in objective fact, it is because of an incompatibility between his self-centered model of reading and the critical practice to which it aspires. Because the transactive model stresses *individual* identity and defines it in terms of a uniquely personal replication, it cannot, rigorously construed, found a critical practice in the traditional sense of the word. The reasons are multiple.

Consider first the work of transactive criticism. Like all interpretation it proceeds by matching: critical reading purports to be an extension and enrichment of the literary work and therefore must show that the structures proposed have counterparts in the target text. However, Holland's theory denies the literary work any intrinsic structure; hence this matching of personal text and other text cannot be shown. Instead, personal text is matched against personal text: the identity theme derived from non-literary data is matched to that derived from literary responses. This makes the referent of the first phase the second phase – and vice versa. The only "work" being enriched is that of a single identity – whether one thinks of that identity as the target reader's, the critic's, or that of the reader of the critical work. Transactive criticism is thus doubly crippled in traditional terms: it cannot claim to enrich understanding of a cultural object; nor can it claim to promote direct interpersonal communication.

In fact, the program's only apparent benefit, that of furthering self-definition, is equally dubious. In order to assert itself, identity must continually confront, absorb, and recreate itself within, new objects. Yet the confrontation which transactive criticism performs is between the identity theme and itself. Doubling back to recreate itself through itself, the transactive critic's experience more resembles narcissism than identity consolidation.[9]

It is to rescue his program from this futile self-enclosure that Holland tries to separate the "fact" of the first-phase identity theme from the figure of the second. Yet the objective logic he imports to this end is more destructive to his theory's truth claims than the ills it seeks to cure. A theory granting primacy to self re-creation has little fear of narcissism; for the negative connotations of that notion derive from an "objectivism" which transactive theory implicitly rejects. However, when such objectivism is imported into the very theory that purports to undo it, the validity of that theory is put into question.

In other words, if Holland himself did not contaminate his theory with objective logic, it could not be criticized from an objective point of view: all reproaches could be dismissed as self re-creations of the detractor. But by not adhering rigorously to the logic of his own system, Holland divides it against itself: the "objective facts" designed to validate it implictly argue against the adequacy of its transactive paradigm; the transactive paradigm in turn puts into question the value of the objective proof. The result is a theory and practice turned against itself.

The problem is not, then, that Holland's theory lacks potential validation principles – I indicated earlier the lines of an argument for intersubjective validation which it could adopt. The problem is that Holland cannot decide between two directly contradictory principles. And this indecision no doubt derives from his desire to maintain a traditional, i.e., objective, version of literary study within the confines of his theory. In this sense, Holland's attempt to defuse the theoretical "impossibility" of knowing the literary work *per se* only opens the door to new problems. By shifting the referential thrust of reading from the text or work to the reader, he makes it easier to know what one's reading is "about," at least in theory. But the lack of an intersubjective model of validation deprives Holland's work of any theoretical consistency or institutional value. His resolutely private notion of identity does not lend itself simply to a theory of shared understanding.

We are now in a position to understand both the failure of trans-active criticism to attract widespread practice and the logic of treating Holland's work in sequence with the phenomenological theoreticians. For his inability to control the relationship between subjectivity and objectivity springs from his recasting of intentionality as a duality.

Like the phenomenologists, Holland grounds meaning in an inter-action between subject and object. But unlike them, he does not understand this interaction as a bilateral unity. Instead, as the early *Dynamics* illustrates, he sees it as a coming together of individual and world. The autonomy he implictly grants each of these monads places him squarely in the tradition of what one might call objectivism – by which I mean the epistemology of those scientists, historians, and others who believe the identity and essence of cultural objects to be independent of our perception of them.

Holland shares this objectivism with his New Critical contem-poraries, who also draw on a "fractured" version of intentionality – but with one important difference. While Holland vectorizes intention subjectively by assuming that meaning originates in the intending subject and is only subsequently conferred upon the object at hand, the New Critics vectorize it objectively, making the textual "object" the source of meaning, but granting the reading subject final auth-ority over that meaning.

This sleight of hand, which we have noted in *The Dynamics of Literary Response*, draws on a distorted version of intentionality that separates the intending consciousness from its object and declares each to have authority over the other. As the single locus of many acts, the text seems an object with a structure and necessity all its own. Since every reader has to contend with this structure, it takes on an originating role. Yet because the work only "means" in reference to some subject's act, its meaning must be contingent upon that subject.

The losers in this scheme are many: most obviously the notion of the author's authority over meaning; less obviously the related notion that a collective can determine with some authority the range and value of the meanings a text can have. When one liberates the notions of intentional object and intending subject from one another, one runs the risk of falling into pure subjectivism, pure objectivism, or both. If a literary work is taken for an autonomous structure, the author's role as arbiter of meaning cannot be maintained. At the same time, since all readings presumably have equal authority, no single critic can arrogate unto himself, or his "reading," the authority denied the author. Meaning becomes a random subjective event triggered by an object beyond knowledge; criticism, an occulted process of narcissism and self-replication.

Misread as the confrontation between determining subject and autonomous object, then, intentionality undermines the very discipline of literary study. Reread from a different perspective, the same principle can furnish the theoretical foundation for just such a discipline – as the work of David Bleich or E. D. Hirsch illustrates. By redefining objective reality as a function of subjective action, subsuming, as it were, one face of intentionality within the other, Bleich integrates his commitment to subjective response into a coherent theory of collective knowledge. E. D. Hirsch achieves quite different ends – the establishment of objective knowledge – through much the same strategy. He postulates that an intentional object indeed requires an intending subject, and the original, and therefore most authoritative, such subject in the case of a literary work is the author. Hirsch thus argues for the recovery of the author's meaning as the first step in literary study. At the same time, the enduring identity of a literary work, the fact that it can exist through a multiplicity of reading intentions, suggests that a coherent and valid discipline of interpretation can be founded on shared intersubjective categories. Meaning, from this perspective, has precious little to do with the idiosyncratic particularities of the individual reader: it is not a private concretization, but a conventional category willed by the author. As such it can be determined with reasonable certainty by the institutions charged with interpreting literary works.

Because both Bleich and Hirsch explicitly redefine particular meaning in terms of larger collectives and shared convention, they make a convenient transition from phenomenological theories of meaning to the later structuralist ideas stressing system over instance. However much they claim to make the case for individual intention, both critics define such acts intersubjectively, thus abandoning the idea of meaning as an image or pseudo-perceptual private vision. In this way, the problem of referentiality is skirted: once meaning and reading are no longer conceived as a presence unto the subject of an imaginational object, literary knowledge, and hence critical truth, need not entail the recuperation of such presence.

The central problem of the earlier theoreticians persists, nonetheless: meaning still exhibits two contradictory faces (phases) when closely scrutinized. Like Ingarden and Holland, Bleich and Hirsch will attempt to cleave the object of their inquiry into separate structures and theoretically distinct phases. And these dichotomies will ultimately work against the theories they are supposed to support, suggesting that a unified theory and practice of meaning may require accepting its irreducible duplicity.

6

David Bleich:
The Dialectics of Subjectivity

Subjectivity through Objectification

David Bleich's avowed interest in subjective response and psycho-analytic approaches puts him squarely in the tradition of Norman Holland. Yet, unlike Holland, Bleich recognizes from the outset the need to redefine objective knowledge and "facts" if one is to shift the focus of criticism to individual response. He therefore elaborates a theory of knowledge that reconciles shared understanding and individual intention by positing truth to be a construct motivated by personal and collective needs. Accordingly, he shifts the goal of criticism from the recuperation of past intention to the formulation of an interpretation adaptive to current needs.

Such ideas build on presuppositions that have gained acceptance only in the wake of structuralism. The most obvious of these is the assumption that shared categories, not material reality, determine meaningful entities. But in contrast to structuralism's institutional bias, Bleich maintains Holland's commitment to the individual reader by subordinating all sign systems to the human need to symbolize from which they arise. Because this does away with any notion of a transcendent structure, what we would otherwise call "objective description" is, from Bleich's point of view, merely an act of resymbolization triggered by a particular need. Subjective criticism thus posits from the outset a conflation of personal motivation and "objective" assessment.

The key to this move lies in what Bleich calls the "subjective paradigm." Drawing on T. S. Kuhn's book *The Structure of Scientific Revolution*,[1] he uses the term "paradigm" to designate "a shared mental structure, a set of beliefs about reality" (*Subjective Criticism*, p. 10);[2] and the "subjective" paradigm he advances believes that "for all practical purposes, reality is invented and not observed or discovered by human beings" (p. 11). In this perspective, knowledge is not a proposition about reality – a statement by subjects about objects – but a subject's response to current needs. So truth is not a state of affairs in the real world, but simply the product of one's current linguistic responses; it has no permanence but is constantly recreated in the face of new motivations: "under the subjective paradigm, new truth is created by a new use of language and a new structure of thought" (p. 18). Defined functionally, then, knowledge is simply an adaptive mechanism assuring the well-being of its creator.

On the one hand, this means there is no such thing as a functionally autonomous object: "an object is circumscribed and delimited by a subject's motives, his curiosities, and above all, his language" (p. 18). On the other hand, the process of validation that marks a particular linguistic response as truth does not depend on referential assessment. Instead, motivated negotiation between subjects determines what is true: "under the subjective paradigm, the common world of thought is established on just such a basis as the common world of sense. The latter world is subjectively determined by extended negotiations among perceivers" (p. 20).

By expanding the notion of reality-creation to encompass the communal enterprise of interpretation, Bleich provides a bridge between Holland's form of subjectivism and criticism's need for objective truth. In Bleich's system, *all* knowledge is interpretation, and it is validated as the satisfactory explanation of current phenomena through intersubjective negotiation. To the extent that situations are shared by individuals, shared knowledge is not only possible but necessary. So while both Holland and Bleich postulate the continual re-creation of reality by subjects, Bleich makes truth a function of *intersubjective* motivation rather than *intrasubjective* self-replication. This in turn allows him to explain the presence of apparently objective knowledge. If something appears objectively so, it is merely because all parties agree that it is so: beyond merely replicating their individuality, people collectively formulate an objective world in accordance with shared motivations.

Central to this notion is predication, defined as the act by which we transform our experience into an object of reflective thought by objectifying it into a concept. For Bleich, this act is an advanced form of infantile "control or management . . . that substitutes a cognitive initiative for an affective frustration," and it "is not simply a linguistic structure" but "the elemental form of conceptual thought" (p. 50). As the "foundation of language" (pp. 66, 237), it involves the assignment of a name to the experience from which we separate ourselves: "the name tells us that something *is*; that is, the name *objectifies* the thing. The mere fact that things have names reifies our sense of the objectivity of things. Our sense of reality depends on our separation between the concept and the experience" (p. 61).

The objectivity of the world is thus a function of naming, and hence of language, rather than the occasion for it. This assumes that language and predication are permanent and necessary functions of the human existence; and for Bleich, such is indeed the case. "All living things, especially animals, actively strive to preserve, protect, and prolong their lives and to enhance the life of the species," he declares (p. 64); and man's principal tool in this endeavor is the ability to objectify experience.[3]

Now to postulate objectification as a necessary component of subjectivity is nothing new: in many ways, Bleich's theory merely states in psychological language ideas implicit in the writings of phenomenologists such as Dufrenne. While Dufrenne correlates objectification to imagining, which in his system mediates between meaning as brute presence and conceptual understanding, Bleich frames a similar dialectic in terms of *symbolization* and *resymbolization*. This distinction is at the core of Bleich's critical program, and it introduces a temporal notion that merits further examination.

Symbolization and Resymbolization

To understand the notions of symbolization and resymbolization in Bleich's theory, one must first understand the importance of motives. If one assumes that "reality is invented" (p. 11) by subjects and that objects are "circumscribed and delimited by a subject's motives" (p. 18), then the only possible object of knowledge must itself be knowledge. And if knowledge is initiated out of current needs or motives, the goal of knowledge must be the uncovering of those motives. In other words, if one views all human discourse as the adaptational objectification of experience, one can best understand any given instance of discourse in terms of the specific motives behind that objectification – the end served.

In keeping with this overall assumption, Bleich is careful not to make the determination of motives optional for the subject. Since we perpetuate ourselves through self-awareness, and since our selves are defined as motivated predications, knowing one's self entails knowing one's motivations. Bleich describes this necessity phylogenetically, in terms of language acquisition:

in the human infant, *the acquisition of language and representational thought transforms goal directedness into the organ of consciousness.* This produces our capacity to view ourselves in terms of unconscious motives, in which we *assume* that all of our behavior is motivated; however, our knowledge of our behavior can become available only through language and thought. We are thus motivated to acquire self-awareness, which in turn gives us the capacity to regulate and to produce further, more complicated, more adaptive motives to govern growth. (p. 64)

In order to take hold of our existence, we must conceptualize – and thus control through objectification – our motives. Our primary motive in knowledge is therefore to know our motives.

This convoluted notion poses problems for the practice of criticism, since it encloses mentation in a regress of self-awareness having no obvious beginning or end point: the motive we uncover beneath our actions and the motive for the act of uncovering will always turn out to be one and the same, namely, to know our motives. Rather than confront such an aporia head on, Bleich elects the strategy of serialization we encountered in the work of Ingarden and Holland: he splits consciousness into an "initial" experiential phase, symbolization, and a subsequent reflective motivation, resymbolization. The latter is defined as the operation by which we assign motives to objectifications: "reality is *defined* symbolically. Reality is *explained* by resymbolization, which is the conceptualization of symbolized objects and processes in terms of subjective motives" (p. 88). In this framework, objectifications are symbolizations – at least in their initial form as simple linguistic designation: "the distinction between symbolization and resymbolization corresponds, respectively, to the use of language as simple denotation and as complex explanation" (pp. 65–6).

With respect to the theories previously outlined, then, symbolization and resymbolization form a serial dichotomy roughly analogous to that of concretization and reflective cognition, or imagination and conceptualization, or, most simply, initial reading and subsequent critical appraisal. It is nonetheless surprising that such a sequence should appear in Bleich's theory, where knowing act and known object are so deliberately intertwined: from a subjective point of view, the dissociation of symbolization and resymbolization can only be aberrant.

In fact, Bleich's assertion that "*the idea of resymbolization is both an explanation of language use and an explanation of explanation*" (p. 65) illustrates by example that the symbolizations one resymbolizes are themselves already resymbolizations. Because his theory is "grounded on the idea of 'development from' as opposed to 'growth toward'" (p. 12), because he sees knowledge as an ongoing adaptation of the intellecting mind to "ontogenetic and phylogenetic developmental demands" (p. 18), Bleich should recognize that every "new" symbolization is to some degree a simultaneous resymbolization of the symbolic objectification system currently held. To suppose the contrary would be to assume predications that are *not* adaptive and that do *not* partake of self-awareness. Bleich asserts that symbolizations are not definitive and that "when we become aware that a symbolic objectification system is unsatisfactory, we try to resymbolize or explain it" (p. 66). Surely, then, it follows that resymbolizations themselves are subject to resymbolization: as explanations become inadequate, they are revised.

In other words, maladaptive resymbolizations are further resymbolized, from which perspective they are mere symbolizations. Conversely, no symbolization can be posited that is so naive as not already to be a resymbolization: the development of new motives on the basis of increased self-awareness must necessarily build on existing self-awareness. In short, every symbolization is also a resymbolization and vice versa; the name one uses depends entirely on one's teleological perspective – whether one considers the moment/ structure in question a beginning or an end.

Bleich's analogy to denotation and explanation means to block the conflation of his two terms, but I think it rather betrays him. Denotation is in no way simply primordial designation: it draws on an extensive, previously established system of linguistic differentiation and designates a phenomenon precisely to the extent that it explains it in terms of pre-existing categories. As the discussion of Holland's work demonstrated (pp. 69–74), one can posit simple denotation only within an objectivist framework, where facts and references displace patterns and figures. In a subjective framework such as Bleich's, no predication can be conceived of that does not integrate experience into one's pre-existing conceptual framework – and that is precisely the definition of explanation.

It is no coincidence, then, that Bleich consistently resorts to the example of the infant when he wants to illustrate rudimentary symbolization. For barring the postulation of a primitive state of pre-linguistic innocence, original symbolization cannot be conceived. Because he is intent on maintaining the distinction between his two notions, Bleich has to argue that "a new experience enters consciousness as a new language system" and that only subsequently does it "automatically undergo motivated resymbolizations" (p. 137); but it is self-evident that if experience were embodied in a truly new language system, it could not enter consciousness – or be experienced – at all. For Bleich's argument to obtain, every instant of symbolization would require a rediscovery of primordial predication and no linguistic competence would accrue. On the contrary, I would argue that by its own logic *Subjective Criticism* conflates denotation and explanation, symbolization and resymbolization, within a paradoxical or non-self-identical notion of meaning whose two faces can best be related through a dialectical model.

Bleich himself indicates how this could be done when he describes "the child's mentation in the storytelling situation as a *subjective dialectic* which . . . represents the prototypical circumstance for subsequent forms of complex *reasoning*" (p. 136). As he sees it, the child listening to a story sets up a dialectic between the language system of that story, as communicated through sensory perception, and that of his own imaginative response. As the child symbolizes the predications of the story into his version of that story, "which he immediately objectifies as 'the story'," he resymbolizes or interprets this objectification, thereby entering into a sort of dialogue with himself (p. 136). And while Bleich maintains that "subsequent responses to this imaginary object are resymbolizations, or interpretations" (ibid.), it is clear that while the reading continues, they are *also* "new" symbolizations of the developing gestalt of the story.

Stated in literary critical terms, this model effectively argues that the distinction between reading and interpretation, or between the experience of a text and its explanation on a higher level of conceptualization, is not one of kind, but of historical perspective. The "new" meanings generated during "experiential" reading are always already reflective conceptualizations according to "old" categories – and vice versa. Every moment of reading is at once the origin and the end of an interpretive fact (of resymbolization) that is always also a naive act (of symbolization).

What is most surprising is that Bleich himself seems unwilling to accept this complication of meaning. His hesitation stems, I believe, from his wish to have an impact on the *discipline* of literary exegesis; it involves, in other words, the problem of translating a theory of subjective criticism into its practice in such a way as to gain widespread acceptance by the existing members of the discipline.

Subjective Dialectic and Intersubjective Negotiation

The dialectic of awareness Bleich advances can be grasped from at least two points of view. Like all the theoreticians covered thus far, Bleich frames reading in a structure of self-confrontation. His version, however, combines features of both Holland's theory of self-perpetuation and the structuralist notion of code change. Because resymbolization is a function of language, the dialectic of consciousness can be framed in terms of language system modification. Because it serves the individual as an adaptational restructuring of reality, it can be thought of as self-perpetuation.

Unfortunately, neither of these perspectives points to the need for any institution of literary criticism. Developed in response to the institutional biases of objectivism, the subjective paradigm dialectically conceived leaves no particular role for the academy within which subjective criticism is supposed to occur. And therein lies Bleich's motive for insisting that symbolization and resymbolization are distinct and isolated operations. Only by separating the two and associating the latter with intersubjective discourse can he build a case for the discipline of literary study and the necessity of the classroom – not to mention his program.

Actually, the association of resymbolization with collective endeavor occurs gradually and obliquely in *Subjective Criticism*. Although Bleich initially states that "the motive for such important changes [resymbolizations of current objectification systems] grows from *personal and communal* subjectivity" (p. 66, my italics), subsequent discussions in his work increasingly associate knowledge with communal subjectivity. He declares, for instance, that "although the resymbolization of a text is usually a fully private affair, it is always done in reference to some communal purpose" (p. 137). The private responses one has to a work are in fact deprived of any meaning of their own: "a response [to a literary work] can acquire meaning only in the context of a predecided community (two or more people) interest in knowledge" (p. 132).

The subjective dialectic notwithstanding, one's experience with a text is apparently not capable, in the absence of intersubjective discussion, of having meaning or constituting knowledge. Rather, Bleich relegates reading to the level of a "preemptory perceptual act that translates a sensory experience into consciousness" (p. 97). This act must in turn be transcribed in a "response statement" if it is to become knowledge: "the practice of formulating response statements is a means for making language experience (hearing, speaking, reading, or writing) available for conversion into knowledge" (p. 132).

Because Bleich sees intersubjectivity as governed by negotiation (p. 137), this conversion of a reading into knowledge can only occur through collective negotiation by a group of people sharing a common purpose. Surprisingly, though, the format and context of such negotiations is not determined on an *ad hoc* basis – at least not in the case of the program Bleich outlines.

First, a decision must be made as to *what* the collective wants to know. This is in accordance with the assumption that knowledge seeks motives and that the motive one assigns the object of knowledge is itself the motive of that knowledge (cf. pp. 68–96). Because the "criterion of adequacy" of knowledge is "the satisfaction of the community of askers and of the community of co-askers" (p. 41), the first procedure in any program must be to determine what needs are to be satisfied.

The second stage in Bleich's program involves the production of response statements – written reactions to a literary work from the individuals concerned. Bleich describes the response statement as "a symbolic presentation of self, a contribution to a pedagogical community, and an articulation of that part of our reading experience we think we can negotiate into knowledge" (p. 167). It is a necessary prerequisite to the collective negotiation that will produce knowledge, and it "tries to objectify, to ourselves and then to our community, the affective-perceptual experience, rather than the story" (p. 147).

Finally, through negotiation, the community of interpreters, usually a class, arrives at a satisfactory collective resymbolization of the response statement, thereby increasing the self-awareness of both the individual respondent and the class. Experience is translated into knowledge, as individual motive merges with collective motive. The advantages of this procedure, according to Bleich, are that it "facilitates full personal involvement in the development of knowledge" while reminding us that "no knowledge is absolute, no matter how it is formulated" (p. 152).

Of course, the former benefit is limited to the actual participants in the classroom negotiation: the response statements Bleich includes in his book are meaningless to his reader precisely because they do not occur in the context of a larger "predecided community interest." They do not correspond to the decision or satisfy the needs of the theoreticians and critics making up American academia, and the person whose symbolization they represent is not available for intersubjective negotiation with the outside reader. Even if Bleich succeeds in persuading the majority of university teachers to accept his methods, the response statements that result will still fall outside of the general reader's negotiative reach, if only because Bleich insists they be made in the vocabulary of personal association rather than collectively sanctioned concept: "a response statement aims to record the perception of a reading experience and its natural, spontaneous consequences, among which are feelings, or affects, and peremptory memories and thoughts, or free associations" (p. 147). Because such associations are "an attempt to abandon customary habits of abstractive definition and replace them with a relaxed imagination" (p. 150), it is doubtful that the document they generate can be accessible to a reader not familiar with the subject or situation in question.

The more general benefit of Bleich's method, that it reminds us knowledge is not absolute, is scarcely unique to subjective criticism. Even the most radical forms of objectivism, such as the "hard" sciences, acknowledge the provisional and adaptational nature of their facts through an ongoing process of revision. As science reformulates its explanations of reality, it invalidates old theories in the process. Because it can be superseded by a "more accurate" account, scientific fact is less absolute than Bleich's type of knowledge, which can never be said to be false. In this sense, the lesson of subjective criticism forms one of the underlying assumptions of objective knowledge, including literary criticism.

My point, then, is not just that Bleich's program falls short of its claims. Rather, I think it can be shown that a biased theory of knowledge such as his cannot be implemented without subverting its claims: the putting into practice of willful subjectivism ultimately promotes its objective counterpart.

Objective Subjectivism

Bleich goes to some length to narrow the range of options open to his practitioners and specify the most effective procedures to be used, including the contexts within which literary knowledge ought to be negotiated in the classroom (cf. pp. 152–67); the kind of associations most desirable in response statements (pp. 168–9, 184–9); and the range of reference to outside reality the response statement must have (p. 169). While he disavows any prescriptive intent (p. 166), the detail of this program suggests an authority which subjectivism explicitly contests.[4] It presupposes a set of procedures that are universally applicable, can be repeated by other teachers at other schools, and will produce predictable results. Ironically, Bleich's own theory convincingly argues that universality, repeatability, and predictability are the criteria of the *objective* paradigm (p. 38).

Yet this is not, I think, a case of deceit or theoretical inconsistency. Rather, the subjective paradigm itself, when put into practice, leads logically to objectivism. More precisely, the historical relationship between objective and subjective paradigms that Bleich adumbrates is, like the relationship of subjectivity to objectification, a dialectic rather than an opposition. Subjectivism cannot banish objectivism from critical practice because they are the two sides of a dialectical unity. When Bleich attempts to translate his theoretical notion into an historical revolution, he enters this dialectic and refutes the subjective paradigm's claim to self-sufficiency.

This dialectic between subjective and objective meaning only becomes obvious if one considers the implications of a widespread implementation of Bleich's program. Practiced on the institutional level, it would require that a large group of people (those studying literature, for our purpose) collectively negotiate the most satisfying explanation possible. Whether one assumes the group in question to consist of six, sixty, or six million negotiators, the principle of explanatory adequacy states that the best or "truest" explanation is the one that satisfies the greatest number of people. Therefore, if one can find a single interpretation that meets the needs of sixty different subjects, that interpretation is by definition more adaptive – more correct – than any of ten others, each of which only satisfies six people. Each group of six people may feel that their more compactly negotiated truth is more satisfying, but if they wish to remain a part of the collective with the other fifty-four, they will have to acknowledge the adequacy of the explanation accepted by all. If one wishes to adjudicate between conflicting explanations – and the negotiation model presupposes that this is the essence of forming new knowledge – one must be willing to seek out the explanation that is best for the greatest portion of the collectivity.

Extended to the level of a national institution, subjective criticism would require negotiating the smallest possible number of interpretations of the "classics" – indeed the single best interpretation of each – so as to consolidate the literary critical community and provide American students with the knowledge that had proved most adaptive in their society. This is, of course, the hallmark of objective paradigms of knowledge – which once again proves that the subjectivist paradigm of negotiation, the assumption that facts are facts by virtue of satisfying a plurality of subjects, leads naturally to the procedures of objectivism. Indeed, we shall see that the difference between Bleich's paradigm and that of the avowed objectivist, E. D. Hirsch, relates more to goal than to net result. It is inevitable that what appears subjectively motivated from the personal level appears objectively true as an accepted fact on the cultural level. Conversely, objective knowledge enjoys its truth status only to the extent that it satisfies the needs of its culture's constituents. Both paradigms, and all knowledge, predicate both objectivism and subjectivism.

Even more than Iser or Holland, then, Bleich exemplifies the difficulty of moving from theory to practice. In all three cases the translation into practice of theoretical principles results in their contradiction. Because Bleich is explicit in his desire to promote subjectivism, it is particularly ironic that his program of criticism should lead to objectivism. But it is also inevitable, for reasons that are becoming increasingly clear. To the extent that meaning constitutes itself as both system and instance, objective structure and subjective act, any attempt to split it into an oppositional dyad necessarily fails: the aspect to which one states one's opposition will always re-emerge within its "opposite."

That this re-emergence coincides with the move into practice underlines only to what extent institutional procedures dictate critical behaviour. Bleich argues for a notion of meaning embracing both structure and gesture; but when he moves into a practical program he adopts an oppositional tack. This is because criticism takes place within an institution whose current conventions predicate a distance between the subjective and the objective (whose needs, Bleich might say, are still best served by the assertion of such a distance). The political privilege and economic subsistence of academia have long depended on the assumption that there *is* a stable order to the world and that proper training will allow one to distinguish it from personal visions and describe it in its essence. Bleich remains loyal to this credo and institution even as he promulgates a new critical practice.[5]

Bleich's inability to implement a truly subjective program has, then, less to do with his particular bias than with the fact that he has one. Like the objectivists he writes against, he errs in forsaking a dialectical notion of meaning in favor of his discipline's oppositional format. Nevertheless, by casting some light on the dialectical nature of meaning and knowledge, his theory makes clearer the extent to which a form of criticism based on subjective meaning would have to be two things at once. It remains to be shown that the same conclusions apply to the opposite tack: those who would argue for the authority of a single, objectively determinable literary meaning, attributable to the unique act of the literary intention's other pole – the author. The most powerful proponent of such a view is E. D. Hirsch.

7

E. D. Hirsch:
Individual Meaning as
Shared Meaning

In the context of this study, the work of E. D. Hirsch complements that of Bleich by showing how a dialectical model of meaning can also ground *objective* knowledge. At the same time, Hirsch shares with Bleich an unwillingness to accept the consequences of his theory. Although his arguments, even more clearly than Bleich's, demonstrate that meaning has a plurality of identities, Hirsch nonetheless eschews dialectical or paradoxical formulations that might convey this complexity in favor of a sequential model that ultimately privileges history over the individual.

Yet this is not immediately evident in his writing. Hirsch's two books on interpretation, *Validity in Interpretation*[1] and *Aims of Interpretation*[2] seem intent on developing a model of meaning that weds private act inextricably to public structure. Their avowed goal is to re-establish the author's meaning as a normative principle for the collective endeavor of interpretation, a goal Hirsch attains by redefining individual meaning, and *a fortiori* experiential meaning, as a shared intersubjective set. But the reciprocity in the relationship between private act and public fact finds no elaboration in Hirsch's work. Rather than confront the possibility that both faces of meaning might communicate between themselves within a single, permanent structure/event of dynamic antagonism, he reiterates Ingarden's tactic by splitting meaning into two consecutive phases and distinct types of knowledge. As a consequence, the ultimate effect of his work is to reassert the primacy of reflective abstraction over imaginational concretization, as well as the individual's subordination to the collective. He thus foreshadows the growing tendency during the sixties and seventies to reduce meaning to a systematic, culture-bound phenomenon.

Thus while his work explicitly draws on phenomenological theory to make its case, Hirsch writes in opposition to those theories that exploit a partial version of intentionality to frame meaning as a subjective event. In Hirsch's eye, to assert that every instance of meaning corresponds to its own unique set of meaning acts is to fall victim to the psychologistic confusion that "mistakenly identifies meaning with mental processes rather than with an object of those processes" (*Validity*, p. 32). In this sense his work stands as an implicit refutation of the work of Holland and Bleich.

To rectify the subjectivism that psychologistic theories have spread, he returns to intentionality to find a principle of authority. Building on the axiom that "a word sequence means nothing in particular until somebody either means something by it or under-stands something from it" (ibid.), he postulates that the cultural institution of criticism requires a criterion for adjudicating divergent meanings, and the most logical choice is the original act by which the author intended a determinate meaning. Thus Hirsch's goal becomes to demonstrate that the shared structure correlated with that act can be recovered by an exegetic program. A first necessary step involves proving that a unique historical act can have as its structural counterpart a self-identical, enduring, replicable meaning.

Meaning as Type

As a preliminary move, Hirsch observes that "my perception of a visible object like Coleridge's table or of a nonvisible object like a phoneme can vary greatly from occasion to occasion, and yet what I am conscious of is nevertheless the same table, the same phoneme" (*Validity*, p. 37). By extending this notion of identity to cover the intentions of different individuals, he concludes that "*an unlimited number of different intentional acts can intend the same verbal meaning*" (*Validity*, p. 38). Although it depends on an individual's act for its production *as a particular instance*, verbal meaning nonetheless exists as a self-identical, enduring category that other subjects can also intend. Thus meaning, as Hirsch defines it, is essentially intersubjective, and the particular meanings an author intends are *shared categories*. At the same time, those meanings derive their enduring particularity from the author's act that originated it. In the absence of this discriminating force, "there would be no distinction between what an author does mean by a word sequence and what he could mean by it" (ibid.). The meaning an author wills, finally, is not a meaning in the sense that Holland understands it – a reflection of the self accessible only through understanding of that self – but rather a willed type, a shared category that may refer to unique entities, but only by means of a typification transcendent of such entities (*Validity*, p. 50).

There are of course limitations to the meanings one can will, but these limitations assure that the meaning can be shared by author and reader alike: "an author's verbal meaning is limited by linguistic possibilities but is determined by his actualizing and specifying some of those possibilities. Correspondingly, the verbal meaning that an interpreter construes is determined by *his* act of will, limited by those same possibilities" (*Validity*, p. 47). The notion of shared meaning as "same possibilities" is thus at the core of Hirsch's argument, and it finds its clearest incarnation in the notion of the *type* or *type idea*.

The type idea serves first and foremost as a bridge between past meaning and present meaning as well as between the author's meaning and the interpreter's meaning. It can best be grasped as a learned superset of meaning possibilities shared by the members of a culture, and having "a boundary by virtue of which something belongs to it or not" (*Validity*, pp. 49–50). At the same time, "since a type can be represented by more than one instance, it is a bridge between instances, and only such a bridge can unite the particularity of meaning with the sociality of interpretation" (*Validity*, p. 71). In other words, because the type willed by the author can be reincarnated in any number of subsequent instances, one's interpretations can theoretically reproduce the author's meaning.

In practical terms, this means that deciding whether a given interpretation is correct will require determining whether the meaning one intends can be considered an *implication* of the author's meaning. This might seem to suggest that one needs to describe completely the type idea before one can commence inter-pretation, but such is not the case. As Hirsch sees it, the relationship of the meaning to its implications (or the type to its traits) is reciprocal, such that the whole can be regenerated from any of its parts. "Precisely because a type can be embodied in more than one instance, it has the apparently magical potency of containing and generating parts of itself which it does not explicitly contain" (*Validity*, pp. 64–5). Thus, even if we have at our disposal only a few parts, the type they embody will be sufficiently defined to reconstitute itself in its entirety: "the peculiarity of a whole meaning is that it retains its integrity and completeness even if all its implications have not been articulated. In other words, the whole meaning is not simply an array of parts but is also a principle for generating 'parts'" (*Validity*, p. 64).

If we take as an example the type "right triangle," the Pythagorean theorem will be part of our meaning precisely to the extent that other people share our knowledge that it applies to all right angle triangles (*Validity*, p. 65). Similarly, knowledge that the triangle involved conforms to the Pythagorean theorem would allow us to infer the other characteristics of the type "right triangle." In short, "when another person has learned the characteristics of the type, he can 'generate' those characteristics without their being given to him explicitly. It is sufficient merely to give him a decisive clue as to the particular type that is meant" (*Validity*, p. 66).

The determination of meaning relies, then, on previous experience and learned conventions. And the same principle that allows us to generate a type from its trait and a whole meaning from a sub-meaning regulates our re-cognition of the author's global meaning, which Hirsch calls the work's intrinsic genre – "the type that determines the boundaries of an utterance as a whole" (*Validity*, p. 89).

Strictly speaking, every work has its own intrinsic genre, consisting not only of its overall meaning, but also of the norms and rules that must be mastered to re-cognize that meaning (*Validity*, pp. 70–1). And like the type idea, of which it is but one variety, the intrinsic genre serves both a heuristic and a constitutive function: one cannot assign any meaning whatsoever to a given text without first making a tentative guess as to the particular type of utterance it is, but as one's interpretation is redefined – or as one's reading continues – this heuristic genre idea becomes increasingly more particularized until finally it constitutes precisely that type which is the whole work (*Validity*, pp. 78–86). At the conclusion of the work, the intrinsic genre that guided us through the text has been displaced by the work's particular meaning, which "arises when the generic expectations have been fulfilled in a particular way by a particular sequence of words" (*Validity*, p. 86). We shall return to this paradigm and its implication that the whole meaning is realigned by the partial meanings whose shape it determines; for this reciprocal constitution is precisely what Hirsch will downplay in his valorization of collective objectivity.

Given Hirsch's theory as outlined to this point, it is not hard to see why he offers no methodology for arriving at correct interpretations. The most crucial step in understanding any text is, finally, the first one, when the reader hazards an initial guess as to the intrinsic genre of the work. And the felicity of this guess, like that of all subsequently postulated submeanings and the final understanding of the work, depends in great part on the past experience of the reader – the conventions he has learned, the types he has mastered. As Hirsch aptly points out, "no possible set of rules or rites of preparation can generate or compel an insight into what an author means. The act of understanding is at first a genial (or a mistaken) guess, and there are no methods for making guesses, no rules for generating insights" (*Validity*, p. 203).

Where then is the practical benefit of Hirsch's theory? It would seem to provide us only with the certainty that an experienced, good reader will have a better chance of recovering the author's meaning than an inexperienced novice. How can it correct the uncontrolled pluralism it set out to remedy? The answer lies in its claim to distinguish valid interpretations from invalid ones, thereby building the interpretive community's insight and increasing the odds that future "first guesses" will be genial, rather than mistaken. This distinction hinges on the operation Hirsch calls validation.

Interpretation, Criticism, and Validation

The notion of validation is particularly interesting for this study because, like Bleich's dyad of symbolization and resymbolization, it both proposes a serialization of meaning and argues against that proposal. In *Validity*, Hirsch first introduces validation as a second-level evaluative operation that takes as its objects the preliminary constructions of meaning produced by understanding: "understanding achieves a construction of meaning; the job of validation is to evaluate the disparate constructions which understanding has brought forward" (*Validity*, p. 170; cf. also pp. 134–6). Although not identical with it, this distinction appears to be derived from the classical hermeneutic distinction between the *subtilitas explicandi* or explanatory phase of hermeneutics, and the *subtilitas intelligendi* or preliminary understanding, which in Hirsch's system advances through implication rather than explication (*Validity*, p. 129).

In fact, this binarism informs every aspect of literary study as Hirsch envisions it. *Interpretation*, for instance, differs from *criticism* in that the former busies itself with simple *meaning*, while the latter is concerned with *significance*. Significance, in Hirsch's system, "names a relationship between that meaning and a person, or a conception, or a situation, or indeed anything else imaginable" (*Validity*, p. 8). Significance is, then, the relating of an author's meaning to something outside of it; it is "meaning-to" rather than "meaning-in" (*Validity*, p. 63). Further, just as interpretation relies on the operation of *understanding*, criticism employs *judgment*, defined as "binding together of any two relata – a 'subject' and a 'predicate' – by some kind of copula which defines the relationship. The act of judging is the construing of this relationship, whether it be that between a meaning and criteria of value or between a meaning and anything else imaginable" (*Validity*, p. 143).

Within this tidy system, validation is something of an anomaly. Not only is it first associated with and then later distinguished from the operation of interpretation, whose "first-level" understanding it is presumed to act upon, but it exhibits a structure and logic that make it difficult to separate from Hirsch's other categories. In its purest form, it involves judgments of probability, based on evidence relevant to the meaning in question. Hirsch defines probability judgments as "informed guesses" about an object that cannot be experienced directly: "they are a rational means of reaching conclusions in the absence of directly experienced certitude" (*Validity*, p. 175). They are of interest to us because they exhibit the same contingency on acquired knowledge and past experience, and involve the same evaluation of a part with respect to a whole, as the construal of an author's meaning or a text's intrinsic genre:

> From the fact that a probability judgment reaches conclusions about something inaccessible to experience (whether that something be in the past or the future), it follows that the judgment must somehow assimilate its unknown object to that which is known. (*Validity*, p. 175)

This assimilation reiterates in its logic the structure of implication. On the basis of perceived traits, we place the object in question in a class with others of the same kind and derive from our knowledge of

that class other possible characteristics of the object. Such procedures hinge on the assumption "that all members of the same class
will tend to act in the same way" (*Validity*, p. 176). And as Hirsch
points out, probability judgment is nothing other than the general
principle underlying understanding:

> in order to determine the meaning of a word sequence it is necessary to
> narrow the supposed genre of the text to such a degree that the meanings are
> no longer doubtful. I called this very narrow and particularized conception
> of the text as a whole its (posited) intrinsic genre. Now this process of
> narrowing the genre is a version of the principle, well known in probability
> theory, of narrowing the class. (*Validity*, p. 178)

This suggests that judgments of probability govern all levels of
inquiry, and that the distinction between understanding (as first-
level construction) and validation is not one of kind. Indeed, Hirsch
acknowledges as much in his subsequent work, where he redefines
understanding as "a validating, self-correcting process – an active
positing of corrigible schemata which we test and modify in the very
process of coming to understand an utterance" (*Aims*, p. 34). Such
schemata conflate the notions of the type idea and the intrinsic
genre, and Hirsch likens them, in his revised conceptualization, to a
continual hypothesis or genre idea, which we form during understanding, and which "provokes expectations that are confirmed by
our linguistic experience, or when they are not confirmed, cause us to
adjust our hypothesis or schema" (*Aims*, pp. 33–4).[3]
   In short, Hirsch is the first to admit the tenuousness of his early
distinctions:

> The universality of the making-matching process and of corrigible schemata
> in all domains of language and thought suggests that *the process of under-
> standing is itself a process of validation*. While this idea was implicit in my
> earlier writings, it has only recently dawned on me in its proper explicitness.
> (*Aims*, p. 33)

This seems to collapse the categories Hirsch set up in *Validity*, and
his admission that such a conflation was already "implicit" in his
earliest theory raises the question of his motivation for ignoring it.
One reason for doing so, I would suggest, lies in the historical,
collective bias evident in his description of literary phenomena.
Meaning, understanding, interpretation, significance, judgment,
criticism, and validation all reiterate in their structure the play
between subsuming whole and subsumed part, but they all also

reinforce a hierarchy of authority that subordinates individual member to larger class. We remember that the whole, in the form of a "type idea," guarantees both the determinacy and reproducibility of the author's meaning. In the guise of "intrinsic genre" and "global meaning," it is both the starting point and the end goal of understanding and interpretation. As the "class" of "that which is known," the whole sets the limits to probability judgments and underlies the process of validation. At the same time, it forms, as "global interpretation," the object of validation: "an interpretation stands or falls as a whole" (*Validity*, p. 172). Finally, as a *consensus omnium* constitutive of the discipline, the whole is quite literally the end of validation.

At all levels, the whole is the seat of power, the principle of authority on the basis of which individual traits can be evaluated or excluded. Naturally, the whole itself is subject to constant modification, but one possibility suggested by Hirsch's theory, namely that a trait might cause a developing schema to be discarded or displaced by another, never seems to surface. Having proven how a single trait can instantiate a type capable of generating its full complement of further traits, Hirsch neglects to explore the subversion of continuity this entails. Rather, it is as if the higher schemata of understanding, by virtue of their persistence throughout the process of dealing with multiple traits and because of their greater level of complexity, are necessarily more authoritative.

Hirsch's description of the procedures for probability judgments reveals the logic of this bias. We remember that understanding requires the progressive determination of the whole, or type, or class, on the basis of class narrowing. To narrow a class is to increase the number of traits an object must possess in order to be a member and, consequently, to reduce the number of instances that fall within that class (*Validity*, p. 180). By increasing the defining traits of a class, one raises the uniformity of that class and hence the likelihood that each of its instances will exhibit the same traits: "when more and more of these traits are identical, the unknown traits of our object will have more and more likelihood of being identical with the known traits of the subclass" (*Validity*, pp. 179–80). And since uniformity becomes more compelling in proportion to its extension, the most relevant evidence will be that which increases the number of members in a class, while at the same time narrowing that class (*Validity*, p. 184).

To illustrate what this means in practice, Hirsch cites the problem of the meaning of "wit" in the eighteenth century. If an instance of the word could not be put in a narrower class than "written in the eighteenth century," one would have to guess its meaning to correspond to that found in the majority of works of that period. If evidence could be found that indicated the author of the text in question, that evidence would be relevant. Indeed, if it turned out that a particular author always used "wit" in a specific and unusual sense, that evidence could overturn one's initial assumption about the word's meaning, precisely because such evidence would narrow the class to that author's works and, in fact, to his uses of the same term. By the same token, evidence that narrowed the class still further, such as the author's other uses of the word "wit" in the *same* work, would be more relevant, all else being equal. Finally, between two equally narrow subsuming classes – such as two distinct uses of the word in the same text – one would weight the one with more instances: if the author used "wit" twenty times in one sense, and only twice in the other, it would be more probable, barring further evidence, that a questionable instance would fall in the former class than the latter.[4]

What is striking about these procedures is that they all demand recourse to a higher class beyond that of the developing whole in question. After a certain point, the class of the meaning under scrutiny can only be narrowed by assimilating its members into a higher, "extrinsic" class. This is because the type/trait conclusions one reaches at any single level of understanding – that of the global meaning of a text, for instance – are based on evidence generated by the very hypothesis under question and therefore tend to be self-validating. "Every interpreter labors under the handicap of an inevitable circularity: all his internal evidence tends to support his hypothesis because much of it was constituted by his hypothesis" (*Validity*, p. 166).

The integration of each successively constituted whole into a higher level of coherence allows for a way out of this dilemma by automatically instigating a narrowing of the class. For instance, on the "lowest" level, that of the type idea shared by all speakers of a language, the class is not a category of consciously elaborated knowledge, and only a very limited number of instances and traits – those in the experience of the reader – make it up. At the other extreme, the highest level of validation necessarily involves an extremely narrow class – say Donne's use of the compass metaphor – with a high number of traits – covering, possibly, his other writings of the same period, other metaphors, the conventions of poetry, circumstances of composition, and so forth – the great majority of which do not derive from personal experience but rather from the collective validations that constitute the critical tradition and canon.

Hirsch's procedure for determining the best of several meanings functions by displacing us into ever more narrowly defined classes of knowledge. We are now in a position to understand why he fragments understanding into so many classes. Only by presuming a qualitative difference between distinct levels of knowledge can one obtain allegiance to the discipline over loyalty to personal intuition. Differentiating between classes of understanding and assuming the class of literary scholarship to be the narrowest or most exclusive allows Hirsch to justify subordinating individual meaning to disciplinary decision: because the understanding achieved at the level of the discipline is presumed to build on narrower, more heavily instanced classes, it can be granted an epistemological superiority over unique intuition. It is, in a word, validated *objective* knowledge, rather than subjective. And the author's particular meaning is, finally, whatever the collective body of academia decides it to be.

Obviously, objective knowledge as Hirsch defines it cannot be thought of as pertaining to the natural world or objects. It derives, rather, from an intersubjective collaboration, and in this sense, objectively valid criticism curiously resembles Bleich's subjective criticism. There is one important difference, however, hinging on the privilege Hirsch grants history.

The Structure of History, the History of Structure

To the extent that Hirsch's fragmentation of meaning never considers how an individual trait in an individual reading might subvert the whole meaning of the work and even the whole class of which the work seems to be a member, it can be thought of as conservative. What it conserves is the text of literary history, the set of classes presumed to furnish us our initial intuitions (intrinsic genre guesses) as well as the narrower subsets that help us refine those intuitions. However, at the same time his theory reinforces history, conceived as a text or structure of pre-existing classes, it neglects the central role history as process or event plays in objectivist epistemology. For history, as both a sequence of events and a structure or code for understanding those events, as both particular instant and generalized class of instances, exemplifies meaning as I (and, I would argue, Hirsch and Bleich) define it. I am suggesting, then, that having so defined meaning (and history), Hirsch forgets his own model and elaborates his epistemology on a serialization or differentiation into levels that depends on differences he takes to be structural, but which are just as clearly "eventual" or historical. This can best be illustrated by returning to his discussion of implication.

We remember that the whole type meaning Hirsch associates with the author's willed meaning encloses within its folds a number of submeanings or implications, which Hirsch characterizes as unspoken or unexplicit meanings that might properly be construed to fall within the domain of the type and hence the author's meaning (*Validity*, pp. 61–2). Yet Hirsch himself argues that words only acquire particular meaning through the will of a subject. Since there is no basis for excluding particular submeanings from this axiom, one can conclude that implications, too, result from particular intentions. This would accord with Hirsch's assumption that all classes of that which is known accrue from prior judgments or "assimilations": implications are implications of some type because they were implied by some subject(s) in the past. "To imply" is a transitive verb, and the *langue* of types, as convention, is generated out of instances and learned through experience: "all types, regardless of their earliest provenance, are learned types – that is, they are type ideas which derive from previous experience and can subsume later experience" (*Validity*, p. 269). That is simply to say that for an implication to be presently (or for some author) a "meaning-in" of a particular type, it has to have previously been generated as a "meaning-to" the array of that type.

It is in this sense that the crucial distinction between meaning and significance is simply one of history, or, if one wishes, of historical perspective. If I view an infolded meaning as already having been folded into the type prior to my apprehension of it, then I consider it an implication.[5] Should I attribute this implication to the author, that is, assume he implied it for the first time by either extending a type or bringing together two separate types, I will consider it part of his particular literary creation and the mark of his artistry (cf. *Validity*, pp. 104–5). If, on the other hand, I assume the implication to pre-date the author, it will appear a mere connotation – a meaning automatically and traditionally assumed under the umbrella of its type.

Significance is in this light simply an "original" implication – the integration of a meaning into a whole or system where we did not previously perceive it as a connotation. Should such an integration achieve wide currency, it too will be retrospectively viewed as an implication of the type in question. A striking example would be the Freudian implications commonly granted slips of the tongue, various objects, dreams, and so forth. Of course, on a smaller scale, the implications of an utterance for any individual subject depend entirely on his past cognitive experience. For the reader of Hirsch's work, the words "interpretation," "meaning," and "criticism" will presumably have implications they do not have for the uninitiated, although according to Hirsch's vocabulary, what *Validity in Interpretation* presents is the *significance* of those terms.

I am not suggesting that Hirsch is wrong when he maintains that one can distinguish between what is implied by an author's meaning and what is not. I am merely underlining that the task of distinguishing between meaning and significance is essentially that of determining who folded what in where – that is, deciding whether a given meaning was already "in" the type at the time of its interpretation (and for its author). In the simplest possible terms, an implication is always perceived retrospectively, as already having been there, while significance is something yet in need of elaboration.[6] In this sense, the task of the interpreter is essentially that of the historian. And as such it is as much conditioned by the text of history – in the form of all that is known about a given author, language, period, culture, and so forth – as by the literary text itself. As I mentioned earlier, Hirsch's theory is essentially a conservative one in the sense that the processes it advocates can only reiterate and consolidate the body of knowledge currently held. It goes without saying that one's belief in the objectivity of interpretations elaborated under this paradigm will be directly proportionate to one's reverence for the established canon of literary knowledge and the methodologies that generate it.

My intention here is not to challenge the authority of this canon, but merely to suggest that, following the logic of Hirsch's system, it *ought* to be put into question. If, as I would argue, Hirsch's serialization of meaning into a variety of successive processes in fact conceals an ongoing dialectic between particular meaning and institutional knowledge, it also implies the need for a further process that would take as its object not the particular meanings of any individuals, but the classes of knowledge used to validate those meanings.

Hirsch argues that "judgments that are accurately made upon explicit criteria furnish the grounds of their own validation and therefore qualify as knowledge" (*Aims*, p. 108), and that "probability judgments bear a necessary relationship only to the evidence on which they are based" (*Validity*, p. 175); but the integrative logic of his whole theory suggests otherwise. While it is true, as I showed in the previous section, that the atomization of meaning into a hierarchy of distinct types assures its own validation, it can also be argued, on the basis of the implicit dialectic between private meaning and shared implication, that the final criteria of validation are themselves in need of validation. The classes of what is known are also continually integrated into higher classes: those of successive generations.

Predictably, Hirsch sees such historical progression as the result of new evidence which causes us to reassess our conclusions (*Validity*, pp. 170–1); but he suggests by omission that this is the only way in which knowledge progresses. On the contrary, new understanding is as frequently as not the result of scrutinizing the methods and criteria of knowledge independently of any evidence such methods may uncover. And it is only a logical extension of Hirsch's own ideas to suggest that a clear understanding of meaning requires that we forego at some point the determination of individual meaning instances in order to consider explicitly the conventions and criteria of the current canon which ground those instances.

Such a course of action, which differs from Hirsch's in its willingness to consider specific conventions at a given point in time, would necessarily provoke and be swept up in a sort of historical regress: current conventions can only be studied from a higher level of analysis, and that higher level would in turn need to be studied by yet another, and so forth. This problem will be studied in the next section, when we turn to structuralist theories concerned with precisely such a task.

In conclusion, Hirsch's fragmentation of meaning can be understood as a response to the threat that a non-simple notion of meaning might pose for the objectivist project. By positing multiple types and levels of meaning he generates differences of kind that seem immune to the necessary regress opened by differences of moment or perspective. By rendering more complex the system of meaning he almost succeeds in obliterating its identity as instance and escaping the dialectic that necessarily unites these two faces in their difference. Were he not committed to the notion of objective knowledge, he would not have to insist on the notion of authorial will in order to provide an enduring identity for meaning, and this in turn might allow for a theory of implication less likely to lead back to the instantial side of meaning. Given the difficulty of developing a theory of objective meaning around the two-faced notion of intentionality, it is not surprising that subsequent theoreticians of intersubjective meaning have chosen to repudiate the phenomenological tradition in its entirety. This move, and its success in simplifying meaning and rendering it more tractable to a systematic practice, will be the subject of the next section of this study.

8

Dialectical Meaning and the Institution

Even as their various strategies form a certain progression, the theories of literary meaning covered thus far display a common ground. Whether they privilege intentional act or textual structure, they all rely on a "self-divided" notion of meaning. The shift from individual identity as the ground of the meaning event (Holland) to an intersubjective vision of collective resymbolization (Bleich) or historically accrued shared types (Hirsch) marks the solution of the referential problem that subject-centered theories bring, but it does not achieve a simplification of meaning. The theories of Holland, Bleich, and Hirsch all deal with the problem of what texts refer to in a different way, but they also all draw on a common model of *meaning as dialectic* that can be traced back to the phenomenological dyad of act and structure.

The phenomenologists, we remember, distinguish between intention as the act of bringing into givenness and as the structure, object, or vision thus intended. Even when they focus on meaning purely as an act of imaginational beholding, they inevitably ground that act in a structure of acquired knowledge (Dufrenne's conceptual knowledge, Ingarden's past experienced aspects, Sartre's *savoir*). Similarly, the critical evaluation of the reader's reading can only occur once that act has been hypostatized into a referential structure – the concretization or reconstruction. Thus, although the literary object can only manifest itself through the intuitive experience of the subject, it is paradoxically inevitable that such experience present itself as an objective structure of reference.

In the work of Wolfgang Iser, this paradox is cast dialectically as the play between the horizon (or structure of the reader's past experiences and reading moments) and the theme (or current instance of meaning which is foregrounded against the horizon). For Iser it is the reader's expectations or repertoire of conventions that generate meaning, but the repertoire itself is the product of the act of reading.

The works of Holland and Hirsch draw on variations of this same paradigm and differ only in the scope of their models. For Holland, every specific meaning in any reading is predicated by an overarching paradigm: as the organizational principle behind the meanings which a reader "finds" in the text, the personality or identity theme of that reader necessarily recreates and perpetuates itself in every critical appreciation. And like Ingarden, Holland apportions meaning into two distinct phases: an initial experiential phase, during which the reader's reaction to a text occurs and is recorded, and a later reflective phase, in which that prior reading act is scrutinized and correlated to the structure of the reader's personality.

The work of E. D. Hirsch transposes this paradigm to the scale of the community or discipline. The notions of meaning as opposed to significance; understanding as opposed to explanation; interpretation as opposed to criticism; all posit the duplicity of meaning as a part/whole dialectic correlated with a two-phased cognitive activity. Each meaning structure in Hirsch's system exists both as an intuited whole and as a part of a larger context, and Hirsch's concept of the type idea does not, finally, differ functionally from Holland's notion of the identity theme. Where Holland locates the subsuming type idea at the level of individual personality, Hirsch attributes it to the conventions of writing as determined by the discipline of literary study. In both cases, the part/whole relationship reiterates the distinction between meaning as subjective event (the particular implications a reader draws from a text) and meaning as a grounding structure (the identity theme or shared type idea). And in both cases, as with Iser, a dialectical formulation of this tension brings the dilemma of the reader-oriented critic into line with the regress of the hermeneutic circle: every instance of meaning is the result – and the anticipation – of an informing context or referential structure; such structures are at once the condition and the result of their instances.

Finally, David Bleich's notion of motivation embodies the paradox most concisely. "Motivation" in his sense of the word embraces both the initial cause of a meaning act and the retrospective attribution of cause, or assignment of motive, that occurs during resymbolization. In this sense, motivation is at once the cause and the effect, the origin and the end, of meaning.

In all cases, then, but most insistently in more recent theories, meaning emerges as two disparate identities that are reciprocally constitutive, if impossible to grasp simultaneously. This lack of self-identity, meaning's difference from itself, feeds directly into a dynamic of growth informing each theory. Whether one envisions such growth as a perpetuation of self, an increase in cultural categories, the development of literary history, or the consolidation of social groups, the growth remains a function of the same motor force: every instance of meaning, every structure of knowledge, refers back to and anticipates its observe self.

In spite of their universal exploitation of a schizoid or duplicitous vision of meaning, the authors treated thus far are nearly unanimous in their repression of that vision (Iser would be the possible exception). While their theories seem to argue at the very least for a dialectical notion of meaning, they all seem intent on fragmenting it into separate, conceptually autonomous categories – phases that can be arranged in a causal hierarchy more amenable to literary historical scrutiny. Although their theories lead to the conclusion that meaning is never fully itself, never fully present, precisely to the extent that its identity is a function of a tension between mutually exclusive notions, the post-phenomenological theoreticians seem determined to reduce it to a consolidation of stable structure by predictable event. As I have tried to show in the foregoing chapters, one comes upon such a perverse conclusion merely by reading the works in question according to their own logic. In a sense, they all emblematize the notion of meaning I am arguing: subjected to the operations they predicate, all of the theories say something other than what they are saying. They all advance a theory of meaning they are unwilling to acknowledge – much less implement; each falls back on the logic of the view it claims to displace.

That the theories in question resist with such consistency their own implications raises the suspicion that a dialectical concept of meaning may somehow clash with the demands of the discipline that grounds their authority. To the extent the writers in question, and particularly Holland, Bleich, and Hirsch, compromise their ideas by settling for a sequential view of meaning-as-consolidation, they betray the influence of a tradition and authority they are unwilling to relinquish. However much they may present themselves as revolutionaries, their work cannot be thought of as revolutionary in any sense of the word. Rather, it serves the institution of literary study in its most conservative sense. To equate meaning with a predictable event that instantiates shared concepts is to place it under the power of those who elaborate and possess, in the form of acquired erudition, the largest number of "facts" or institutionally validated categories. As long as one accepts that facts are different from events, there is little danger of their repudiation: separated from the "authorities" that intend them, they are also immune to subversion by outsiders to the discipline. One can either accept the framework within which they hold authority – and then one is no longer "outside" but a member of the discipline – or challenge it, at which point one's act, precisely because it is "outside" the discipline, will be disqualified or, more likely, ignored.

Divided notions of meaning wreak havoc on this system, by repudiating causal hierarchies, stable structures, and privileged events. Whether one assumes certain "facts" to be facts by virtue of their utterance by a privileged subject (which is generally the case in non-empirical disciplines, and frequently elsewhere as well!) or whether one privileges them because they correlate to a revered system, a program that challenges such distinctions from the outset and recasts all meaning and knowledge as an inconceivable tension between act and fact will necessarily itself seem inconceivably subversive. If every meaning is at every moment and place another (an other) event and structure, then its identity cannot be stabilized, and no person or group of persons can claim it as their creation or possession. In this scenario the meaning of a text becomes not just the privilege of every reader, but his plight. Authority cannot persist where history and canon lose their invulnerability.

We shall see in coming chapters how such a complete subversion is "in fact" inconceivable precisely because we cannot divest ourselves of the institutional affiliation that motivates critics like Hirsch and Bleich. For now it is enough to note the inseparability of meaning theory from the political side of academic criticism, and the degree to which the "perversity" in question can be understood as the mark of a tradition that cannot admit a divided notion of meaning.

Finally, what sets the writers of the preceding section apart from the phenomenologists as well as their structuralist and post-structuralist counterparts is their ambivalent awareness of this relationship. Like the phenomenologists, they retain a strong sense of the individual's role in making meaning. At the same time, they demonstrate an increasing awareness of the social dimension of any meaning act and of the extent to which particular action can be subsumed within collective norms. I have tried to show how the thrust of Bleich's and Hirsch's work in particular is towards a collective vision of meaning, in spite of their explicit bias for the authority of the individual subject. And it is to their credit that they do not succumb to a more reductive perspective. The same cannot be said of the structuralists, whose rigorously systematic approach to meaning carries to an extreme the subordination of instance, self, and act to grounding structure.

Part Three
Structuralism and Semiotics

9

Jonathan Culler:
A Structuralist Poetics

Meaning as *Langue*

The easiest way to relate the structuralists to the theories of meaning that precede them in this study is to consider their ideas an extension of the "shared" identity of Hirsch's type idea to the exclusion of its role as willed instance. The implicit assumption of the structuralist, or his more general counterpart the semiotician, is that events, phenomena, and objects are culturally functional only to the extent that they have meaning, and objects that have meaning are by definition social phenomena best understood in terms of the shared structures through which that meaning constitutes itself. Virtually all notions of such shared structures, whether they be called conventions, codes, rules, or linguistic competence, are based on the Saussurian concept of the *langue*.

As the ground of meaning, *langue* is neither physical essence (presence), nor originating intention (cognitive activity), but rather a set of institutional conventions forming codes. These codes are possessed as linguistic competence by the members of the culture or group in question, and their practice does not depend on the existence of any corresponding objects in the "real" world. This means that questions of reference or the relationship of meaning to subjective presence are of little interest to the semiotician:

> within the framework of a theory of codes it is unnecessary to resort to the notion of extension, nor to that of possible worlds; the codes, insofar as they are accepted by a society, set up a "cultural" world which is neither actual nor possible in the ontological sense; its existence is linked to a cultural order, which is the way in which a society thinks, speaks and, while speaking, explains the purport of its thought through other thoughts.[1]

Because in most of its avatars structuralism likes to seize this cultural order synchronically – that is, as a stable network of codes existing at a single moment in time – it has as little interest in the historical causes behind meaning as in the objects or subjects that meaning may refer to. Unlike aesthetic criticism, it attempts to go beyond identifying *what* one experiences in reading a literary work to explain *how* one can derive from texts the meanings one does. This explanatory goal does not, however, imply any recovery of historical causes, or, as in the case of Holland, personal motivations. Like its parent discipline, linguistics, structuralism in its most rigorous form

does not try to explain why an individual uttered a particular sequence at a given moment, but it shows why the sequence has the form and meaning it does by relating it to the system of the language. . . . one attempts to show why a particular action has significance by relating it to the system of underlying functions, norms, and categories which make it possible.[2]

Thus, the "author's meaning" to which Hirsch devotes his attention simply ceases to be problematic for the structuralists. This is because, on the one hand, they are not concerned with objective knowledge and therefore do not need a stable criterion for validation, and, on the other, do not consider the subject to be constitutive of meaning. Within the framework of communication that structuralism presupposes, meaning is only meaning to the extent that it is codified. As Jonathan Culler puts it, "a speaker's utterances are understood by others only because they are already virtually contained within the language. (*Structuralist Poetics*, p. 29 – unless otherwise indicated, all citations from Culler in this chapter are from this work).[3]

From this rigorously systematic point of view, the act of will that invests a sequence with meaning in Hirsch's system seems purely ancillary; meaning can be expressed entirely in terms of shared, pre-existing categories. Even the "self," because it must be expressed through semiotic units, can be thought of as a conventional construct – a function of the codes that ground it. Naturally such a "self" cannot be synonymous with consciousness, since one is not necessarily conscious of the conventions shaping meaning; neither can it serve as the origin of meaning: "once meaning is explained in terms of conventional systems which may escape the grasp of the conscious subject – the self can no longer be identified with consciousness. It is 'dissolved' as its functions are taken up by a variety of interpersonal systems that operate through it" (p. 28). In particular, the self can no longer serve as the source of origin of meaning (p. 30) – but then again, meaning no longer *need* have an origin, since it consists entirely of an intersubjective system having no beginning or end. There can be no originating act of meaning behind a system that is itself the precondition for such acts.

Not only does this reasoning invalidate the notion that meaning is something given a word sequence by an individual, it eliminates the traditional object of literary study – the author's meaning – as well as the activity of interpretation that object entails. In its place, the structuralists propose a discipline concerned with the description of the structure of rules and conventions underlying various texts. Because such codes cannot be unique to a single text, this discipline must take the form of a poetics – that is, a general description of the ways in which meaning is made by literary works of various types – rather than an exegesis. Nevertheless, because a poetics, like any system of conventions, changes with time, the structuralist poetician must limit his analysis to a specific set of codes operative at a given moment in time. One can no more define the conventions of literature for all periods at once than postulate a single *langue* for all of the cultures in history.

The choice of a synchronic perspective is in this sense a theoretical as well as a practical necessity. Reconstruction of the *langue* governing utterances of a given type can only be achieved if the system described is historically circumscribed, yet broad enough in its sweep to seize an entire shared competence rather than an idiosyncratic usage. As Saussure bluntly puts it, "the language is not complete within any single brain, it exists perfectly only in the collective mass."[4]

One might argue that the only way to avoid the particularities of individual utterances (*parole*) would be to limit the synchronic investigation to the *langue* one shares with one's contemporaries. That is the only system of conventions we can be certain is shared, and the only one whose discussion will transcend the interpretation of specifics. Finally, one might observe that diachronic descriptions that portray historical modifications in a *langue* can do so only by charting different instances of the "same" code or convention. Such instances can never be assumed to represent the entirety of the *langue* and they contaminate the rigor of the systematic approach by introducing particular evidence. For this reason, rigorously structuralist studies must adopt a synchronic perspective on their object and limit themselves to the description of relatively current systems of conventions.

Such is in fact the goal of Jonathan Culler's *Structuralist Poetics*, which sees a poetics of reading as a prerequisite to any discussion of literary phenomena: "to discover and characterize structures one must analyze the system which assigns structural descriptions to the objects in question, and thus a literary taxonomy should be grounded in a theory of reading" (p. 122). In fact, this theory takes up only a portion of the work, much of which is devoted to evaluating various structuralist approaches to literature and to justifying the systematic approach to meaning. Nevertheless, Culler's concise argument is particularly accessible and provides an excellent example of the problems posed by the structuralist strategy.

Reading as Competence

The keystone to Culler's theory of reading is an analogy with the notion of linguistic competence. Culler reasons that "the context which determines the meaning of a sentence is more than the other sentences of the text; it is a complex of knowledge and expectations of varying degrees of specificity, a kind of interpretive competence" (p. 95). This knowledge, and the operations it oversees, constitute the central object of his inquiry, and, as such, would seem to indicate a certain communality of interest with the phenomenologists. However, Culler's interest is not in the sequence of pseudo-perceptual or imaginational acts that draw on knowledge during reading; and his version of knowledge is at once more abstract and less personal than that of Ingarden or Dufrenne.

Above and beyond a mastery of their language, he asserts, readers bring to literature a whole bank of tacit assumptions and anticipations: "expectations about the forms of literary organization, implicit models of literary structures, practice in forming and testing hypotheses about literary works – is what guides one in the perception and construction of relevant patterns" (p. 95). The ensemble of such experience and expectation forms an "internalized competence which enables objects to have the properties they do for those who have mastered the system" (p. 120); from the structuralist point of view, this competence not only governs the production and apprehension of meaning, it also constitutes the institution of literature as we know it.

Understanding reading, within this framework, requires only that one systematize the conventions that make up literary competence. And because this *langue* of conventions is theoretically embodied in the interpretations that have been accepted by the community, one should be able to extrapolate from the canon a set of generative principles accounting for it and for the range of meaning the discipline will currently tolerate. This procedure is in keeping with that of linguists, who begin with known effects – well-formed utterances – and work towards structural explanations for those effects (cf. pp. 68–9, 73–4, 120–30).

Naturally, Culler's theory runs the risk of depending on *parole* for the generation of its *langue*, but this danger is mitigated by the certainty that the interpretations in question are at least "acceptable utterances" for the critical community. Similarly, Culler proposes generalizing from a large number of interpretations and taking a middle course which can skirt "an experimental or socio-psychological approach which would take too seriously the actual and doubtless idiosyncratic performance of individual readers, while still avoiding on the other hand the dangers of a purely theoretical approach, whose postulated norms might bear little relation to what readers actually do" (p. 258).

Two other assumptions govern Culler's decision to extrapolate his model of competence from current interpretations. In the first place, his primary goal is to promulgate the procedures and advantages of the structural approach; thus the truth value of his model is less crucial than its exemplification of a way of thinking: "there is little reason to worry initially about the validity of the facts which one sets out to explain; . . . the important thing is to start by isolating a set of facts and then to construct a model to account for them" (p. 128). In the second place, working with interpretations from one's own tradition will at least have the advantage of compelling self-awareness about the way one makes meanings. I shall return shortly to this second advantage. The former one is most interesting as a contrast to the assumptions of the theoreticians considered up to this point.

In a sense, Culler's argument makes explicit Hirsch's implication that integration into the known constitutes validation. If we can construct an explanation for a "set of facts," which coherently integrates those facts into that which is already known, we will, in a sense, have objectively explained those facts – providing, of course, that the integration has been into shared, not idiosyncratic, classes.

This characteristic of Culler's approach also liberates its practitioner from ontological speculation: "one need not struggle, as other theorists must, to find some objective property of language which distinguishes the literary from the non-literary but may simply start from the fact that we can read texts as literature and then inquire what operations that involves" (p. 128–9). Of equal indifference to Culler are Ingarden's concretizations. Since the individual subject has been absorbed into a matrix of shared conventions, any singular construct he might generate during reading is either entirely constituted in shared concepts or, from the structuralist point of view, meaningless. To the extent that concretizations, in the Ingardenian sense, are intrapersonal, they cannot be communicated to other subjects and have for Culler little value: "analysis of the activity of reading becomes worthwhile only if we assume that it is an interpersonal process and that meaning is not an individual creation but the result of applying to the text operations and conventions which constitute the institution of literature."[5]

Culler is by no means unaware of the exclusions he performs, however. Recognizing the potential conflict between his approach and that of the phenomenologists, he assigns his work a complementary role that presupposes much of the theoretical ground covered by the latter: "structuralism must take place within phenomenology; its task is to explicate what is phenomenally given in the subject's relation to his cultural objects" (p. 27). But he also insists that meaning, as it is understood by academics, cannot refer to individual experience; it must be a conceptual category resulting from recognitive consideration of the text: "the meaning of a poem within the institution of literature is not . . . the immediate and spontaneous reaction of individual readers but the meanings which they are willing to accept as both plausible and justifiable when they are explained" (p. 124). Here again, he extends the authority of the tradition, to which Hirsch alludes, to its logical conclusion: the author's meaning is what the interpretive community agrees it to be.

Finally, *Structuralist Poetics* reiterates, in cultural terms, the dialectic of self-discovery and the revision of norms that Iser outlines. On the theoretical level, Culler maintains that "an awareness of the assumptions on which one proceeds, an ability to make explicit what one is attempting to do, makes it easier to see where and how the text . . . leads to that questioning of the self and of ordinary social modes of understanding which has always been the result of the greatest literature" (p. 129). And even more than Iser, Culler insists than the "expansion of self" afforded by literature must occur through an "awareness of the *interpretive* models which inform one's culture" (p. 130, my italics). This increased awareness of interpretive conventions is a major justification for Culler's project; and to inaugurate such awareness, Culler proposes a preliminary taxonomy of the central convention of *naturalization*.

Naturalization and Irony

To naturalize a text is to give it "a place in the world which our culture defines" and for Culler as for Hirsch this means assimilating it into the classes of the known: "to assimilate or interpret something is to bring it within the modes of order which culture makes available, and this is usually done by talking about it in a mode of discourse which culture takes as natural" (p. 137).

There are two important shifts involved in this definition. First, Culler assumes that naturalization involves more than recognition or perception of a familiar object. It requires that one articulate that perception in one's own language. This implies that understanding involves more than a mute intuition: it must invoke the conceptual categories of shared language. Culler's theory, like Hirsch's, reflects an historical trend in meaning theory of the late sixties: the intimacy and alienation from "another" consciousness that characterizes Blanchot's and Poulet's descriptions of reading is relegated to a position of obscurity and meaninglessness, as concerns for objective knowledge and stable understanding displace interest in subjective experience.

Secondly, Culler's "naturalization" rephrases in purely linguistic nomenclature the process of referentialization that other theories cast as a relationship to reality. As in every definition of reading, we have here a process of exchange or correspondence; but what the theoreticians of pre-structuralist persuasion consider a correlation between text and world or text and subject, the structuralist sees as a link between texts – that is, between the literal text of the work and the figurative texts of inherently legible discourse that define our culture. One does not naturalize a work by relating it to known objects but by translating it into a more familiar mode of discourse.

In the case of literature, such discourse is represented by other, previously read works, such that meaning can be more specifically defined as the result of an intertextual exchange: "a work can only be read in connection with or against other texts, which provide a grid through which it is read and structured" (p. 139).

Under the general rubric of naturalization, Culler further discerns five different levels at which the correspondence with known texts occurs. On each successive level – and there is a sort of hierarchy organizing them – a different "text" serves as the correspondent to which the read text is correlated. On the first level, there is what Culler calls "the socially given text, that which is taken as the 'real world'" (p. 140). This is the version of "reality" that our cultural language defines, and correlations between it and the literary text explain the mimetic quality of literature.

On the second level, correlations are made to a text explicitly recognized as having its origins in our culture. This Culler calls the "general cultural text: shared knowledge which would be recognized by participants as part of culture" (ibid.). Under this category, he includes the stereotypes and commonplaces specific to a particular culture and period, the generalizations that are not necessarily shared by all people and are recognized as generalizations rather than "facts."

The third level of naturalization involves an even narrower class of text: that constituted by the literary tradition itself. This text takes the form of generic conventions, the set of specifically "literary norms to which texts may be related and by virtue of which they become meaningful and coherent" (p. 145).

The fourth level brings into play what one might call the text of nonconformity or unconventionality, in which the text of the third level is specified negatively as the set of conventions *not* to be invoked in naturalizing. Works that try to dissociate themselves from the conventions normally attending their genre, such as epistolary novels that claim not to be fiction, depend for their comprehensibility on this fourth level of convention. Since the repudiation of conventions implies a claim to natural simplicity, Culler terms this fourth level that of "the conventionally natural" (p. 48).

Finally, on a fifth level, we have the "complex *vraisemblance* of specific intertextualities, where one work takes another as its basis or point of departure and must be assimilated in relation to it" (p. 140).

It is on this last level that Culler locates the conventions of parody and irony, and it is considerably more complex than the other four, if only because it thematizes and suspends the very process of correlation they invoke. While the fourth level of naturalization allows one to correlate a given text with the conventions it cites – and therefore to obtain a higher understanding of how literature works in general – the fifth level suspends that type of recuperation by refusing both identification with and repudiation of general codes. Instead, it cites a particular text to which it must be correlated, but in relation to which it can neither be merged nor set in opposition. One might say that the fifth level of naturalization thematizes the very structure of difference and similarity which correspondence implies.

In the case of parody, this thematization contrasts the conventional way the parodied text was "meant" to be read to the "literal" way the parodying text rereads it (cf. pp. 152–3). As Culler puts it, "parody involves the opposition between two modes of *vraisemblance*, but unlike the fourth case its oppositions do not lead to a synthesis at a higher level" (p. 154). Parodic meaning cannot be generalized to all literature because the conventions it cites are specific to one text and its relationship to those conventions is one of dependency and repudiation at the same time.

Irony, in Culler's system, also involves the explicit thematization of incompatible naturalizations. But because it relies on "semantic rather than formal effect" (p. 154), and because meaning cannot be as narrowly correlated to a single level of conventions as can the formal aspects of a text that parody targets, the juxtapositions of irony cross over many levels of convention. In the case of *Madame Bovary*, for instance, Culler isolates four distinct levels of convention that go into the ironic *vraisemblance* we oppose to Emma's attitudes (p. 157). Irony also seems to put more things into question than parody, up to and including the very process of naturalization itself: "once expectations are established . . . we can undertake ironic readings which lead to no certainty or 'true attitude' that can be opposed to the apparent statement of the text but only to a formal *vraisemblance* or level of coherence which is that of ironic uncertainty itself" (p. 158).

Thus the fifth level of naturalization dominates the other four by its ability to challenge their procedures for making sense; it also stands out in its reflexivity and its rejection of closure. In this sense one might say that Culler's ultimate form of recuperation states the uncertainty of ultimate recuperation. And it does this by underlining the conventionality of the meanings we possess as certainty. This points to one of the more interesting characteristics of conventions: their necessary exemption from thematization. Conventions can only make the unnatural natural if they are allowed to work unnoticed. For the natural is by definition precisely that which cannot be identified as an arbitrary, transitory cultural construct. If a convention is exposed as such, the "naturalness" of the constructs it grounds comes into question and it loses its cultural functionality. (Clearly, the theoretical commonplace which states that the natural is founded in conventions does not itself expose any convention in particular.)

That such an implication should surface in Culler's work is of particular interest, in that it addresses the impact of the project he sets himself. The exposure and interrogation of specific conventions presupposes – indeed, posits – further conventions to regulate such a gesture. Carried to its logical conclusion, semiotic reflexivity implies an infinite regress. It is to arrest this regress that Culler makes his final level of recuperation ironic: irony is itself invulnerable to ironization because it proposes no closure that could be questioned, but rather "the action of irony itself as a means of hesitation" (p. 159). The ultimate "level" of naturalization is not a text at all, then, but an act of suspension that refuses correlation with any single "correlate text." However, to the extent that Culler's work itself is not ironic, his theoretical solution to regress does not apply to *Structuralist Poetics*, whose impact and goal must be reconsidered in the light of its own theoretical claims.

The Historicization of Convention

If one suspends conventions by thematizing their specific activity, the status of a book like *Structuralist Poetics*, and more particularly of the program it promotes, becomes problematic. To the extent that thematization defuses conventions, Culler's project can pretend no innocent descriptive goals. The very conventions he would unmask would find themselves, by virtue of that unmasking, dysfunctional. While one might exempt his general theoretical descriptions from this accusation, the implementation of his program would certainly involve irony – indeed, multiple ironies.

In the first place, Culler insists that naturalization is not only inevitable (p. 159) but beneficial and necessary: "the strange, the formal, the fictional, must be recuperated or naturalized, brought within our ken, if we do not want to remain gaping before monumental inscriptions" (p. 134). From this perspective, anything which disturbs or calls into question one's mode of naturalizing is necessarily to be avoided. Yet this is exactly what Culler's program would do: by drawing the public's attention to the conventions underlying their understanding, it would contribute to a reinstatement of that detrimental strangeness.

That this could not occur is self-evident: one would simply formulate new conventions capable of making natural that which appeared strange. Here again, though, Culler's program is pitched into irony. Its avowed goal of making explicit the conventions operative for a given genre and culture would be thwarted by the success of his venture. Once explicit, the conventions he brought to our attention would no longer be operative and hence no longer those that needed attention: "the study of any set of semiotic conventions will be partially invalidated by the knowledge which results from that study" (p. 251). The uncovering of conventions only precipitates more conventions, which in turn need to be uncovered, and so forth. Again, infinite regress. Self-awareness, particularly on the cultural level, is not something that can be achieved once and for all.

Culler is obviously aware of this, and he obliquely alludes to the real value of his program, which would be to catalyze change in the ways we interpret texts. A program of convention description would promote the development of new knowledge by making obsolete old ways of understanding: "the possibility of change depends on some concept of identity . . . there must now be operative conventions for the production of meaning if they are to change tomorrow" (pp. 253–4).

There is yet a third kind of irony in Culler's gesture, however. The underlying presupposition of structuralism is that all meaning can be reduced to a structure, or *langue*, and that one can attain a higher kind of objectivity by moving the study of meaning to the metacritical level. The explicit goal of a structuralist poetics – to chart the conventions of reading – carries with it implicit effects: the displacement of interpretation by theoretical description, and the generation, at the metacritical level, of a new series of rules for studying the notion of meaning. An entire critical discipline and tradition is thus implicitly hypostatized into a stable language of conventions constitutive of a knowledge more removed, and hence objective, than that which our intuitive sense of how we make meaning can give us.

Put in historical perspective, this redefinition of the discipline can be read as a reaction to the scientific ethos of our times. Just as Hirsch felt compelled to recoup objective knowledge from the vagaries of subjectivism, so too do the structuralists emulate the methods and principles of scientific investigation. The irony is that this attempt to reinvest literary study with the prestige of science advances a dialectical model of meaning-as-process that undermines its synchronic vision. By choosing irony as the final stage of recuperation and citing historical change as the end of his work, Culler implicitly reinstates the dialectic of act and structure structuralism presumes to arrest. Although the dialectic thus reopened involves an entire cultural institution, rather than an individual, it nonetheless reiterates a pattern of self-representation that is by now quite familiar.

In *all* of the models of reading we have considered thus far the reading self is assumed to benefit from an expansion and reorganization. Holland, Bleich, and Hirsch distribute the process into two distinct stages, Iser sees it occurring as a continuum from initial perception to final discovery, and Ingarden locates it entirely within the initial, experiential phase of reading. For Ingarden, experiential reorganization occurs prior to conceptualization; for Culler, conceptualization is the precondition of such reorganization.

That the same process can be framed according to such different causal sequences and on so many different levels suggests that no localized explanation can adequately enclose it. Indeed, Iser's and Hirsch's theories, with their emphasis on holistic gestalten and the inseparability of instance and system, argue rather convincingly that self-confrontation and reorganization occur constantly on both the individual and the collective levels, because particular meaning and conventional system are mutually determinative sides of a single phenomenon. In other words, instances are the actualization of conventional systems that can themselves only be actualized as instances necessarily grounded in further systems, and so forth. Put somewhat differently, reading entails conceptualization in categories that can only manifest themselves as particular meanings – even as they are modified by the instances they ground. And to the extent that the "self" shares this divided identity, it necessarily exists through and within the same dialectic.

All of this points to a further question: is a structuralist poetics necessary? Texts like Culler's, which purport to provide us a necessary tool for the expansion of our cultural awareness, may not furnish us with anything we do not already have. All reading (and *a fortiori* all writing) must be to some degree self-reflective, and contribute to some degree to the ongoing development of conventions, or we would still be reading and writing according to the conventions of our ancestors. In this light, Culler's proposed program seems less an innovation than an acceleration of historical process.

Yet this is not the role *Structuralist Poetics* envisions for itself. Rather than a key moment *in* history, it wants to organize the text *of* history, by mapping out all the conventions in every genre of the literary tradition. Through a proliferation of classes and distinctions, such a history of meaning could cover all possible ways of making meaning – or *écritures*, as Culler calls them:

> One can, of course, multiply the number of *écritures* until one produces as many distinctions as seem necessary to account for the different ways in which texts may be read, the different contrasts which the institution makes available. Such distinctions must take account both of the historical changes from one period to another and of the differences between genres in any given period. (p. 135)

By defining itself as the one master class that subsumes such distinctions, a history of meaning attempts to remove itself from the flux of history. But since further codes would be necessary to read such a history, it can scarcely hope to outstrip the dialectic it portrays. The historian's dream of controlling change by transforming it into objective knowledge is incompatible with Culler's model of meaning. The theory of *Structuralist Poetics* invalidates its practice.

In sum, Culler's model of naturalization posits a final recuperative move whose ironizing power points to a dialectic of meaning rather than a static *langue* of conventions. This dialectic exists only in an incipient form in his work, but it is cited as the primary justification for his project and forms a further variation of the theme of self-expansion so familiar to reading theory. Ironically, this same dialectic undercuts the historical claims of Culler's program as well as the original structuralist premise that meaning can be seized most effectively as a synchronic grid of rules, conventions, and codes. Like Hirsch, Culler obliquely argues a notion of meaning that could account for the supersession of one code by another – that could grasp meaning simultaneously as process *and* structure, instance *and* system.

If such a model never receives explicit endorsement in *Structuralist Poetics*,[6] it is because it poses a conflict with the fundamental structuralist assumption that meaning can be studied as a *langue*. If instances of meaning continually modify the codes that inform them, no study of conventions can forego the consideration of message production as an event, no study of reading can omit the role of specific readings and texts. This is the underlying premise of another theoretician who has attempted to provide a structural description of the dialectical nature of meaning. That theoretician is Umberto Eco, who attempts to outline a global theory of meaning and apply that theory to reading and criticism.

10

Umberto Eco:
The Reading Process as
Code-Structure

Communication and Code

Umberto Eco's *A Theory of Semiotics* and *The Role of the Reader*[1] state two distinct yet complementary projects. The first work does not limit itself to literature but attempts a general theory of all sign systems and communication processes, while the later *Role of the Reader* is concerned only with the semiotics of reading and its application to critical practice. Nonetheless, the general theoretical work furnishes a precise description of the difference between literary and other semiotic works, as well as a discussion of the unique role of the former in the enrichment of our cultural universe. Because the *Role of the Reader* builds on these ideas I shall postpone its discussion until after I have outlined Eco's general theory.

Central to Eco's work is his recognition that any theory of meaning involves a theory of processes as well as one of structures. His brand of semiotics is thus two-pronged, stressing on the one hand signification, and on the other, communication: "a semiotics of signification entails a theory of codes, while a semiotics of communication entails a theory of sign production" (*A Theory of Semiotics*, p. 4 – unless otherwise indicated, all citations of Eco refer to that work). This distinction corresponds to the distinction between system and instance, competence and performance, or *langue* and *parole*: "there is a signification system (and therefore a code) when there is the socially conventionalized possibility of generating sign functions. . . . There is on the contrary a communication process when the possibilities provided by a signification system are exploited in order to physically produce expression for many practical purposes" (p. 4).

In keeping with the Saussurian valorization of *langue*, Eco initially grants signification precedence over communication: "a significa-tion system is an autonomous semiotic construct that has an abstract mode of existence independent of any possible communicative act it makes possible. On the contrary . . . *every act of communication to or between human beings . . . presupposes a signification system as its necessary condition*" (p. 9). This assertion epitomizes the structural-ist bias and explains the tendency to treat individual texts as code systems rather than specific meanings: by treating each text as an individual *langue* unto itself, structuralist discussions purport to explain meaning on a more fundamental level than that of individual understanding.

Yet Eco's central thesis in *A Theory of Semiotics* quickly undoes this assumption. He is concerned with what he calls *unlimited semiosis*, a concept that introduces the idea of process into the structure of meaning. Crudely paraphrased, Eco's thesis is that the cultural content of an expression can only be defined in terms of conventional abstractions, or interpretants, as Peirce called them, that are themselves in need of further definition by further cultural units, *ad infinitum*. Meaning is the correlation of an expression unit and a content unit, the value of which can only be given through a further unit, itself a similar correlation, depending on a further unit, and so forth. This correlation Eco calls a sign-function, in order to underline its status as a temporarily encoded relationship, rather than a permanent structure. As sign-function, "signs are the pro-visional result of coding rules which establish *transitory* correlations of elements, each of these elements being entitled to enter – under given coded circumstances – into another correlation and thus form a new sign" (p. 49).

This formulation does not just reiterate the standard structuralist assumption that meaning is a cultural unit whose value is determined relative to other such units. It also implies that (1) each interpretant is potentially linked to all others in the semantic system, forming a vast metonymic aggregation, and (2) meaning is an ongoing process of code reorganization having no ultimate referent or closure: once one posits the need for a further interpretant, "there begins a process of unlimited semiosis, which, paradoxical as it may be, is the only guarantee for the foundation of a semiotic system capable of checking itself entirely by its own means" (p. 68).

From a practical point of view, this means that one cannot

describe the entire semantic field of a given text: any meaning unit is capable of linking up with any other via a potentially endless string of interpretants. We shall see that Eco shrinks back from this conclusion, since it would close the door on practice. From a theoretical point of view, unlimited semiosis puts into question the pre-eminence of the code over the act of sign production. If the code is neither "*a natural condition of the Global Sematic Universe nor a stable structure underlying the complex of links and branches of every semiosic process*" (p. 126), but rather a momentary "magnetization" of cultural units that arises out of usage, its value as the end of all semiotic analysis is difficult to maintain – as is the objective superiority of such analysis over more traditional forms of inquiry.

In fact, as "subcode," a given meaning such as one of Hirsch's "implications" is in this perspective neither stable structure nor natural law but merely an historical event – "a comparatively transitory phenomenon which it would be impossible to establish and describe as a stable structure" (p. 126). Nevertheless, because he feels that "the restricted number of pertinent items and combinational rules" (p. 128) makes the semantic analysis of a particular message more feasible than the obviously impossible task of describing our Global Semantic Universe, Eco proposes that "a semiotics of the code can be established – if only partially – when the existence of a message *postulates it* as an explanatory condition" (pp. 128–9). This proposition literally reverses Eco's original bias: as it turns out, the code is not the ground of meaning, but merely "a purely temporary device *posited* in order to explain a certain message, a working hypothesis that aims to control the immediate semantic environment of given semantic units" (pp. 126–7).

If this sounds like a fairly apt description of literary interpretation, it is no coincidence. For just as Eco must reverse his stand and redefine the semiotics of the code as "an operational device in the service of a *semiotics of sign production*" (p. 128), so too does he subordinate the description of conventions to the study of individual meanings: "the description of fields and semantic branches can only be achieved *when studying the conditions of signification of a given message*" (p. 128). If this is the case, the structuralist transcendence of the particular, and specifically Culler's goal of displacing interpretation through a poetics of reading, would seem ill-starred. Indeed, Eco assigns to interpretation the very role of catalyzing change that Culler attributed to his own project; in his own theoretical terms, Eco makes interpretation the bridge between his theory of signification and his theory of communication.

Interpretation as Culture Enrichment

The role of aesthetic texts, in Eco's opinion, is to enrich our codes, and they do this through a process of *extra-coding*, which in turn consists of overcoding and undercoding. These are quasi-inferential processes by which we extend present codes to cover new circumstances, thereby modifying those codes and enriching our overall code – presuming, of course, that our extensions are accepted and become habitual (pp. 131–3). Overcoding consists of either the application of pre-existent conventions to cover new situations or the assignment of additional values to "macroscopic strings" of minimal coded expressions such as iconographical representations (pp. 133–4). Undercoding occurs when "in the absence of reliable preestablished rules, certain macroscopic portions of certain texts are provisionally assumed to be pertinent units of a code in formation" (pp. 135–6). To the extent that the division of a text into "macroscopic portions" can hardly be presumed to occur in the absence of some code, this distinction seems to me spurious: undercoding is contingent on overcoding, which term I shall retain to designate code extension in general.

Although overcoding presumably occurs whenever one is faced with a new semiotic object, Eco places the major burden for code changes on aesthetic texts. For Eco, an aesthetic text is characteristically ambiguous, and thus self-focusing, precisely because it violates the rule of the code (p. 262) and thereby draws attention to its expression and content planes and their correlation (pp. 263–4). Like Iser, Eco assumes that the reader confronts challenges to his norms by subjecting them to direct scrutiny and reassessment. But unlike the phenomenologist, Eco locates the dialectic of self on the metalinguistic level: the reader questions not his personal assumptions or habits, but the scope and function of semiosis itself.

The exact mechanism of this reassessment is quite simple. Aesthetic variations in the use of sign-vehicle *matter* such as rhyme and rhythmic patterns make such matter interesting and elevate it to the level of an "aspect of the expression form" (p. 266). This in turn causes the addressee to isolate further categories and subdivisions within the material continuum and to assume – because "there is a strong relation between the segmentation of the token matter of a given sign-vehicle and the further.segmentation of the expression plane of an entire semiotic system" (p. 268) – that such complexity finds its counterpart in the expression and content planes of the code. More simply, "the aesthetic experience, by revealing that within its basic matter there is a further space in which sub-forms and sub-systems can be isolated, suggests that the codes on which the aesthetic sign relies can likewise be systematically submitted to such further segmentation" (p. 268). Reading an aesthetic text thus triggers an inflation in the overall complexity of the addressee's semantic universe: it quite literally increases one's culture.

In keeping with his loyalties to the semiotic approach, Eco also redefines aesthetic rapture in terms of this ongoing "complication." Because the logic of his own system leads to the conclusion that all works of art can have meaning in excess of any one code imposed on them, and exist "as a magic spell that is radically impermeable to all semiotic approach" (p. 270), Eco postulates "an underlying system of mutual correlations" (p. 271, a single design or "systematic rule" by means of which the text's many messages can be consolidated. This he calls the work's idiolect, and its contemplation is the source of aesthetic rapture:

> The semiotic notion of an aesthetic idiolect explains the vague expression of 'cosmicity' that the addressee feels when contemplating a work of art. Insofar as every one of its levels is semiosically interconnected, the aesthetic text continuously transforms its denotations into new connotations; none of its items stop at their first interpretant, contents are never received for their own sake but rather as the sign-vehicle for something else. (p. 274)

Since this deferral of closure focuses the reader's attention on semiosis itself, the aesthetic experience brings about a reconsideration of the way we make meaning in general: "the addressee becomes aware of new semiosic possibilities and is thereby compelled to rethink the whole language, the entire inheritance of what has been said, can be said, and could or should be said" (p. 274).

This account of code modification correlates the development of new conventions with an increased awareness of current ones in much the same way that Culler's theory does. But Eco awards the central role in this process to the *aesthetic* text, read by the ordinary addressee. He thus explicitly bypasses the metacritical enterprise promoted by Culler. While Culler posits the need for a separate discipline in order to reveal the conventions of reading, Eco subsumes the metacritical *prise de conscience* in the general process of reading. This seems much the more defensible position, if only because it explains past code evolution in the absence of a structuralist poetics. Specifically, Eco explains how the systematic rule of a text can be hypostatized into an idiolect, extended to other works of the same author, other authors of the same period, or even a whole culture, ultimately to be inscribed as history (p. 272). All of this occurs at the hands of the literary exegetes and historians, with no help from semiotic poeticians.

Unfortunately, Eco compromises his system's general applicability by making a generic distinction that is clearly aberrant from the structuralist point of view. He distinguishes aesthetic texts from all others on the basis of their ambiguity and self-focus. But it seems self-evident that if ambiguity and self-focusing derive from the violation of norms, *any* text can be made code-inventive simply by reading it according to conventions it seems to violate. Code enrichment does not depend on formal structures alone, but on processes of meaning production as well.

Equally contestable is Eco's assumption that overcoding increases the complexity of the code at the expense of the text. The design of the idiolect consolidates the many semantic units and levels of the text into a more economical figure, which in turn can be combined with other such figures from other works by the same or different authors, in order to reduce semiotic complexity into historical simplicity. While Eco's perception of the solidarity between various components of the work does to some degree justify this metaphoric totalization, his comparison of the work with a *langue* (p. 271) should alert him to his blindness: to the extent a work is like a language, it is not reducible to an historical fact or stable pattern; if it is a code, it is a never-ending process of structuration, and the "magnetization" of cultural units the historian might record as its idiolect is only a transitory state in its being.

More obvious still: to the extent that a work succeeds in transforming the "common codes," it will succeed in modifying its own identity, since that identity is inseparable from those codes. In other words, any reading of an aesthetic text necessarily invalidates itself and requires a rereading productive of further code changes, and thus another rereading, *ad infinitum*. That such a dialectic reproduces in microcosm the play of *parole* and *langue*, or performance and competence, is underlined by Eco's own contention that the idiolect, which he initially identifies as a code, is to be understood (two paragraphs later) in terms of an abstract model "which constitutes the performance of an underlying competence" (p. 272).

Under the apparently tidy dichotomy of signification and communication, then, *A Theory of Semiotics* flirts with a model of meaning that merges performance and competence, code and message, in a single complex notion. Clearly, to the extent that this merger argues against the possibility of studying one in the absence of the other, it also invalidates the structuralist claim to rigor and objectivity: if a system cannot be isolated from the instances that constitute it, structuralism can pretend no more distance or generality than any other literary undertaking. It is perhaps for this reason that Eco introduces questionable notions such as the stable idiolect and shrinks from a full-blown dialectical approach to theory. His closest admission of the inseparability of signification and communication comes in the last pages of the work, where he accords semiosis a "double (systematic and processual) aspect." But in the next breath, he quickly reasserts the semiotician's dream of reducing everything to a determinate structure: "semiotics treats subjects of semiosic acts in the same way: either they can be defined in terms of semiotic structures or – from this point of view – they do not exist at all" (p. 316).

This is perhaps the most forceful expression of the structural brand of what I call objectivism: the assumption, on premises similar to those elucidated by Hirsch, that objectivity is attainable, that it is determined by intersubjective accord rather than propositional veracity, and that knowledge, like all linguistic phenomena, is conditioned by the *langue* within which it is cast and can therefore best be understood as a shared interpersonal structure of meaning units. Such a conceptual bias results when one severs the notion of intention, such as informs Hirsch's work, from that of the shared codes which intentions invoke. The authority for this severance is, of course, Saussure in the case of the structuralists; but we shall see in the coming chapter that other authorities can provide equally compelling grounds for completely different notions of objectivity.

The important point here, however, is that the structuralist desire to assimilate meaning processes into structural paradigms poses certain problems for the study of reader response. Eco's second

American work, *The Role of the Reader*, emblematizes these problems and the general limitations of the structuralist reduction.

Reading as Textual Structure

Given Eco's conviction that semiosis must be described as a structure, it is not surprising that he inaugurates *The Role of the Reader* with a pictorial schema outlining all of the acts a text might elicit in terms of textual structures. The initial chapter of this collection of essays[2] diagrams reading through a single chart, each of whose ten interconnected boxes marks both an operation performed by the reader and a component of the textual structure. Although these boxes are not arranged in a rigid hierarchy, it is clear that they interact with one another along certain lines. The first three boxes, consisting of the codes and subcodes (box one), the circumstances of utterance (box two), and the linear text manifestation (box three), can be distinguished from the remaining seven, all of which represent portions of the actualized text content.

The most basic unit of actualized content is the *discursive structure* (box four) that results when "the reader confronts the linear text manifestation with the system of codes and subcodes provided by the language in which the text is written" (*Role*, p. 17). Circumstances of utterance such as historical and biographical information about the author, his period, social context, and so forth, inform this confrontation. During the production of discursive structures, the reader must actualize not only those semantic properties explicitly manifested in the text, but also those implicit in its lexemes – its words individually considered – and relevant to the work (*Role*, p. 23). For instance, the lexeme "man" brings with it a number of anatomical properties the reader can either "blow up" or "narcotize," depending on their relevance. If the man in question is running, the property of having legs will be blown up, while that of having a pancreas (for instance) will be narcotized (*Role*, p. 23).

Eco calls this process the implementation of semantic disclosures and further specifies that it depends on a textual operator or topic. The topic is the general frame of reference of the text, and it regulates the formation of unified levels of sense, or isotopies, by imposing limits on the semantic disclosures. In other words,

the textual topic helps the reader to select the right frames, to reduce them to a manageable format, to blow up and to narcotize given semantic properties of the lexemes to be amalgamated, and to establish the isotopy according to which he decides to interpret the linear text manifestation so as to actualize the discursive structure of a text. (*Role*, p. 27)

Once this is done, "the reader knows what 'happens' in a given text" (ibid.).

Out of the elementary discursive structures, the reader next constructs the *narrative structures* or *fabula* (box six): "the basic story stuff, the logic of actions or the syntax of characters, the time-oriented course of events" (*Role*, p. 27). This concept is close to the Russian formalist notion, but Eco specifies that it "need not be a sequence of human actions . . . but can also concern a temporal transformation of ideas or a series of events concerning inanimate objects" (ibid.). Further, it does not always represent a condensation of the discursive structures but can just as easily expand them – as is the case when the text provides a fragmentary dialogue out of which a reader must extrapolate a series of events (*Role*, pp. 28–9).

To elaborate the *fabula*, the reader must infer its outcome, that is, forecast on the basis of intertextual frames what will happen next. In other words, the reader extends the incipient propositions of the *fabula* to "a still-bracketed possible world" (*Role*, p. 31) and hazards a hypothesis about the direction the *fabula* is taking. Because the reader draws on intertextual frames and has "to 'walk,' so to speak, outside the text, in order to gather intertextual support (a quest for analogous 'topoi,' themes, or motives)" (*Role*, p. 32), Eco christens this hypothesis formation *inferential walks* and locates it on the extensional side of his chart in box seven.

The possible world to which such hypotheses contribute forms another extensional box (number ten), while the bracketed version of the same possible world (which has not yet been confirmed by the text) forms box five. The final possible world of box ten represents the concretization of the text and, as such, the portrayal of "what the text accepts and mentions as 'actual' and what has to be recognized as a mere matter of propositional attitudes on the parts both of the reader and of the characters of the story" (*Role*, p. 37). It is thus the stage at which decisions of credibility and verisimilitude are made, on the basis of a comparison between the "real" world and the text's world (ibid.).

An intensional version of this same category, dealing with ideological structures such as "Good vs. Bad, Positive vs. Negative, True vs. False, or even . . . Life vs. Death and Nature vs. Culture" (*Role*, p. 38) forms box nine; but Eco concedes it may be reducible to box ten, which he specifically formulated to deal with ideological problems in an extensional perspective. Finally, box eight covers the actantial structures or roles to which one can reduce the *fabula*; but Eco makes little use of this category in his discussions.

One cannot help but notice the affinities between Eco's schema and the ideas of prior theoreticians of reading. Like Ingarden, Eco has reading culminate in the constitution of a world structure based on one's intertextual knowledge and semantic universe. The process of inferential walking reiterates Iser's notion of recognition, expectation, and gestalt formation, while the mechanics of semantic disclosure approximate those of implication, as described by Hirsch. Likewise, the generation of narrative structures on the basis of intertextual codes accords with Culler's overall thesis of naturalization.

But Eco's rendition of these ideas is remarkable in its transcendence of the opposition between textual structure and subjective act. Each of the "boxes" in his scheme at once marks a structural component of the literary text as it is actualized by the reader *and* an activity of the reader as elicited by the text. Since the text's structure cannot be actualized as such in the absence of the reader's performance, which is in turn dependent upon the textual "score" to guide it, Eco's model eludes reduction to causal paradigms. Reading is neither a production of textual structures nor a response to them, but both at once.

The most explicit formulation of this entanglement comes under the rubric of the text's *subcode*. This notion covers not only (1) the rules of the parent language upon which the text draws, and (2) the particular literary competence the reader brings to his reading, but also (3) the rules governing the specific interaction of reader code and textual code that occurs during the reading of that text. In other words, the competence necessary to read a particular text is not just the sum of two extrinsic codes but the result of a process of structuring that takes place during the act of reading: "a well-organized text on the one hand presupposes a model of competence coming, so to speak, from outside the text, but on the other hand works to build up, by merely textual means, such a competence" (*Role*, p. 8). In this sense, competence is not merely a matrix of conventions that can be conveniently listed, but also the process of their development.

An anthropomorphic version of the same notion is Eco's concept of the Model Reader. Unlike its more historical counterparts, the Model Reader Eco describes is entirely a product of the reading process that elaborates it. Conversely, "the text is nothing else but the semantic-pragmatic production of its own Model Reader" (*Role*, p. 10). In the light of Eco's overall theory of semiosis, one might say that the text as subcode is the product of its reading – a transitory structuration in an unending process – while the reader's activity is nothing more than the event of that subcode's development.

The circularity of this formulation is seductive, if only because it avoids the pitfalls of both pure objectivism and pure subjectivism: it neither says the text is just anything one might make of it (as does Holland, implicitly), nor does it argue that the text is an immutable structure of class relationships, transcendent of individual instance. On the other hand, it is a theory that seems to close the door on practice. If the competence underlying a text's proper reading is generated automatically by that text, one need only read the text and reflect on one's reading to become aware of that text's particularity. Only by reneging on the dialectical promise of his theory and postulating a textual structure transcendent of reading acts – indeed, to some measure inaccessible to the uninitiated – can Eco reinstall his epistemological privilege and justify his authority. This is, in fact, precisely what he does.

The Subversion of a Theory

That Eco's theory has hit an impasse in the translation to practice is first manifest in his ambivalent treatment of the Model Reader. Although his identification of this notion with the textual subcode clearly implies that *every* text has a Model Reader, whether or not that Model Reader be explicitly acknowledged, another theoretical notion suggests just the contrary. On the basis of a dubious generic distinction between "open" and "closed" texts, Eco divides all literary works into two groups: those that acknowledge, invite, and thematize the activity of the reader, and those which merely "aim at arousing a precise response on the part of more or less precise empirical readers" (*Role*, p. 8). By correlating the Model Reader with the former kind of text, he confuses his theoretical category with the more mundane idea of a thematized reader. The reasons for this confusion are not immediately obvious.

It is possible that Eco's roots in the structuralist tradition lead him to assume that implementing his theory requires the location and description of a Model Reader in the texts he studies. This is not the case, of course, since his own theory suggests that any interpretive reading will manifest a Model Reader through its determination of the text's subcode. In fact, his conflation of the Model Reader and that subcode suggests that *only* an interpretive reading can describe a Model Reader: a distanced structural analysis of the text would not be able to "perform" the development of a competence.

Nonetheless, Eco persists in "looking for" his reader in the form of a visible thematic component. Obviously, in many cases, including the detective stories, comic books, and spy novels that Eco favours, "one can at most guess what kind of reader their authors had in mind, not which requirements a 'good' reader should meet" (*Role*, p. 19). In such cases the description of the Model-Reader-as-theme cannot get off the ground. These texts seem indeed closed to Eco's program, but the fact that we can nonetheless read them – and presumably actualize their subcodes – suggests that the Model Reader is perfectly accessible. It is Eco's confusion of that notion with the idea of a thematized reader that denies him this same access: although he purports to describe a universal phenomenon, the only exempla he can find are those of unconventional texts. In short, his theory seems plausible enough, but it does not seem to correlate to a distinctive practice.

The import of this stricture is graphically illustrated by the closing chapter of Eco's work, where he finally does perform – at great length – a reading of sorts. While it is clear that every text generates a Model Reader – in the dialectical sense of the term – and that therefore *any* text would serve to perform/illustrate it, Eco selects a short story by Alphonse Allais remarkable only for its aberration. Written in 1890, *Un Drame bien parisien* presents a short sequence of barely adumbrated events which, according to Eco, draw the reader into making erroneous assumptions that the text first repudiates and then, in a perverse turnabout, builds upon.

In Eco's terminology, *Drame* lines up a number of discursive structures sufficiently vague to cause its reader to make some questionable inferential walks and to generate, on the basis of intertextual frames, a *fabula* and possible world at odds with those explicitly revealed by the final passages of the text. Specifically, the reader is led to believe that a jealous married couple, Raoul and Marguerite, are the characters in disguise at a masked ball, and that each has assumed the disguise of the other's presumed lover in hopes of catching his or her spouse in the act. The text does not directly authorize any of these assumptions and ultimately reveals the couple to be not Raoul and Marguerite but total strangers to each other – a fact that causes them no small surprise when they unmask. Nevertheless, the last portion of the story informs us this little incident had a profound and salutary effect on Raoul and Marguerite, who lived happily ever after.

A traditional reader-oriented critical approach – Iser's, for instance – could account for *Drame*'s teasing in an interesting way. One is thus entitled to ask what particular virtues Eco's model can exhibit. Since the translation of the story into his vocabulary and categories takes an inordinate amount of discourse and involves digressions into modal logic, theories of possible worlds, and formalaic representations of the plot (all of which are informative but superfluous to the task at hand), one might expect it to provide a proportionately richer enactment of the text's subcode/Model Reader and an insight into reading semiosis in general.

In fact, the results are rather disappointing. Focusing primarily on the final "box" of his chart – the possible world constructed by the text in conjunction with its reader – Eco states as his central thesis that "when one imagines a set of individuals (and of relations among them) that the text cannot finally admit, one in fact resorts to opposing to the world of the text a possible world not accessible to it" (*Role*, p. 217). This seemingly tautological conclusion carries with it some highly questionable presuppositions.

For one thing, it implicitly redefines reading in terms of an opposition between text and reader. For another, it implicitly renounces a paradigm of meaning generation for one of meaning evaluation. Eco's thesis is that the reader forms hypotheses or tentative possible worlds, which he then verifies or abandons through a true/false decision. There is no room in this process for a compromise: when a reader imagines a world the text cannot admit, he must simply "get rid of his world so as to accept the state of affairs established by the *fabula*" (*Role*, p. 245). Not only does this imply that the state of affairs established by the *fabula* is completely determinate, it also negates the dialectic of mutual determination between reader and subcode:

between the world of the *fabula* and the world of the reader's *wrong* forecasts, there is no accessibility. If they are wrong it is so because the reader has imagined individuals and properties the world of the *fabula* could not conceive of. When the reader realizes his mistake he does not manipulate his possible (wrong) world to come back to the story. He simply throws it out. (*Role*, p. 246)

Such a repudiation of one's beliefs may occur, but only on the level of the superficial "events" of the *fabula*; and it is only visible in the trick texts that fascinate Eco. To the extent that one's relationship with the more complex and ideological aspects of the *fabula*, such as projected moods, sentiments, thoughts, ideas, and so forth eludes reduction to a mere true/false decision, Eco's model cannot hope to account for even the most traditional complex works of fiction – much less any of the other genres. Its value as an exegetic tool is limited, and as a portrayal of the reading process it does injustice to the complexities of Eco's theoretical description. In fact, the true/false paradigm proposed by Eco does not even have the virtues of its closest counterpart in this study, Hirsch's idea of validation. For while Hirsch grounds validation in shared classes and acknowledges these classes to be the products of interpretation – and hence uncertain or subject to modification – Eco makes his form of "validation" a simple matching with an immutable structure. And he attributes this structure to the *fabula*, as if to imply that the *fabula* was not itself the product of the reader's work.

On the contrary, Eco's original theory clearly subordinates the *fabula* and the possible world it grounds to the hermeneutic progress of the reader. He insists that the possible worlds in question are "'pregnant' worlds of which one must know all the acting individuals and their properties" (*Role*, p. 218). But properties are determined through semantic disclosures that are regulated, according to Eco, by the textual topic. And that topic stands in relation to the individual lexemes, with their potentially infinite number of sememes – embedded properties or submeanings – in much the same way that the hermeneutic "horizon" stands in reference to its "theme." Thus to uncover the requisite properties, one must single out the pertinent lexemes and sememes, which in turn requires the formulation of a topic that itself derives from a selection of pertinent lexemes.

The hermeneutic circle is thus thoroughly embedded in Eco's model of reading. Each successive portion of a text evolves against the horizon (according to the topic) of those which precede it. As each new "part" of the text emerges against the "whole" thus far constituted, it modifies that whole, such that the topic, like the subcode it helps develop, can be thought of as one face of a dialectic between structure and act. The important thing to retain is that at no point is the topic simply "thrown out." Like Iser and Holland before him, Eco argues for a holistic notion of meaning – and thus disputes the logic of his own practical application. Readers do not throw away their readings, if only because those readings are not stable structures, but evolving structurations; one cannot discard the possible world one has constructed, because, by Eco's own theory, that possible world is not given in a mode stable enough to permit disqualification.

It is because he suppresses this conclusion that Eco does not recognize the shift in his program from the logic of semiotic description to that of evaluative criticism. When he phrases his description in terms of possible worlds the "text cannot finally admit," he displaces the concern of his investigation from significance to admissibility. Rather than depicting semiosis "in action," he tries to isolate a deviation from textual prescription and thus introduces, on the heels of a theory stressing the transience of codes, the notion of an immutable code. The reemergence of this concept vitiates much of his theoretical achievement by reasserting an objectivist perspective and reducing the role of semiotics to that of traditional evaluative criticism.

Along similar lines, the notion of a stable code reintroduces the spectre of the autonomous textual object that not only Eco's theory but semiotics in general has rejected. If one can reduce the text to a restricted message (see *Role*, p. 206) and the possible worlds it projects to a stable formal structure and limited "semantic encyclopedia," such that "accessibility (and compatibility) are not a matter of psychology, but one of objective and formal comparison between two cultural constructs" (*Role*, p. 225), then one has effectively hypostatized the literary work as historical fact. And that is but one step from granting it the status of a natural object.

Ironically, this objectification of the text – which carries with it a concomitant redefinition of the Model Reader as some unspecified third party distinct from both Eco and the text – opens the way for some amusing subjective readings on Eco's part. If the above citation is to be believed, he intends to mark a higher degree of objectivity by reifying the textual structure; but such reifications always carry with them the assumption of a literal level of meaning, and Eco is not exempt from confusing that supposed meaning with his own idio-syncratic response. As "objective" analyst of a stable structure, he never questions the universality of his reading.

For instance, in reading *Drame*, much of Eco's thesis rests on the episode where the two masked figures, having rendezvoused for a night of passion, unmask and discover they do not know each other. For Eco, their surprise can *only* be explained by the fact that they are not Raoul and Marguerite – that is, the characters' surprise *must be* a function of the reader's: "were the Templar and the Pirogue Raoul and Marguerite, they would have recognized each other. *Were they not, they would not have reason to be astonished*" (*Role*, p. 254, my italics; see also p. 247). At no point does it occur to Eco that the sememe "stranger" is not necessarily synonymous with "not Raoul" or "not Marguerite." Presumably, his own cultural encyclopedia does not code as astonishing the discovery that one's companion in an intimate situation is not in fact the person one thought it was.

I am not suggesting that Eco's reading is wrong, only that his (unconscious) belief in a transcendent structure has led him to accept as literal or self-evident meanings that by his own definition can never be. We must remember, however, that this confusion results from his desire to implement theory with practice. Since his theory of semiosis attends to the role of particular acts of communication, he naturally aims at a practice capable of dealing with individual texts. Yet his practical application violates his theory. The theory may in fact declare all codes to be the product of an ongoing dialectic between performance and competence; it may indeed merge the reader of a text with the subcode of that text; but when it comes to practice, Eco cannot refrain from postulating a permanent underlying code.

And in a sense, he has no choice. For one of the implicit thrusts of his theory as I have extended it is to dissolve the distinction between the semiotic analyst and the interpretive critic. If the description of a subcode can only be achieved through its performance as interpreta-tion, the distanced and objective analysis of such a structure can only be a delusion: were Eco to extend his theory to its logical conclusion, he would have to concede that from a practical point of view there is no particular function for the semiotician as regards individual texts.

So if Eco cannot bring himself to take the final step and *perform* through his own reading the thematization of the Model Reader, it is because such a move would acknowledge the gratuity of his gesture: if any well-argued reading will disclose the Model Reader of a text, the reading of a skilled semiotician has no claim to distinctiveness. Likewise, the truth value of a traditional interpretive performance in one sense exceeds that of a structural description, since the interpreter, like any performer, can embody the artistic work and animate its structure without hypostatizing it in a static abstraction. The structuralist description, on the other hand, is powerless to render the work's structure as structuring process, at least insofar as it does not put into question its final configuration.

There is a sense, however, in which the interpretive performance is also inadequate. Because it does not explicitly acknowledge its function as embodiment of semiosis, it cannot be relied upon to provoke the reassessment of text and code that Eco's theory invites. Only when the understanding of a particular work expands to an awareness of semiosis in general as well as an awareness of its own dialectical constitution does it attain the higher level of insight necessary to code change. This would suggest that while Eco's approach to reader-response criticism may not attain its goals, neither is a reversion to pure interpretation warranted. What seems to be needed is a theory and method that retain the theoretical insights of the semiosic model while at the same time transcending its objectivist delusions; that is, an approach to meaning that would not feel compelled to maintain an absolute distinction between theoretical analyst and lay exegete, between "objective" structural description and "subjective" interpretive act, in a word, between theory and practice.

11

From Structuralism to Post-Structuralism – Derrida's Strategy

The writings of the structuralists demonstrate that the process/ structure of meaning is beyond simple description, both in general and in particular. Even viewed dialectically, it cannot be controlled by a concept both because it cannot be reduced to a structure, and because the event of conceptualization assumes a further grounding structure – and thus puts into question its own "conclusion." This stricture holds *a fortiori* for particular instances of meaning: to the extent that it can *mean* in the absence of its author (and that is the condition of conventional meaning) a specific meaning cannot be enclosed in an originating intention, nor can it ever be fully present in any event of communication; it necessarily presents itself within another (an other) instance and structure of meaning.

A critical gesture adequate to this paradox would have to re-nounce exegetic and theoretical closure – and the distinction between the two. In the preceding chapters I have tried to show how various authors resist that move, elaborating critical programs loyal to the discipline's tradition of closure, but at odds with the dialectical meaning their theories advance. Structuralism demonstrates to what extent the same discord arises when one tries to dislocate the structure of the event (theoretical description) from the event of structure (interpretive act). The structuralists renounce interpretive particulars specifically to overcome the idiosyncrasy of instance, but their axiomatic separation of poetic theory from interpretive practice leads to no stable science, if only because by their own definition even theoretical discourse instantiates and realigns conventions – and thus transforms the object it purports to describe. We have seen how this constant deferral of a system's identity saturates general descriptions of meaning as well as its particular instances.

Even theory that deliberately disqualifies itself as an instance of particular meaning cannot *not* be a semiotic event. To the extent that it means *any thing*, even the most apparently neutral "description of a system" inaugurates a disruption of that system: because it can always mean *some thing* to someone else, each instance of meaning contains as a structural possibility an infinite number of further systems, the inscription of which marks it from the outset as a structure of non-identity. Thus, the structuralist project, if taken seriously, requires the postulation of a structure that encloses within its identity an infinite history and future of other, different, meanings. If one insists on reducing meaning to a single constitutive paradigm, that paradigm must be one of self-difference. In this sense, the structuralist agenda feeds directly into the *post*-structuralist paradox of identity as the possibility of otherness.

This paradox can be phrased historically. To account for *all* the semiotic events under its aegis, a systematizing theory must configure the eventuality of its own disruption or invalidation; the inclusion of that eventuality *as a structural characteristic* builds self-suspension into the theory (as illustrated by Culler's inclusion of irony in his description of "competences"). The synchronic analysis that would step out of history itself constitutes a further moment in history and assures a further theoretical matrix to ground that moment. It thus remains unavoidably "inside" the history it purports to enclose. The structuralist principle of isolating theory from instance leads to a post-structuralist dissolution of that boundary. Theory and practice, momentary instance and permanent truth, the structure of meaning and its instantiation, are each within and without each other. Every semiotic fact is an act, every history of events an event in history, not just on(c)e, but all (ways).

Such formulations may appear contrived, but they are useful for expressing/enacting the "meaning" in question. Coinages that contest themselves and resist stabilization into any single meaning resist, if only momentarily, the reduction to *any thing*, and thus convey, albeit too cutely, the complexity of the matter that occupies them. It is from this perspective that one can most comfortably grasp the strategy of word-play most infamously exemplified by Jacques Derrida, whose enormously influential writings occupy a spot too central in the current polemics not to merit at least brief consideration in this study.[1]

Although he is frequently treated as an original moment in contemporary thought, Derrida's work in many respects simply extends to its logical conclusion the ongoing attempt to "know" meaning that we have charted throughout this book. He shares with his predecessors the desire to portray semiosis in its complexity, but he profits from their shortcomings by recognizing at the outset that strategies of fragmentation are not up to the task. Rather than overcoming discipline- or tradition-bound hierarchies, such oppositions perpetuate them and prevent the emergence of meaning in its alterity:

> an opposition of metaphysical concepts (e.g., speech/writing, presence/absence, etc.) is never the confrontation of two terms, but a hierarchy and the order of a subordination. Deconstruction cannot be restricted or immediately pass to a neutralization: it must, through a double gesture, a double science, a double writing – put into practice a *reversal* of the classical opposition *and* a general *displacement* of the system.[2]

This gesture at once steps into history and pulls back from it, provoking and accelerating the displacements and regresses of meaning with such rapidity (density) that they seem to cohere in its very structure. In other words, meaning's "identity within difference" is *enacted into* its structural definition, such that the possibility of its various "other" meanings, in other places and other times, becomes the condition of its identity. Spatially figured in the language of phenomenological hermeneutics, the horizon(s) grounding meaning must be rethought as part of the theme: the outside circumstances are already inside meaning; meaning can only mean by virtue of the outside, the "other" it contains as its possibility of functioning.

The difficulty we have in thinking such notions points to a major difference between Derrida and the more properly literary critics we shall be looking at in the rest of this study. His work does not limit itself to literary meaning *per se*, and it does not just define by example but through the direct formulation of paradoxes drawn from the key concepts of western thought. While critics such as Paul de Man or Stanley Fish work to redefine meaning from within the critical traditions that formed them and generally extrapolate their arguments from the *narrative* of an "original" text, Derrida organizes his arguments around a single conceptual locus, which he posits as problematic – and then problematizes, by tracing its various identities (and the arguments they undermine or ground) through a variety of texts. Because they exist only in reference to such constellations of texts, Derrida's "ideas" owe no allegiance to particular disciplines or traditions but manifest themselves as embedded in all texts in general.

To achieve this "ungrounding," Derrida has to assimilate in his writing a widely dispersed selection of philosophical, social, scientific, and literary texts, each of which carries its own set of marked terms and concepts. By emerging from "everywhere at once" the theory carries the proof of its universality and the confirmation that it is not itself the product of any specific conceptual structure. But by the same token, it must be articulated in a variety of vocabularies, the totality of which the average reader is unlikely to master. Accordingly, many find the density of the Derridean text and its simultaneous exploitation and subversion of crucial yet unfamiliar terms simply too high a price to pay. Be that as it may, his strategy of "definition within a (non)concept" offers a powerful alternative to the more tractable versions of dialectical criticism that emerge in the wake of structuralism to champion the notion of meaning we have seen foreshadowed.

Crudely speaking, Derrida's strategy consists in taking apart key philosophical terms or assumptions and elaborating the contradictory structures and arguments they conceal. His goal is nothing less than to deconstruct the entire tradition of western metaphysics, with its postulation of a self-identical unified presence of meaning as distinct from the secondary, derivative inscription of that meaning in written language – a tradition and attitude Derrida calls "logocentrism." Within the context of this study he shares with the three "dialectical" critics I shall be treating the explicit conviction that meaning as presence or act and meaning as structured and structuring inscription are reciprocally constitutive notions, neither of which can be granted priority over the other. The structures and moments of opposition that mark western thought, then, must be rethought as mere derivative traces of a more elusive "meaning," that cannot itself be located or occur, since it is the condition of possibility of acts and structures, of the temporalization and spatialization of experience. This more elusive notion assumes a variety of guises in Derrida's work, such as *différance, supplément,* or *brisure* (fold, or cleaving), all of which function, I would argue, to designate in its absolute alterity the (no)thing of *meaning*.[3] Derrida's treatment of the Saussurian subordination of writing to speech provides a familiar and accessible instance of how such "concepts" emerge.

Saussure's two central postulates are that within any language (1) the correlation of a given signifier, or acoustic image, with its associated signified, or concept, is purely arbitrary (there is no reason the sound "cat" should designate an animal), and (2) correlatively, the value of a signifier or signified cannot be determined by its counterpart but must be grounded in the difference between that signifier (signified) and all others – the value of the color maroon exists only to the extent that it can be differentiated from red, brown, sienna, burgundy, and so forth; to function fully, the sound "bat" need only *not* be confused with "pat," "mat," "fat," etc. – it has no pure identity. (For Saussure's discussion of these two principles, see *Cours de linguistique générale*, pp. 155–66.)[4]

From the first of these postulates Derrida concludes that all speech has as its condition of possibility a prior inscription or encoding. If the relationship of signifier to signified is arbitrary, there can be no natural hierarchy between them; thus the fact that correlations of sound to concept *do* exist implies an institutionalization or inscription. In that sense, writing is not a secondary representation of the spoken word, it is its prerequisite: "the very idea of institution – and hence of the arbitrary sign – is inconceivable prior to the possibility of writing and outside of its horizon" (*De la grammatologie*, p. 65).[5]

Likewise, Saussure's definition of writing as a representative image goes against his own thesis: if writing is the signifier of spoken language's signified, they must be *arbitrarily* related, and no natural resemblance or image can be posited. In this sense, writing is at once "more external to speech, no longer being its 'image' or its 'symbol,'" and more internal to speech, which is already in and of itself a writing" (*Grammatologie*, p. 68).

At the same time that speech turns out to be derivative of the structure of inscription it was said to ground, meaning finds itself deprived of presence and self-identity. Language cannot be reduced to a configuration of full terms that could guarantee the stability of meaning by their identity and hence subordinate it once again to a "present," precisely because, as Saussure himself argues, "in language there is nothing other than differences" (*Cours*, p. 166). Because linguistic value is a function of differentiation, not full identity, one cannot locate the origin of meaning, much less of concepts, any*where* within language: "the signified concept is never present in itself, in a presence that would refer only to itself. Every concept is by right and necessarily inscribed in a chain or system within which it refers to the other, to all other concepts through a systematic play of differences" ("La Différance," p. 11).[6]

The identity of meaning is constantly deferred, then, through the play of differences that constitute it. This play, however, cannot simply be grasped as a system, since it is precisely not a concept, but that which makes concepts possible: "such a play, *différance*, is no longer simply a concept but the possibility of conceptuality, of the conceptual process and system in general" ("Différance," p. 11). To convey such a (non)concept, Derrida coins the term *différance*, a (non)word that simultaneously exists (in writing) and doesn't (in speech), as noun and gerund, state and act, difference and deferral, yet is none of these things alone. Because it displaces meaning as stable structure or full origin with a play of differentiation and deferral having no beginning, no end, and no presence, *différance* disqualifies the truth of its own originality. It is not the "source" of meaning precisely because it deconstructs the idea of source; it cannot be understood, because it closes the door on closure:

That which is written as *différance* will be therefore the movement of play that "produces," by that which is not simply an activity, these differences, these effects of difference. This does not mean the *différance* that produces differences is prior to them, in a simple, unmodified, indifferent present. *Différance* is the non-full, non-simple "origin," the structured and differing origin of differences. Consequently, the name of origin no longer pertains to it. ("Différance," p. 12)

Derrida's strategy now becomes easier to put into perspective. In contrast to prior theoreticians, he focuses explicitly on the self-difference of meaning and tries to condense its inexpressibility into a "single" (non)term. Deconstructive criticism always enacts and states the paradox of meaning by both conceptualizing it and then putting the truth value of such conceptualization into question, but Derrida's strategy defeats the sequentiality of that "then" by playing on both sides of meaning at the "same" time, "within" the "same" term – whose apparent simplicity unravels into a web of aporias that, taken collectively, allegorize *différance*. That is, Derrida breaks down apparently monadic concepts into myriad constellations of further (and former) moves. From out of a single term comes a sequence of reversals, the history of which Derrida envisions as a structural characteristic of the concept in question, which thus becomes an emblem or version of *différance*.[7]

Iterability, which he elaborates in his discussion of Austin and speech acts, provides an easy illustration of this process. Reasoning that it is a necessary quality of an utterance that it mean something even in the absence of its utterer, Derrida concludes that one must rethink the structural definition of speech acts to include this eventuality: "[the] unity of the signifying form only constitutes itself by virtue of its iterability, by the possibility of its being repeated in the absence not only of its 'referent,' which is self-evident, but in the absence of a determinate signified or of the intention of actual signification, as well as of all intention of present communication" ("Signature," p. 183). A structural description of meaning, in other words, must necessarily account for all the possible events it can give rise to: "even if this (eventual) possibility only occurred once, and never again, we would still have to account for that one time and analyze whatever it is in the structural functioning of the mark that renders such an event possible" ("Limited Inc," p. 195).

Whatever eventual acts or ideas a meaning might ultimately trigger are from this perspective already "in" the meaning as a structure of possibility. Yet as an object of knowledge, meaning is always already out of any conceptual closure we might build for it: "what is valid for intention, always differing, deferring, and without plenitude, is also valid, correlatively, for the object (*qua* signified or referent) thus aimed at" ("Limited Inc," p. 195). This formulation does not do away with intention or the act of meaning any more than it denies its structure(s); rather it brings these two faces together to mark a further step in the logic of meaning we are charting: "we will be dealing with different kinds of marks or chains of iterable marks and not with an opposition between citational utterances, on the one hand, and singular and original event-utterances, on the other" ("Signature," p. 192).

Merging potential meaning event into the structure of iterability in general, Derrida conflates history as interpretive act and history as theoretical structure. To the extent that it eludes the dichotomy of theory versus practice, such a complex field/gesture seems to clash with the traditional concerns of literary criticism. But as I have tried to show in preceding chapters, its groundwork already exists in a long series of previous attempts to wed dialectical theories of meaning with exegetic programs. Derrida's contribution to this realignment is to conflate particular exegetic meaning and general theoretical truth, by grounding both in a structure of eventuality exceeding the control of either. The plight of the individual reader is thus absorbed into the structure of meaning in general, which necessarily reiterates an agenda of self-difference and dialectic reversal.

In practical terms, this means that post-structuralist writing must espouse a self-suspending itinerary of dialectical reversal. Yet to the extent such works retain the disciplinary format of effacement before an "original" literary text, they necessarily modify Derrida's strategy. Before deconstructing any key terms into sequences of aporias, they must extract the key terms from the sequence of the literary text. Where Derrida unravels the histories woven into the (non)concept, these critics transform the literary work's history into a series of propositions that ultimately culminates in a complex (non)concept of meaning.

Fidelity to traditional formats also aggravates these critics' relationship to history, which, as the collective embodiment of dialectical meaning, increasingly moves to the foreground of their speculation. Because post-structuralists see history as a structure within which all events are already inscribed, as well as an infinite sequence of events linked to endless structures, they are torn between the limitless possibilities of action and the pre-limitation of structure, between their ability to control history and history's ability to control them. Naturally, not all critics react similarly to this predicament. In an attempt to illustrate the various forms which dialectical criticism can assume, and to dispel any suspicions that a dialectical or self-differing vision of meaning locks literary study into a particular stance, I have chosen to examine the work of three disparate yet consistently dialectical critics: Stanley Fish, Roland Barthes, and Paul de Man. Each is in a different field, concerned with a different historical period, and the product of a different background. Each has done his most influential work on a different genre and publicly affiliated himself with a different movement (or rather dissociated himself from a different tradition). And each, in my opinion, conceptualizes *and* performs the infinite regress of meaning in a different fashion. For Fish the thematics of meaning merge with those of belief, and the regress he traces in his best-known works finds relief in an ultimate transcendence. Barthes' notion of meaning valorizes the very loss of certainty that Fish denies as a possibility. Eschewing transcendence for institutional subversion and the erotics of self-disruption, Barthes exploits the self-difference Fish transcends. For de Man, finally, the question is primarily epistemological and concerns man's ability to control history through his knowledge and its expression. Accordingly, it is in rhetoric that de Man finds his grounding tradition and the master tropes of allegory and irony.

Part Four
Three Models of Dialectical Criticism

12

Stanley Fish:
Supersession and Transcendence

Stanley Fish is not normally associated with post-structuralism, and his work scarcely exhibits, in its most recent incarnation, the infatuation with uncertainty and non-closure we associate with that school. On the other hand, Fish does resist, from *Surprised by Sin*[1] up through his volume of collected essays, *Is There a Text in this Class?*,[2] the separation of (1) spatial construct from temporal activity, (2) underlying context from particular instance, or (3) subjective experience from objective artifact. He thus achieves a more complete merger between theory and practice than any of the theoreticians covered thus far. And while it may seem unconventional to affiliate him with the deconstructive school of criticism, his sustained effort to formulate a notion of meaning transcendent of the subjective/objective opposition does culminate in a historical version of Derrida's iterability that displays most of the hallmarks of post-structuralism.

Considered in its development, Fish's work reflects the shift in theoretical approaches to meaning of the past quarter-century. From an early stance that focuses on indeterminacy as a catalyst for reader responses, to a subsequent fascination with the role of interpretive context, to a final position where the distinction between interpretive matrix and the event of understanding ceases to exist, Fish traces much the same itinerary we have outlined in our study of meaning from phenomenology through structuralism to post-structuralism. And he is the first author covered thus far to make the slipperiness of meaning, the ability of a sentence always to mean something different than what it means, the very armature of his theory and exegeses. He differs from what we normally call "post-structuralists" only in that the dialectical displacements of his thought culminate not in an irony (de Man) or ecstasy (Barthes) of suspension, but in a state of transcendent certainty that acknowledges the theoretical necessity of its undoing but cannot instigate it. To grasp the relationship he draws between dialectical meaning and transcendence, we must return to Fish's earliest works.

What the Text Does to Us

Fish's preoccupation with the dialectics of meaning first surfaces in his well-known study of *Paradise Lost, Surprised by Sin*. In this work, he founds his interpretation on the distinction between what he calls the ways of the reader – and by extension of all mankind since the Fall – and the Way of the Lord. His thesis is that Milton recreates in the mind of his reader the drama of the Fall by repeatedly tempting him into erroneous moves, forcing him to recognize the inadequacy of his knowledge and the source of that inadequacy in his fallen state, and finally bringing him to renounce his analytic pretensions and to accept a belief – and revelation-based knowledge. In other words, by experiencing the poem, the reader becomes aware of the "superfluousness of the mold of experience – of space and time – to the perception of what is true" (p. 351).

This edification entails a sequence of reversals of the reader's judgment. By tempting him into making a number of inappropriate or obviously erroneous figural comparisons (pp. 23–30), chronological arrangements (pp. 30–6), moral judgments (pp. 93–103), inferred connotations (pp. 128–42), and analytical partitions (pp. 142–57), Milton forces his reader to accept the inadequacy of his way of knowing. Specifically, the reader learns the futility and error of interpreting the Fall in ways that cast a favorable light on mankind's disobedience to the Lord; he comes to "resist the temptation to submit it to the scrutiny of reason, just as Adam and Eve must maintain the irrelevancy of reason to the one easy prohibition" (p. 244).

From his experience the reader of *Paradise Lost* learns to "affirm the primacy of revelation against the claims of present circumstances as they are urged by the affections and interpreted by reason" (p. 245). And with this affirmation comes a unity in the way of knowing, in that which is known, and in the union of these two now-transcended categories. The way of knowing is unity because it overcomes the analytic partitioning of reality with the belief that there is but one Truth, one thing to be known: "what the reader must learn is that the analytical intellect, so important to the formulation of necessary distinctions, is itself an instrument of perversion and the child of corruption because it divides and contrasts and evaluates where there is in reality a single harmonious unity" (p. 143). By contrast, when man gives himself over to illumination from within, his mind becomes congruent with the object of its desire and is absorbed within it: "the reader labours consciously to recover a lost unity of vision, which, when found, absorbs and nullifies the consciousness" (p. 328).

It is tempting to read this unified vision as an allegory of meaning in its undifferentiated identity as both intentional event and codified structure. Indeed, in the collection of essays that follows *Surprised by Sin*, the paradigm of self-transcendence is extended to the work of literature itself, giving rise to the notion of the *self-consuming artifact* for which the volume is named.[3] If "the insight that God's word is all is *self*-destructive, since acquiring it involves abandoning the perceptual and conceptual categories within which the self moves and by means of which it separately exists" (*Artifacts*, pp. 156–7), it follows that the text motivating such an insight destroys itself as well: "a dialectical presentation succeeds at its own expense; for by conveying those who experience it to a point where they are beyond the aid that discursive or rational forms can offer, it becomes the vehicle of its own abandonment" (*Artifacts*, p. 3). In *Self-Consuming Artifacts*, then, the dialectical theory of meaning provides a paradigm for reading in general, which can no longer be thought of as a mere intuitive beholding, nor the revelation of conceptual truth, but must rather be grasped as the moment/structure in which each of these notions becomes at once the ground and the end of the other. To understand what this means in practice, one must look at Fish's critical procedure.

Fish's readings all have this in common: they describe a series of reversals in the reader's experience of a text. To demonstrate these reversals the critic must focus on the flow of the text, which in turn requires a new definition of meaning that can bypass thorny notions such as connotation and implication by associating the meaning of a literary work with the experience it elicits. Instead of asking "what does this sentence mean?", Fish asks "what does this sentence do?" ("Literature in the Reader: Affective Stylistics," p. 125),[4] and he suggests as a critical goal the "*analysis of the developing responses of the reader in relation to the words as they succeed one another in time*" ("Affective Stylistics," pp. 126–7).

→The advantage of this method is that it works even when no clear meaning for a sentence is available: an ambiguous sentence, or even a "meaningless" one, has, like any other sentence, a definite effect on the reader, which, according to Fish, can always be charted. However obscure a work, one can always "make it signify: first by regarding it as evidence of an experience and then by specifying for that experience a meaning" ("Interpreting the *Variorum*," p. 468).[5]

This methodological principle would seem at once to emphasize the notion of meaning as an experience and to sanction the reduction of that meaning to a conventional concept. Yet Fish directs his polemical sally against this very reduction. Insisting on his method's valorization of the *temporal* side of meaning, he maintains "the basis of the method is a consideration of the *temporal* flow of the reading experience, and it is assumed that the reader responds in terms of that flow and not to the whole experience" ("Affective Stylistics," p. 127). The formalist, against whom Fish writes, takes the opposite tack and "transforms a temporal experience into a spatial one . . . steps back and in a single glance takes in a whole (sentence, page, work) which the reader knows (if at all) only bit by bit, moment by moment" ("Affective Stylistics," pp. 140–1).

In other words, Fish sees his critical program as a rectification and inversion of the normal exegetic serial: he views meaningful structures (texts) as events (reader experiences), and dismisses as ancillary the conceptual paraphernalia critics might hang on such experiences: "it is the experience of an utterance – *all* of it and *not anything that could be said about it*, including anything I could say – that is its meaning" ("Affective Stylistics," p. 131, my italics). Since interpretation is a mere conceptual abstraction of "our immediate linguistic experience," it cannot help but degrade that experience's meaning: "the meaning of any utterance, I repeat, is its experience – all of it – and that experience is immediately compromised the moment you say anything about it" ("Affective Stylistics," p. 160).

One could scarcely find a more forceful expression of the notion of "*meaning as an event*, something that is happening between the words and in the reader's mind" ("Affective Stylistics," p. 128), and a denunciation of the text's objective status. For Fish, the text or sentence that seemed autonomous to the New Critics is "no longer an object, a thing-in-itself, but an *event*, something that *happens* to, and with the participation of, the reader" ("Affective Stylistics," p. 125).

Were this bias towards meaning-as-event to remain unexamined in Fish's work, one could simply classify him as the antithesis of the structuralists in whose heyday he wrote "Affective Stylistics." While continental theoreticians were busy trying to confine meaning to ubiquitous shared structures, Fish was attempting to prove it an ephemeral event the very discussion of which marked its loss. Yet the frequency of personification in Fish's analyses of "what the sentences do to us" suggests not only that texts have autonomous properties but that structure plays a role in meaning which he is suppressing for the sake of polemic. For just as the texts he studies "force" us to do things and "generate" expectations which "impel" us forward, so do they "promise," "stabilize," "give potential form," and "turn on us" as well ("Affective Stylistics," pp. 126, 130).

Such tropes suggest that the "event" of meaning is in fact a response to stable textual patterns. Although Fish does not admit to such a structure in the text *per se*, he confirms its presence in the text of the reader's interpretive experience: "in my method of analysis, the temporal flow is monitored and structured by everything the reader brings with him, by his competences; and it is by taking these into account as they interact with the temporal left to right reception of the verbal string, that I am able to chart and project *the* developing response" ("Affective Stylistics," p. 143). In short, having specified meaning to consist entirely in an *event*, Fish turns around and grounds it in a "regulating and organizing mechanism, pre-existing the actual verbal experience" ("Affective Stylistics," p. 143).

Fish admits that such a mechanism "would be a *spatial* model in the sense that it would reflect any system of rules pre-existing, and indeed making possible, any actual linguistic experience" ("Affective Stylistics," p. 141, my italics). Indeed, the metaphor he chooses to express this system's relationship to the event of meaning is not that of competence to performance or system to instance, but that of deep structure to surface structure. And it is in his explanation of this metaphor that the dialectic character of meaning emerges most clearly:

in . . . the actualization of meaning, the deep structure plays an important role, but it is not everything; for we comprehend not in terms of the deep structure alone, but in terms of a *relationship* between the unfolding, in time, of the surface structure and a continual checking of it against our projection

(always in terms of surface structure) of what the deep structure will reveal
itself to be. ("Affective Stylistics," p. 144).

Although this formulation explicitly casts reading in terms of a
hermeneutic dialectic, Fish's own gesture of self-reversal furnishes an
equally compelling, if implicit, argument for a self-suspending notion
of literary knowledge. If the later sections of "Affective Stylistics"
seem to contradict the early ones, by subordinating the event of
meaning to an overarching structure, it is only because they attempt
a unified vision of reading that transcends the opposition of space
and time, subject and object, with which Fish begins. By applying the
method of the essay to the reading of the essay, and reporting its
meaning in terms of the sequence of propositions about reading
presented, one can understand that meaning is as spatial as it is
temporal, as much a structure of past experience as an event of
current intuition. More importantly, experiencing the theoretical
reversal of the essay persuades us of the ephemerality of propositional truths.

It is, in fact, the constant reiteration of this ephemerality – and the
constant refusal to accept it – that saves Fish's work from paradox.
As the persistence in his writings of words like "inquiry," "search,"
"progression," and so forth indicates, Fish's method assumes that
meaning is propositional and the goal of reading is truth about
extra-textual reality. In *Surprised by Sin* and *Self-Consuming
Artifacts* this assumption translates into the mind's desire to comprehend the Supreme Good or Truth, but it informs every step of
Fish's analysis at even the simplest level.

In "Affective Stylistics," for example, Fish opens his discussion of
the sentence, "that Judas perished by hanging himself, there is no
certainty in the Scripture," with the observation with "this particular
sentence has the advantage of not saying anything. That is, you can't
get a fact out of it" ("Affective Stylistics," p. 124). Assumed, of
course, is that *facts* are what one reads for. And Fish underlines this
assumption by parenthetically stating that "in constructions of this
type 'that' is understood to be shorthand for 'the fact that'"
("Affective Stylistics," p. 124).

Later on, Fish characterizes the prose in question as "continually
opening, but then closing, on the possibility of *verification* in one
direction or another" ("Affective Stylistics," p. 125, my italics).
What the sentence does is "give the reader something and then take it
away, drawing him on with the unredeemed promise of its return"

(ibid.); the something that is promised and withheld is certainty or knowledge of an extraliterary fact.

The paradigm of propositionality has the advantage of enclosing the spatial and temporal versions of meaning within a single expression. As a conceptual structure designating an existing state of affairs, a proposition is a permanent structure – it does not vary from individual to individual or fluctuate in time. On the other hand, propositions are always subject to invalidation, as new data or evidence call for better explanations of their designata. Considered as an ongoing process, propositional knowledge – of which scientific explanation is the most striking example – is always knowledge *to a point in time*, and the latest stage of that knowledge necessarily supersedes all previous understanding. Supersession, temporality, and sequence are thus built into propositional meaning: like reading, it *advances*.

At the same time, however, since any stage in this progressive approximation of truth refers to a presumably enduring reality, propositional knowledge also presents itself as an atemporal structure. Each successive stage in the development of knowledge may "advance" us, but the goal of this quest is nonetheless congruence with an "original" unchanging state of affairs: the object or phenomenon that provoked our need to explain in the first place. To this extent, propositionality transcends time; its end is always its origin.

Because it is suspended between temporal supersession and structural permanence, propositionality gives Fish a powerful vehicle for his expression of reading dialectics. To the extent that it posits the attainment of an ultimate truth, it dovetails elegantly with the theological themes of the target text; to the extent that any proposition is vulnerable to supersession in a way that fictional meaning is not, the articulation of reading as the quest for propositional truth ensures a series of reversals and, therefore, an incarnation of the dialectics of meaning.

One must keep in mind, though, that Fish's valorization of the proposition is no simple response to observed literary characteristics, but rather a developing experience that culminates in a conviction transcendent of – indeed, in conflict with – traditional conceptualizations of meaning. In fact, by suppressing the imagistic notion of meaning, Fish disputes the single most widespread convention of literature, namely that whatever else they may do, literary texts do not, by convention, refer to real people, objects, or events. Fish maintains that the advantage of his approach lies in its ability to account for virtually any kind of phrase. Since *"every linguistic experience is affecting and pressuring,"* even the banal sentence "there is a chair" can be made to yield fascinating results if we ask the crucial question "what does this do?" ("Affective Stylistics," p. 128). Yet because questions of imaginational givenness cannot be accommodated within a propositional framework, Fish must pass over them in favor of referential assessment: "thus the utterance (written or spoken) 'there is a chair' *is at once understood as the report either of an existing state of affairs or of an act of perception* (I see a chair). In either frame of reference it makes immediate sense" ("Affective Stylistics," pp. 128–9, my italics). But clearly, the operations such a phrase might provoke in a *fictional* context – such as the visualization of a chair, its constitution in an image or concretization, the recollection of a capital event associated with a (this) chair, the assignment to the chair of a symbolic value, etc. – not only exceed referential reduction, they *exclude* it.

Ironically, then, just as he overcomes categorization, Fish falls back into the "original" sin he decries: to assume that literary language is understood as "the report either of an existing state of affairs or of an act of perception" is to realign literary interpretation with the recovery of an original referent, to reassert the necessity of asking "what does this sentence mean?"

In other words, the experience of meaning as a proposition engenders a proposition about *all* reading, namely, that it is propositional. Yet this very proposition, because it reduces reading to referential assessment, invalidates the truth it states. As with the model reader he describes, the origin of Fish's fall is the fall itself: he is the source of his own sin, and his ways of knowing lead to their own refutation. Acceding to Divine Truth, the theoretician–critic finds the vehicle of his understanding inadequate to its task. Just as Milton's reader must fall back into man's ways, so too must Fish, in his very transcendence of the conceptual tradition, fall back into conceptualization: promoted to the level of theoretical truth, his quest for an intuition unmediated by reference charts its own undoing.

Such reversals are intrinsic to a self-differing performance of meaning. As the catalysts for still further experiences, they mark the theoretician's inability to outpace the dialectic. Since Fish himself sees the gesture of *exegesis* as the reiteration of that dialectic –

"experience is immediately compromised the moment you say anything about it" ("Affective Stylistics," p. 160) – it is only logical that
he focus next on *critical* experience and discourse *per se*.

What We Do to the Text

One of the assumptions fundamental to Fish's early version of
dialectic meaning is that it entails "involving the respondent in his
own edification" (*Sin*, p. 49), which can only occur to the extent the
subject is made aware of his own actions: "instruction is possible
only because the reader is asked to observe, analyze, and *place* his
experience, that is, to think about it" (*Sin*, p. 21). We have seen how
this self-attentiveness forces Fish into a theoretical analysis of his
model that precipitates the "fall" back into conceptuality. It remains
to be shown how the subsequent stages of this self-scrutiny attempt
to rectify the "errors" of the initial proposition and reattain the unity
of meaning that is Fish's goal. The first move of reunification focuses
on the assumption, implicit in "Affective Stylistics" in spite of its
anti-formalist stance, that the literary work enjoys structural integrity
and modulates through that structure the responses of the reader.

If his early theory seems to leave the notion of textual autonomy
intact, it is because Fish concentrates almost exclusively on the
affective side of meaning. Not surprisingly, his next essays correct
this bias by stressing that meaning is in fact an effect – the correlate of
an intention that generates it willfully. Invoking the model of the
speech act, with its implicit rejection of "the positivist assumption of
a 'brute fact' world and a language answerable to it" ("How
Ordinary is Ordinary Language," p. 53),[6] Fish argues that utterances be "regarded as instances of purposeful human behavior;
that is to say, they refer not to a state of affairs in the real world, but
to the commitments and attitudes of those who produce them in the
context of specific situations" ("Ordinary Language," p. 50). In
other words, meaning in the absence of a specific contextual motivation is a theoretical aberration: texts have no properties: they receive
them from their users.

If this is true, the organization of the text which presumably
orchestrated the reader's response in *Surprised by Sin* and *Self-
Consuming Artifacts* can only be a delusion. The stages in the
reader's revelation do not reflect spaces in the textual sequence, but
impose upon that sequence its structure: "my unit of analysis is

interpretive or perceptual, and rather than proceeding directly from formal units of language, *it determines what those units are* . . . is formed (or forms itself) at the moment when the reader hazards interpretive closure, when he enters into a relationship with a proposition."[7]

This description paraphrases Fish's own experience as a theoretician to the extent that it correlates the birth of a textual structure – and hence the resurgence of a dichotomy between textual object and reading subject – to the fall into propositionality. It also indicates the direction he will take in order to re-establish the unity of meaning: alienated from his own experience by the textual structure it precipitated, he must do away with that structure by relocating its ground in the activity of reading.

As a first step in this direction, Fish does away with his own preconceived notion of intention as a purely authorial gesture in opposition to reader understanding. Again, the model of the speech act serves him:

> intention and understanding are two ends of a conventional act, each of which necessarily stipulates (includes, defines, specifies) the other. To construct the profile of the informed or at-home reader is at the same time to characterize the author's intention and vice versa, because to do either is to specify the *contemporary* conditions of utterance. ("*Variorum*," p. 476)

In short, when we speak of understanding or intention, we describe the conventions of meaning shared by *both* parties to the text/utterance. This definitional constraint states the difference between Fish's thought and subjectivism: his theory has no room for an autonomous, idiosyncratic self to the extent that it postulates any self engaged in meaning as a function of shared conditions or contexts.

By the same token, the "formal features" of a work are merely those structures or forms which our critical conventions or interpretive strategies, as Fish calls them, allow: "rather than intention and its formal realization producing interpretation, (the 'normal' picture), interpretation creates intention and its formal realization by creating the conditions in which it becomes possible to pick them out" ("*Variorum*," p. 477). In short, "formal units are always a function of the interpretive model one brings to bear; they are not 'in' the text" ("*Variorum*," p. 478) any more than are "the 'facts' of grammar," which is to say that they "*are* there, but only as a consequence of the interpretive (man-made) model that has called them into being" ("*Variorum*," p. 480).

The propositional format that shapes most of Fish's early readings is now revealed to be a product of his interpretive act and not a formal characteristic of the texts in question at all. In a disarming gesture of persuasion, Fish illustrates this with a personal example: "in the analysis of these lines from *Lycidas* I did what critics always do. I 'saw' what my interpretive principles permitted or directed me to see, and then I turned around and attributed what I had 'seen' to a text and an intention" ("*Variorum*," pp. 477–8).

However, as this final citation illustrates, Fish has not entirely overcome the dichotomy he set out to transcend. While it is true that the notion of interpretive strategy unites writer and reader, reading act and textual structure, under a single conceptual umbrella, it nonetheless retains a vectorization that works against unified meaning. From origin of our response, the text has become its end, but it still persists as an empty, separate domain, awaiting the collective intention that will fill it. There remains the implication (which would be an erroneous and premature reading) that – as the metaphor of an interpretive strategy suggests – meaning hinges on a very conscious, sophisticated, and deliberate endeavor carried out by a limited group of people. While the arguments of "Ordinary Language" do not tend in this direction, those of "*Variorum*" do suggest interpretation to be a particular cognitive activity of certain people – which conclusion would drive a wedge not only between criticism and reading, but between meaning in general and interpretation.

In his next major article, "Normal Circumstances, Literal Language, Direct Speech Acts, the Ordinary, the Everyday, the Obvious, What Goes without Saying, and Other Special Cases,"[8] Fish sets out to correct this misapprehension and to overcome the last vestiges of a distinction between meaning as literary work and meaning as event/ structure of understanding. Like many of Fish's titles, this one states its thesis: "a normal context is just the special context you happen to be in, although it will not be recognized as special because so long as you are in it whatever it permits you to see will seem obvious and inescapable" (pp. 640–1). This formulation again tends toward a structural bias, by making context something one is "in" rather than a strategy one elects, but it also does away with the aberrant distinction between critical knowledge and everyday understanding which the notion of "strategy" promotes. Moreover, the structural bias of context is only superficial: it is not a question of a context we adopt or select, or away from which we might stand; Fish's notion of context is permanent and inseparable from that of meaning-event:

> A sentence is never not in a context. We are never not in a situation. A statute is never not read in the light of some purpose. A set of interpretive assumptions is always in force. A sentence that seems to need no interpretation is already the product of one. . . . No sentence is ever apprehended independently of some or other illocutionary force. ("Normal," p. 637)

From the viewpoint of this study, the most important of these statements are the first two, which are really one, and the fifth, which renders temporally the paradox of dialectical meaning as it applies to the discipline of criticism. Context and situation (which must be read in the existential sense) express essentially the same notion: every experience (structure of meaning) is a function of a spatio-temporal and cultural–historical structure. We have seen in previous sections of this book on just how many levels that structure can be defined – grammatical, historical, semiological, psychological, and sociological, just to name the most evident. What Fish adds to the theories of his predecessors, however, is the notion of absolute identity between the event and the informing structure of meaning. Because he retains a slight structural bias, he casts the context or situation of meaning as the *informing* face, but he is careful to note (1) that this face is co-present and coextensive with the event it predicates, and (2) for this very reason, and because the event of intuition cannot, in the moment of its beholding, behold the structure grounding it, that structure remains unknowable in the very moment of its function. In other words, because there is a specific situation associated with every instance of consciousness, there will indeed always be a meaning capable of excluding all others in its self-evidence; but to the extent that it is self-evident, its ground cannot be found in some external order, or indeed perceived at all:

> we are never not in a situation. Because we are never not in a situation, we are never not in the act of interpreting. Because we are never not in the act of interpreting, there is no possibility of reaching a level of meaning beyond or below interpretation. But in every situation some or other meaning will appear to us to be uninterpreted because it is isomorphic with the interpretive structure the situation (and therefore our perception) already has. ("Normal," p. 631)

This definition does away with both objectivism, or the notion that there exists some permanent, normative meaning, and subjectivist pluralism, or the idea that any meaning is possible: "a sentence neither means anything at all nor does it always mean the same thing; it always has the meaning that has been conferred on it by the situation in which it is uttered" ("Normal," p. 644).

The notion of "situation" encloses the event of meaning as well as its contextual ground, the present state and permanent identity of the subject – whose identity is a function of his interpretive strategies or competences – as well as that of the object, which "has" the structure we perceive only to the extent that it is embedded in "our" situation. The "subjective" act and the "objective" fact of a word's "literal" meaning merge within a single notion – which is neither a structure nor an event, but that which makes the retroactive position of events and structures possible.

Meaning thus defined necessarily eludes critical location. It cannot be found "in" any structure, since it has already to have occurred for there to "be" a perceived structure. Meanings (structures) that seem incontestable or obvious, and therefore appear to exist independently of any interpretive gesture, only confirm, by their very self-evidence, that interpretation has already occurred: "there is always a literal meaning because in any situation there is always a meaning that seems obvious in the sense that it is there independently of anything we might do. But that only means that we have already done it" ("Normal," p. 631). Naturally, this applies to the situation as well. There is no way we can know our situation directly, that is, independently of the interpretive force it represents. Nor can we inhabit a situation in the sense of coming into an objectively independent framework that was awaiting us: "being in the situation means that [one has] already construed it" ("Normal," p. 630).

Unlike Fish's theory of reader response, which predicated a definite critical methodology, the concept of situation does not correlate to any specific program, nor can he locate it in any specific reading. As the condition of consciousness itself, situation is by definition everywhere and always; meaning requires no particular apparatus for its revelation, because it only "exists" as that revelation. It is not some "thing" to be found, for it is itself the finding – and that finding can only occur to the extent that it already has. This may sound willfully oxymoronic; it in fact only restates in a linguistic–intentional format the theme that dominates all of Fish's work: belief.

What We Believe in/What Believes in Us

Belief is the name we give certain knowledge that does not derive from the categories and historical vicissitudes of conceptual proposition. It is the name we give to that state where the opposition of subject to object, intuition to structure, simply does not obtain. It is the name we give to those convictions that exceed justification and communication for the very reason that they are already widely held. And it is finally the term that most accurately characterizes the transcendent unity of meaning Fish stipulates. Because we cannot distance ourselves from the situation determining our understanding, to see beyond what appears to us a literal meaning, we can never validate our understanding. On the other hand, to the extent we *believe* it to be the case, it requires no validation: "no one can achieve the distance from his own beliefs and assumptions which would result in their being no more authoritative *for him* than the beliefs and assumptions held by others, or, for that matter, the beliefs and assumptions he himself used to hold" (*Is There a Text in this Class?*, p. 319).[9]

Thus even as he shifts his focus from religion-specific transcendence to a more generalized model of belief, Fish privileges the final order of certainty that, as the ground of all knowledge and understanding, cannot itself be understood. This ultimate incarnation of meaning provides (1) a solution to the dichotomy of objective and subjective meaning, (2) a template for assuring critical accord, and (3) a program for assimilating the potentially subversive designs of post-structuralist thought into the institution of literary criticism. The first of these achievements is the easiest to grasp.

As belief, understanding is neither subjective nor solipsistic. This is because

an individual's assumptions and opinions are not "his own" in any sense that would give body to the fear of solipsism. That is, *he* is not their origin (in fact it might be more accurate to say that they are his); rather it is their prior availability which delimits in advance the paths that his consciousness can possibly take. (*Is There a Text*, p. 320)

To the extent that the individual is understood by anyone, those beliefs are by definition shared; the self in Fish's system is "a social construct whose operations are delimited by the systems of intelligibility that inform it" (*Is There a Text*, p. 335). Thus Fish overcomes the opposition between subjective and objective criticism while appropriating the claims of both.

[meanings] will not be objective because they will always have been the product of a point of view rather than having been simply 'read off'; and they will not be subjective because that point of view will always be social or institutional. Or by the same reasoning, one could say that they are *both* subjective and objective: they are subjective because they inhere in a particular point of view and are therefore not universal; and they are objective because the point of view that delivers them is public and conventional rather than individual or unique. (*Is There a Text*, pp. 335–6)

The advantages of a belief-based notion of meaning seem obvious. It transcends the nagging conflict between discipline and individual (history and interpretive act, community and self, canonic truth and personal conviction) that we have seen repeatedly enacted, and it reconciles, for the literary critic, the inalienable rights of personal meaning with the absolute authority of the canon. It allows for a nearly limitless number of "new" readings that will by definition reinforce the canon out of which they arise. It provides for the reinvigoration of texts, the discovery of new truths, without having to posit the abandonment of the discipline's values or rigor. Finally, it brings together absolute exegetic freedom and unfailing disciplinary allegiance and does away with the necessity of electing one or the other.

Such gains are not without their price, however. Fish admits that criticism loses its distinctiveness under his system, becoming merely a reiteration of a general model of *persuasion* associated with any belief modification. To persuade someone, one need merely "back up to some point at which there [is] a shared agreement as to what [is] reasonable to say so that a new and wider basis for agreement could be fashioned" (*Is There a Text*, p. 315). Validation, in the sense of a shared but unprovable belief in what a text says, will occur automatically through back-tracking to the point of self-evidence. Criticism is thus reduced to a generalized gesture of persuasion: "this is the whole of critical activity, an attempt on the part of one party to alter the beliefs of another so that the evidence cited by the first will be seen *as* evidence by the second" (*Is There a Text*, p. 365).

Strangely enough, this happy vision allows for permanent certainty, but it also imprisons the subject in a blind present that can only know itself historically, as past error. This is because Fish has elevated the idea of belief or interpretation or situation to a point transcendent of scrutiny. It cannot lead to a dialectical regress or suspension of self – as does the more widely known post-structuralist meaning – because it cannot be contemplated, grasped, or in any way conceptualized, even in its inconceivability. Thus while Fish asserts as a general benefit of his approach that "institutional assumptions . . . can themselves become the objects of dispute" (*Is There a Text*, p. 367), his frequent reiteration of the invisibility of final conventional sets would seem to argue the contrary. Although it clearly provides for the modification of conventions *in the abstract*, his theory precludes explicit discussion of the only set of conventions that really counts: those we are not already aware of, the "set of overarching interpretive principles that are not themselves the object of dispute because they set the terms within which disputes can occur" (*Is There a Text*, p. 294).

Moreover, in his latest work, Fish associates the belief system with the institution (in this case, criticism), stressing that anything we can understand must already somehow have been accounted for by the procedures and conventions of the discipline, which *cannot* be challenged because, like God, they will always be further removed, as that which allows any perceptions at all. Even doubt, from this perspective, is blind to its disciplinary foundations: "the ability to be uncertain is an institution-specific ability, and rather than being evidence of the freedom of our minds, it is evidence of the way in which the operations of our minds, no less than the texts those operations call into being, are enabled by institutional assumptions."[10]

What is most interesting about this redefinition is the way it provides for the assimilation of new understanding while nonetheless rendering the discipline invulnerable to subversion from without. By redefining any theory that can be understood to be already within, and in a sense a product of, the interpretive community of the person doing the understanding, Fish defuses subversion of its claim and appropriates its energy for the tradition. In this way, he demonstrates how a dialectical notion of meaning that is essentially post-structuralist in its logic can be used to bastion the institutions and traditions which post-structuralism is generally assumed to subvert.

From Fish's point of view, for example, (non)concepts like Derrida's iterability only restate – in what Fish calls a "vexing use of the term" – the founding status of belief ("With the Compliments of the

Author: Reflections on Austin and Derrida," p. 703).[11] Fish's preference is for what one might call "arche-interpretation," a belief-like version of reading so fundamental as always already to underlie or precede any perception of structure one might have:

> Iterability, then, stands for the general condition of having-to-be-read . . .
> iterability is another word for readability, not as a possibility but as a
> necessity. . . . the interpretive gesture which threatens to infect the center
> (that is, presence) is responsible for the very form of the center and of
> everything it contains, including persons, their messages, and their very
> worlds. That outside is its inside, the very force and law of its emergence.
> ("Reflections," p. 704)

This displacement of the "infection" of meaning-as-iterability by the "force and law" of meaning as arche-interpretation accords with Fish's exclusion of the "other" of meaning – or more precisely with its domestication into a historical moment that always appears an inconceivable, and hence harmless, error. In contrast to critics like Barthes and de Man, Fish excludes the moment of doubt, suspension, or regressive uncertainty from his schema: the displacement or suspension of one belief system by another can never be known, if only because one can only be in the grip of a single belief at any given moment. Fish states that "unless someone is willing to entertain the possibility that his beliefs are wrong, he will be unable even to hear an argument that constitutes a challenge to them" (*Is There a Text*, p. 299), and while this seems to leave the door open to mutual understanding (except for those too stubborn to "entertain the possibility" that their beliefs are wrong), it in fact states the unshakeability of faith. To the extent that the assumptions of belief cannot be perceived, there is no way one could be brought to "entertain the possibility" of their wrongness. To do so would be to be in the grip of a new belief system already: the entertainment would have ended before it started.

What I am arguing is that Fish's theory obtains its elegant unified vision of meaning at the expense of the self-initiated dialectic of learning that so fascinated him in his early works. Postulating a reader incapable of seeing the ground of understanding and thus of losing his balance, Fish proposes a stasis of certainty that makes the individual an object of history rather than its agent. Always already assimilated by a further set of conventions we cannot know, we are swept forward in a regress that cannot be grasped as such, but only as a sequence of past moments – a conceptual structure that offers us no control over our destiny precisely because it derives by definition from a belief system beyond consciousness. As a body into which one is absorbed rather than an arm one might wield, meaning as belief also precludes self-interrogation. Imprisoned in our convictions, incapable of stepping outside of the institutions that define us, we can never know the differing from oneself so frequently associated with literary experience: "the fact that a standard of truth is never available independently of a set of beliefs does not mean that we can never know for certain what is true but that we *always* know for certain what is true" (*Is There a Text*, p. 365). To this I would add, alas, we *will always* know for certain, regardless of what it is we happen to know.

What is lost, then, in Fish's transcendent belief, is the wavering between knowledge and doubt, power and impotence – and the rapture of infinite regress that accompanies it. Fish's reader knows no anguish, can provoke no change in himself. Theoretically capable of persuading others, he can never outflank the beliefs of the institutions that define him; he can trigger no revolutions: the discipline will always have already understood, assimilated, indeed produced, any arguments for its realignment he might generate. And the experience of his evolution he may know will always be doubly diluted: first, by the fact that any beliefs he isolates are by necessity former, dead beliefs; second, by the certainty that his perception of them is mitigated by a further belief system which he can never know in its actuality. Fish's reader, finally, can neither escape nor know himself.

If I insist on the grim side of Fish's most recent vision, it is not in the hopes of devaluing it: indeed, I shall argue in the concluding chapter that this model in some respects most closely accounts for the institutionalization of post-structuralism we are currently (even in the gesture of this book) witnessing. Rather, I wish to underscore the contrast between the self-enclosed (perhaps even self-satisfied) vision of knowledge Fish underwrites and the more self-negating version of Roland Barthes, who derives from a similarly dialectical notion of meaning a theory and practice equally intertwined, yet diametrically opposed to Fish's in their insistence on the subversive erotic side to losses of certainty and disruptions of belief. In contrast to Fish's quest for transcendence, Barthes courts ecstasy or orgasmic rapture. And he does so by provoking his own undoing.

13

Roland Barthes: Subverting History/Suspending the Self

If Fish's implementation of a unified theory of meaning seems intent on transcending the regress of historical awareness, the writings of Roland Barthes exploit history as the source of their vitality. For Barthes as for Fish, meaning is dialectical, and one cannot help but read his successive works as the performance, over a quarter-century, of that dialectic. Pitting closure, conventional wisdom, and continuity against historical change, paradox, and disruption, his writing ceaselessly works at exposing the assumptions, encoded operations, and ideologies that are embedded in language and reiterated or disrupted by texts. However, where Fish transcends meaning's self-difference through the unity of belief, Barthes aggravates that difference to provoke disruption of the self's reassurance. If Fish aspires to a state undivided, a single truth uniting institution and individual, Barthes delights in the plurality of meaning as a means of outpacing the canon that would absorb it.

Barthes' strategy, then, is to exploit the boundlessness of meaning as a lever for historical change. In his program, the absolute "otherness" of meaning, its potential to mean something else, is used to disrupt history and advance it, to dismember the corpus of received ideas and to reconstitute it. Ultimately, however, this political use of paradox gives way to an erotics of reading that exploits the same paradigm on the personal level of sensual pleasure. In this final avatar of paradox, the self's pleasure at re-membering culture is correlated to its ecstasy in dismemberment, or loss of solidarity, in a way that exceeds the dialectical model Barthes' early writing promotes.

The first steps along this itinerary can be found in *Le Degré zéro de l'écriture*,[1] where Barthes elaborates the notion of *écriture*, or writing as a suspension between moment and duration, instance and history. An author's *écriture* is that tone, ethos, and affiliation to a marked order of language (*Degré zéro*, p. 55) which, as distinct from his personal style and inherited linguistic matrix, define his work's particular vision of its own literarity, that is, its relationship, as an institution, to society (*Degré zéro*, pp. 7, 14–15). "Writing is thus essentially the ethic of form, the choice of the social domain within which the writer decides to situate the Nature of his language" (*Degré zéro*, p. 15). As such, it results from the author's free choice of a function and social role for his discourse, and it opens a dichotomy between the individual writer's gesture of free will and the historical determination that engulfs him.

Because the writer's choice necessarily occurs within a framework of possibilities determined by history – that is, all past writings – his *écriture* emblematizes the tension within meaning between past uses and present function. In this sense, writing can be defined as "that compromise between a freedom and a memory, . . . that remembering freedom which is only free in the gesture of the choice, but already no longer in its duration" (*Degré zéro*, p. 16).

This formulation divides the burden of historical continuity between the word and its use, while placing a negative accent on the concept of duration, as opposed to disruption. The quasi-originary choice of the author that invests writing with its innovative power is quickly reabsorbed into the flux of history. And this occurs because writing tries to *sustain* itself: "I can no doubt choose for myself today such and such a writing, and in that gesture affirm my freedom, lay claim to a freshness or a tradition; but already I can no longer develop it in a duration without becoming gradually the prisoner of the words of others and even of my own words" (*Dégre zéro*, p. 16). The gesture of innovation succumbs in time to the institutionalization and rigidity it originally proposed to remedy: "it is impossible to develop a negation in time without elaborating a positive art, an order that must be destroyed anew" (*Dégre zéro*, p. 31).

Such a metamorphosis of negation into affirmation characterizes the story of writing Barthes adumbrates in *Dégre zéro*, where he demonstrates that history can defuse even the most self-conscious attempt to found a neutral voice – a "zero-degree writing" that would be "free of any servitude to a marked order of language"

(*Dégre zéro*, p. 55). For Barthes, even an author like Camus, who rigorously purges his language of received forms, will ultimately be hypostatized into a "classical" formula by history:

> automatic reflexes develop on the very spot where first there was freedom; a network of hardened forms constricts the primal freshness of the discourse. . . . The writer, attaining the status of a classic, becomes the imitator of his early creation; society makes a mannerism of his writing and returns him a prisoner of his own formal myths. (*Dégre zéro*, p. 57)

History's petrification menaces the critic as well. Because writing vitrifies with repetition and the inevitable assimilation into an economy of social exchange, the critic's activity both institutional-izes the writer's innovation *and* lays the groundwork for further disruptions by uncovering petrified orders. Barthes particularly values the disruptive function and calls for a *fuite en avant* or escape into the future, away from the stereotypes and shared opinions upon which ideologies depend. In his vision, newness becomes the principle value: "all old language is immediately compromised and all language becomes old the moment it is repeated" (*Le Plaisir du texte*, p. 66).[2] The automatic association of key terms into commonplaces prompts their immediate rejection: "nausea arrives as soon as the connection between two important words goes without saying. And as soon as a thing goes without saying, I desert it" (*Plaisir*, p. 70).

Repulsed by precisely that state of assurance that Fish deems permanent, Barthes prescribes a course of criticism that would outpace its own beliefs by a continual self-negation. Because even the most revolutionary desertion of the commonplace becomes in time a stereotype requiring further repudiation, the responsible critic must espouse a course of self-contradiction that can free him from the oppression of his own authority. In his retrospective autobiography for the "Ecrivains de Toujours" series, Barthes phrases his own dialectic of self-suspension in terms of movement from existentialism through structuralism and textualism to a Nietzschean hedonism of discourse. The paradigm underlying each shift in this itinerary remains constant: "a *doxa* (a common opinion) is established, intolerable; in order to free myself from it, I postulate a paradox; then that paradox itself becomes mired, becomes a new concretion, a new *doxa*, and I have to go further to a new paradox" (*Roland Barthes par Roland Barthes*, p. 75).[3] A continual self-undoing thus subtends the theoretical/critical enterprise; and it depends on a particular method of reading which we might, following Barthes' example, call paradoxical reading.

Paradoxical Reading

To constitute a paradox, a reading must counteract the stereotype of received opinion by supporting its antithesis. More precisely, one must uncover this antithesis within the very folds of the writing that advances the *doxa*. One must show that a particular discourse does not mean what it ostensibly claims to mean, or that it means far more than it admits. A primitive version of this quintessentially deconstructive procedure can be found in Barthes' early collection of essays, *Mythologies*, where he exposes the myths underlying the cults, institutions, and publications of post-war France.[4] Each text he examines reveals a new meaning or mythic significance apparently at odds with the surface logic of its language. Unlike Fish, however, Barthes does not present this tension in terms of propositional reversals; rather, he postulates a vertical layering of meaning in which each synthesis of understanding itself serves as a simple meaning unit in a higher-level synthesis.

This vertical theory of meaning hinges on the functional duplicity every "mythic" signifier displays. The first meaning that results from the correlation of signifier to signified can in Barthes' system become in turn the signifier in a second-level correlation to yet another content unit or signified. This second-level correlation produces a myth rather than a sign, and the function of the myth is significance rather than mere meaning. To the extent that the mythological signifiers are the simple meanings of natural language, Barthes' idea resembles Hirsch's concept of significance and reveals their common heritage in phenomenology. But unlike Hirsch, Barthes acknowledges the double identity of the mythical signifier, which functions at once as a *sens* or meaning (on the first level) and a form (on the second, or mythic, level). The same "entity" is at once the full meaning resulting from the correlation of signifier to signified on the level of elementary meaning, *and* the signifier that will be correlated to a further signified on the level of mythic meaning or significance (cf. *Mythologies*, p. 202).

It is clear that the integration into a higher level does not stop with the identification and analysis of the myth, since that analysis can itself become the signifier (form) for a higher-level recuperation concerned, for instance, with the ethical dimensions of mythography (cf. *Mythologies* pp. 222–3). The vertical play of meaning allows a dissimulation of one's ideologies under the guise of the "natural." As a first-level meaning, the mythic signifier carries an entire history of accepted usage and presupposes prior readings: "the meaning is already full, it assumes a knowledge, a past, a memory, a comparative order of fact, ideas, and decisions" (*Mythologies*, p. 202). This full content is pushed aside or obscured to make room for the new signified the myth appends, but it does not disappear. Hovering in the background as a source of assumptions, "the meaning will be for the form an instantaneous reserve of history, like a subordinate wealth that it is possible to recall and dismiss in a sort of rapid alternation" (*Mythologies*, p. 203).

In this reverberation of inherited meaning we find Barthes' first approximation of the deconstructive conflation of history and structure. Barthes claims the myth "steals" language and its meanings in order to naturalize its own concepts (*Mythologies*, pp. 217–18), but from a structuralist perspective it can only steal that which it already "has" as a structural possibility. Rather than phrasing this paradox in terms of structure and event, Barthes depicts it as the interface between history as text and history as textuality – or, more simply, between a "vertical" notion of meaning formation and a more "horizontal" one.

To the extent that meaning can always be integrated into a further level of significance, it provides access to a semiotic "piling up" in which no natural or final term can be isolated. Every meaning is but one layer in an endless *feuilleté* whose accumulation cannot be reduced to a causal chain. Although Barthes takes simple linguistic meanings as the fundamental stage in his analysis, he also frequently reiterates the fallacy of an origin and of Nature, as in this resumé of his career:

In order to foil the origin, he first culturalizes Nature completely: nothing natural anywhere, nothing but the historical; then (persuaded like Benveniste that all of culture is merely language) he relocates this culture in the infinite movement of the idioms, each erected on top of the other (and not engendered) as in the game of "hot hands." (*Barthes*, p. 142)[5]

As the trace of culture and language, history exhibits a doubled structure that can be grasped as the tension between synchronic and diachronic determination. Considered diachronically, each meaning imposes itself upon those beneath it, appropriating, distorting, and feeding upon the meanings it supersedes. Such a paradigm implies no causality, for it is precisely the mark of accrued meaning that it empties prior meaning in order to create a form for its own expression. From an intentional point of view, one might say that each new layer of meaning signals an exploitation and effacement of prior meaning according to present intentions – but those intentions can never be shown to arise from the distorted meaning. History seems thus an incessant revisionism, a remaking of meaning according to present needs.[6]

On the other hand, "successive" layers of meaning do not cease to exist simply because they are not currently in the foreground. Rather all layers coexist at all moments as the irreducible plurality of the text. As the metaphor of the hand game shows, the play of language fascinates us because of the continual surfacing of submerged signifieds, the constant accumulation of new levels of meaning, all of which are in a sense "already there."

Language, culture, and by extension every individual act,[7] thus mark the convergence of two versions of history: history as continual supersession, revision, innovation, or naturalization; and history as an all-encompassing permanent vortex of meaning; history, in short, as text and textuality. And true to the paradox, each of these identities leads to and cancels out the other. This is best dramatized in *S/Z*, where Barthes blends the closure-inclined diachronic text with its determinedly pluralistic textuality.

Infolding and Unfolding

On the simplest level, *S/Z* depicts a traditional interpretive activity in pursuit of a final meaning, a totalization or reduction of the text to a single pattern or message – not unlike the activity Holland outlines in *5 Readers Reading*. At the same time, however, an inversion of this activity in Barthes' work disrupts the text's sequential development by multiplying the layers of meaning and revelling in the text's plurality. These two contradictory impulses are reflected in *S/Z*'s format: three distinct type faces and narrations, which correlate to (1) Balzac's short story *Sarrasine*, (2) Barthes' progressive analysis of the story's components as he reads it, and (3) Barthes' theoretical speculation and analysis of his own reading. *S/Z* thus formally thematizes the tension of paradoxical criticism by incorporating two distinct reading gestures: that of *Sarrasine* by Barthes and that of Barthes by Barthes.

The opening pages of the work present a manifesto for a new, active reading – a reading that engages in the process of historical reordering and meaning formation with as much freedom as writing, a reading that can "attain, and give itself over to, the spell of the signifier, the voluptuousness of writing" (*S/Z*, p. 10). The goal of such reading would be not to assign a meaning to the text, but to "appreciate the plural of which it is fashioned" (*S/Z*, p. 11); and such an appreciation requires of the reading what Barthes terms a topological function:

my task is to animate, to relay systems whose course neither stops at the text nor with me. (*S/Z*, p. 17)

reading however does not consist in halting the chain of systems, in founding a truth, a legality of the text . . . it consists in engaging these systems not according to their finite quality, but according to their plurality (which is a state of being, not a quantification). (*S/Z*, p. 18)

Topological reading underscores the text's palimpsestic play of meaning at the expense of its sequentiality. Renouncing the traditional critical goal of synthesis, it proposes a casual unravelling of the fabric of codes knotted around each textual element. Barthes has in mind no final systematization of the text, no reduction to a single proposition or mechanism (as in Eco). And in contrast to Fish, he seeks no sublime unity through reading. Texts do not lead to their abandonment in favor of an all-embracing truth. If we are awed by meaning it is because the text engages us in its infinite plurality, its refusal of simplicity and teleology: "no *construction* of the text! Everything signifies continually and multiple times, but without any mandate for a final unity, for a supreme structure" (*S/Z*, p. 18; see also p. 21).

The actual mechanics of Barthian reading involve the exploration "within" every unit of the text of those strings of meaning that various codes would underwrite – code being understood in this context not as a finite structure of decryption but as "a perspective of citations, a mirage of structures" (*S/Z*, p. 27) similar to the layers described above. At the heart of this process is the idea of *connotation*, which reiterates the model of signification encountered in *Mythologies*. One derives a connotation by correlating a new signified meaning to a form that results from the emptying of a prior denotation. To the extent that the connotation is immanent in the denotation it will be one of the layers in that meaning's palimpsest of inherited meanings, and it will mark, for those who pursue it, "the point of departure of a code (that will never be reconstituted), the articulation of a voice that is woven into the text" (*S/Z*, p. 15). Nevertheless, connotation is not just a function of vertical layering, but also of the text's *espace séquentiel* or seriality, such that it involves petrification. As we read, the connnotations we unearth become, through their duration and repetition within the reading, denotations from which further connotations need to be derived.

This familiar paradigm finds yet another restatement in Barthes' treatment of naming, a gesture he considers central to the notion of reading. For Barthes, naming functions both as an act of closure and of reopening, and as a process, it restates the history latent in textuality:

> To read is to find meanings, and to find meanings is to name them; but these named meanings are swept away towards further names; names invoke each other, come together, and their conglomeration calls out to be named anew; I name, I unname, I rename: thus passes the text: it is a nomination in the becoming, a tireless approximation, a metonymic project. (*S/Z*, pp. 17–18)

Allied with the synchronic model of connotation, naming under-scores the diachronic dimension of association and the concomitant processes of condensation and expansion that are structured into meaning. In his description of the name as it pertains specifically to literature, Barthes elaborates this idea: "in the realm of the fictional (and elsewhere as well?) it is an instrument of exchange: it permits the substitution of a nominal unity for a collection of traits by positing a relationship of equivalence between the sign and the sum" (*S/Z*, p. 101). By substituting a single generic term for a plurality of textual units, the reader makes the text "mean" or fit into his cultural categories. And the efficacy of the name in imposing closure depends on its relative expansiveness: "the meaning is a force: to name is to subjugate, and the more generic the nomination, the stronger the subjugation" (*S/Z*, p. 136; cf. also p. 160).

In its stress on the unavoidability of assimilation, this version of reading makes explicit history's subsumptive power. Grouping and naming according to institutionalized categories, we consolidate and enclose the text in spite of ourselves. Were Barthes to rest with this model, his work would differ only slightly in its political implications from that of Fish. Once again the institution would emerge as the all-powerful analog of history: it could never be subverted, if only because the act of subversion – while conceivable in the abstract – would, in its reliance on naming, reinforce the *doxa* it sought to undo.

Not surprisingly, however, Barthes doubles this version of reading with a contrary mechanism that stresses the infinite regress implicit in naming. He conceives of this regress as a constant dialectic between the *infolding* we have seen above and an inverse force of *unfolding* that draws on each name's limitless potential for sending us off into new directions. "What is a series of acts?" he asks, but "the unfolding of a noun" (*S/Z*, p. 88), and he postulates that every noun such as "entrance" can be broken down into a sequence of individual actions that are either constitutive of its field ("knock," "open the door," "step into the room,") or merely associated with it ("say hello," "remove one's coat"). Reading consists of such "unfoldings" of nominal groups as much as it consists of the infolding of nomination. Indeed, infolding triggers unfolding by constituting the names that dis-integrate during reading. The construing of meaning can thus only be grasped as a double movement: "it is going from name to name, from fold to fold; it is folding the text into a name and then unfolding the same text along the new creases of that name" (*S/Z*, p. 89).

This double movement embraces both meaning as personal association, as outlined by the phenomenologists, and the reductive determination of implications performed by Hirsch and Eco. It posits reading as a simultaneous implosion and explosion, a continual contraction and expansion. The consolidating name with which one subjugates the text to culture in turn falls victim to the dissemination of meaning from within its folds. A text's meaning can no more be defined in terms of its denotative thrust than in terms of a finite number of code lists. Each infolding/unfolding marks a further codal nexus permeated by countless strings of further associations that can always be pursued out beyond the text or back into it. Textual meaning cannot be explained in terms of structure alone, but only as a continual structuration. As Barthes puts it, "the meaning of a text cannot be anything other than the plural of its systems, its infinite, circular 'transcribability'" (*S/Z*, p. 126).

Such a formulation eludes subordination to the institution and

tradition of literary criticism by positing meaning as its own disruption, as a continual aggregation and dispersal that cannot be
subsumed under any rule, because it thwarts its own accumulation
and uses the certainty of its conviction as a springboard into an
infinite constellation of "other" understandings. In contrast to Fish,
whose dialectic reversals culminate in a transcendent unity, Barthes
finds in textuality a permanent suspension between closure and
opening, structural layering and dialectical displacement, the circle
of textuality and the cycle of history. From this suspension he
generates a third avatar of reading and meaning – one that substitutes for the play of totalization and dispersal an absolute
disjunction productive not of meaning, but of erotic fascination and
rapture.

Of Rifts and Rapture

The dialectic that informs Barthes' early work and grows into a
full-blown theory of reading in *S/Z* undergoes a radical reformula-
tion in *Le Plaisir du texte*. Here reading is no longer centered on
accrued meaning, innovation, and appropriation, as in *Mythologies*,
or *Le Degré zéro de l'écriture*; nor does it hinge on the dialectical
tension of infolding/unfolding of *S/Z*. In fact, meaning *per se* is no
longer the question. Rather, Barthes encloses all of his previous
versions of reading under the rubric of text-as-pleasure, which he
opposes to the text-as-knowledge. Within the general field of pleasure,
however, there emerges a more marked state he terms *jouissance*,[8]
and it is correlated with a specific kind of reading and text (*Plaisir*,
p. 34).

The difference between *jouissance* and pleasure cannot be reduced
to a simple dialectic or opposition. They stand as parallels that
cannot be brought together, opposing forces in a struggle, unable to
communicate with one another and resistant to any accretional
history or "pleasing dialectical process of synthesis" (*Plaisir*, p. 36).
And the rift between pleasure and *jouissance* entails a correlative
division of the reading subject. As pleasure, the textual experience –
which involves all of the dialectical complexities outlined above –
generates "euphoria, fulfillment, comfort (a feeling of satiety that
culture permeates freely)" (*Plaisir*, p. 34). As *jouissance*, however,
the reading event is a shock, an unforeseen upset, a loss of continuity
and ground – and by extension a loss of the self.

As if to trigger this loss of footing, Barthes employs his key term, pleasure, in conflicting and not always systematic ways. In a general sense it refers to "an excess of the text, that which, within it, exceeds all (social) function and all (structural) functionality" (*Plaisir*, p. 34). This pleasurable excess of the text is precisely what cannot be controlled through models of meaning or knowledge; it seems somewhat akin to the institutional matrix that ensures Stanley Fish's reader his certainty by remaining beyond his grasp. Within this general field, the more particular pleasure of *jouissance* occurs whenever there is a radical disruption, a gap between the reader's historical, cultural, psychological foundations and the sense of the text he feels not in his intellect, but in his whole corporeal being (cf. *Plaisir*, pp. 25–6, 31). When the reader's social idiolect fails him, he is swept off into *jouissance*, which is not necessarily a violent, aggressive movement, but rather one of self-abandonment (cf. *Plaisir*, p. 33). The enraptured reader loses his identity, his intellectual, cultural self, with all its values, memories, and preconceptions. He exists primarily as a feeling body. At the same time, there persists the comfort and gentler euphoria of pleasure in general, reasserting the reader's cultural identity, such that he appears truly different from himself and "at once takes pleasure, through the text, in the consistency of his self and its fall" (*Plaisir*, p. 36).

Two points are worth noting. First, *jouissance* does not come of mere negation, but of suspension in the abyss between continuity/consistency and its negation. Secondly, since continuity delineates the subject, what is at stake is the erotic fascination that self-destruction holds for self-construction: the erotic potential of meaning situates itself in the hesitation between "me" and "not me." The first of these points forces a reassessment of the critical/theoretical text's format; the second reopens the problematics of reading as an auto-referential structure/moment.

If, as Barthes maintains, "neither culture nor its destruction are erotic; it is the fissure or crack in the one and the other that becomes so" (*Plaisir*, p. 15), then *jouissance* precludes conceptualization (or naming, in Barthes' terms). That which is constituted by a rift or gap is literally atopical and cannot be related or shown. Only negatively, by bringing forth the two extremes that call it into being, can the critic elicit the spark of *jouissance*. The culturally validated canon and its subversive disruption become handmaidens in the service of critical hedonism (cf. *Plaisir*, pp. 14–15). Thus the description of textual hedonism that would go beyond a dialectical or paradoxical view of textuality must necessarily reinstitute that view (cf. *Plaisir*, pp. 31–2), in the hopes that somehow, between the extremes of its terms, a sense of disjunction will occur and trigger *jouissance* on the part of the reader.

The exact prerequisites for this event remain unclear. Barthes suggests that the reader "pervert" the text by actively seeking to turn it against itself through the revelation of its fissures, self-contradictions, and discrepancies (*Plaisir*, pp. 31–2). To the extent that all texts partake of textuality, this would seem to grant the reader authority over his own pleasure. If one reads *Le Plaisir du texte*, for instance, for the "excess" of meaning it provides, giving oneself over to the drift of *jouissance* when it occurs, one ought to attain the same erotic benefit as with any more rigorously "literary" text.

Yet Barthes shrinks back from this possibility. Perhaps because erasing generic distinctions would deprive the critic of his special bailiwick, Barthes does not challenge the notion of social classification as a criterion of textual distinction. He in fact correlates pleasure to two different types of text, the *texte de plaisir* and the *texte de jouissance*. The former offers its readers the general pleasure of cultural euphoria, while the latter actively cultivates disruption and the *dérive* (drift, loss of footing) of *jouissance*. And Barthes provides a prescription for the second of these types.

To provoke *jouissance*, writing must first shed its identity as a historical *écriture* by means of a program of extenuation. The goal of this process is not to gain a superiority over other texts and languages – which would only reiterate the pattern of all historical *écritures* and precipitate a further example of the class it claims to supersede – but to attain "that unheard of state, that incandescent metal, beyond origin and communication" where it becomes "*language* and not *a* language" (*Plaisir*, p. 51). To reach this state, the text must relinquish all metalanguage or reliance on scientific or institutional doctrine; destroy, through the cultivation of contradiction, its own discursive category or generic status; and attack "the canonical structures of language itself" on both the syntactical and lexical levels, through the abolition of logical units and sentences, and the introduction of exuberant neologism, transliterations, and equivocal, multilayered words (cf. *Plaisir*, pp. 50–1).

To a large extent, *Le Plaisir du texte* itself follows this prescription, such that one might well term it a *texte de jouissance*. It is not written in the form of an essay or theoretical argument, but rather as a loose collage of aphoristic speculations arranged in alphabetical order according to the first word of their ostensible topic. Barthes uses no consistent metalanguage or scientific terminology and does not valorize any single methodology such as semiology, historical classification, psychoanalysis, or structuralism. Most remarkably, *Le Plaisir* multiplies the discrepancies between the "cultural" and "disruptive" identities of its own discourse by introducing numerous ambiguities, digressions, and contradictions. Barthes himself signals his confusing use of "pleasure," which alternately merges with, encloses, or is opposed to *jouissance*, depending on whether an opposition is established between non-hedonistic "scientific" reading and its erotic counterpart, or between pleasure in general and *jouissance* in particular.

In a similar vein, the metaphor of the fissure or fault line occurs both as emblem or "location" of a general erotics and as an asymptotic relationship relating pleasure to *jouissance*. In other words, the same figure describes both the oppositional *constitutive* relationship out of which pleasure is born *and* the discontinuous non-relationship of pleasure to *jouissance*. This ambiguity is particularly fascinating, since it provides for a second-level fascination (Barthes'? ours?) triggered by the asymptote relating *jouissance* to pleasure: even if we attempt to contain the two notions in a happy synthesis, the disruption of the one by the other is likely to set off a further erotic pleasure on the metacritical level. The theoretician of literary hedonism, and his reader, risk being caught up in the regress they describe – literally getting their own drift.

Risk, however, is at the heart of *jouissance* and must not be negatively marked: it merely reinforces the erotic potential of the text. One might say that for Barthes the object of control becomes the loss of control, a willfully perverse thesis that finds performance in its own praxis. When Barthes defines the procedure of extenuation and thus lays out the practical guidelines to be followed by the erotic text, he breaks his own rules and situates both his text and his "program" in the abyss of paradox. To the extent that they derive from a rule-bound program for hedonistic writing, the texts he calls for can in no respect be said to be "beyond" the realm of particular language – which is precisely what they are supposed to be aiming for. Having repeatedly shown how pleasure occurs with the falling away from the normative use of language, Barthes draws up the rules for a *texte de jouissance*.

The contradiction is blatant, and so it *must* be, by its own logic: a program that calls for continual contradiction must first and foremost contradict itself, and it necessarily does so by the fact of its self-promotion as a program. That the *Plaisir du texte* "programs in" its own contradiction – and thus contradicts its own program – only demonstrates more strikingly that the erotic discrepancy occurs not between two units of the text, but between a unit and itself. In this case, the same passage (the prescription for extenuation) stands as both the embodiment and the antithesis of the work's thesis, as both the denial of spontaneity and the event of its disruption; it has, in short, a gap "between" itself.

Along the same lines, it is clear that one's (my) ability to make sense of Barthes' contradictions (or consistency) is contradictory and irrelevant to the text, which, after all, addresses not the question of understanding, but of pleasure. Whether or not one can reconcile the program of extenuation with itself matters only in terms of the pleasure, or lack thereof, that effort entails. Should one succeed in levelling all the contradictions of this text, one might well claim to have understood it, but that claim will disprove itself to the extent that understanding the text is precisely not the point. To a lesser degree, the same holds true for my treatment of *Le Plaisir du texte*, which attempts less to minimize its contradictions than to pursue them. As the reading of extenuation shows, when one pursues textual difference very far, one risks losing one's footing and sliding into the *dérive* of pleasure. Conversely, to the extent one gets no pleasure from Barthes (or my reading of him) it is unlikely one will pursue either text very far.

If one were, out of perversity, to come to the point here, it might well be that in an asymptotic as in a dialectical world, the spreading of the text, its *jouissance*, requires and provokes constant perversion in both directions: the apparently normative or conservative text must be read in terms of its disruption just as deliberately as the Barthian text must be read for closure – and vice versa. Ecstasy is no more the result of willed passivity than of headstrong activity, neither the effect of the text nor its cause. It is, in short, neither an "element" of the text nor a decision of the reader, but rather, at all times, *imprévu* (unforeseen) and *atopique* (nowhere) (cf. *Plaisir*, pp. 11, 39). Nor is it a happy combination of the two, but rather the (non)moment/place beyond both where each reaches its highest degree of coercion and most intimate sense of both self and other.

Metaphoric couplets like these could be multiplied endlessly, unfolded and infolded, in an attempt to bring *jouissance* under control, but they would be justified or efficacious only to the extent that their will to knowledge became so antithetical to Barthes' text as to produce a massive loss of continuity and the *dérive* of pleasure, at which point, *jouissance* might come of itself and no longer need to be known.

Thus, like Fish, Barthes interprets and performs his theory as he theorizes on interpretation, subjecting his discourse to its own logic and that logic to a further discourse. The end result is a reading/writing neither theory nor practice, nor even "both," since it baffles any attempts to maintain that dichotomy. The impact of such a creature is, for those dissatisfied with mere erotics, to reopen the question of its own value. Fish transcends the opposition of discipline to individiual by absorbing the latter into the former. Meaning as belief overcomes the anxiety of authority by blinding itself to the belief systems that authorize it – and it does so by merely believing itself to be blind. But this puts the reader/critic in the position of a passive (retro)spectator as regards the collective regress of meaning we call history.

For Barthes the primary anxiety is history, perceived both personally and communally as the diachronic petrification of lived meaning into received opinion (negative revolt into positive dogma), or (synchronically) as the originless layering of meaning upon meaning, myth upon myth. Just as Fish finds his solution to the constraints of structure within a structure of constraint, so does Barthes find his weapon against history in the structure of history: because it is a linguistic construct, every closure of history (or his story) brings a new opening, every infolding an unfolding, every *doxa* a *paradoxa*. Certainty is transformed into the catalyst for its own undoing – and that of institutional dogma. Rather than the product of a history he inhabits with comfort, Barthes' reader/writer is the agent of the process that dogs him.

Yet Barthes ultimately goes beyond the activist meaning that dialectic proposes, by shifting the axis of reading from epistemology to hedonism. In so doing, he implicitly relinquishes the tactic of outpacing petrification through contradiction. Instead, he sidesteps the dialectic by making fortuitous suspension the end of meaning.

This marks a more vigorous implementation of post-structuralist meaning than Fish's theory of belief, if only because it attempts to forestall its own institutionalization. By *flirting* with infinite regress, rather than extolling it as the ultimate truth, Barthes' hedonism refuses both the petrification of the *doxa* and the similar fate of the *paradoxa*. He refuses to be in or out of the tradition, knowing that both are the same.

One could go no further in this direction without reneging on the hedonistic model: to fling oneself into the abyss — rather than slipping in — would require abandoning the notion of self-abandon itself in favor of a model more intent on control. This model would be ironic to the extent that the abyss it leapt into would be that of its own control, cast as a permanent division against itself. And the critic/theoretician most drawn to such irony is Paul de Man.

14

Paul de Man:
The Irony of Deconstruction/
The Deconstruction of Irony

Perhaps more than any other American critic, Paul de Man has come to symbolize for the conservative literary-critical community all that is inaccessible, nihilistic, and subversive in interpretation. He is the leading – one might argue the only authentic – practitioner of deconstructive hermeneutics writing in English, and his work is steeped in philosophical traditions that further alienate him from the mainstream of "close-readers." He would seem, then, to have little in common with critics like Fish and Barthes, much less Holland and Bleich; indeed, deconstructive criticism has been widely branded as the antithesis of all that is worthwhile and wholesome in the study of literature. I would argue nonetheless that his theory of meaning and reading builds on the notions elaborated earlier in this book, and his exegetic practice only carries these notions to their logical conclusion – albeit in a rather unsettling way.

Like that of Barthes and Fish, de Man's work charts an itinerary of self-interrogations, but it does so more systematically and along a narrower axis. Whereas Fish finds inner contentment in the certainty of belief and Barthes derives erotic pleasure from the disruption of his beliefs, de Man's dialectic of meaning culminates in a vertiginous apotheosis of irony.

This crucial notion of irony must be read both structurally and historically, as the suspension of one's meaning between two identi-ties, and as the relentless putting into question of that meaning by the very categories it calls into play. For unlike Fish, the structuralists, or even most of his own epigones, de Man eschews that transcendent moment when the conviction that stable meaning is impossible displaces the practice of that impossibility, when the logic of belief – even negative belief – overcomes the critic's belief in logic. Early on, de Man's work discovers that unswerving adherence to *any* concept, from the structure of literature, to history, to the self, will lead to the dismantling of that concept's truth claims. The statement that linguistic structures (and acts) are unreliable is itself unreliable, and necessarily so, since it uses linguistic means to arrive at its conclusion.

In this way, de Man's exegeses attempt to push beyond the moment of renunciation and faith that Fish foregrounds. At the very moment where Fish transcends and abandons proof by analytic means and thereby proves his point, de Man opens his analysis of such an abandonment in its own terms: those of rhetoric.

Similarly, the erotic slippage or groundlessness that is randomly provoked in Barthe's hedonism of writing occurs in de Man's work only as the result of a painstakingly rigorous analysis. Loss of control is directly proportionate to the amount of control the exegesis imposes. This is perhaps the most troubling aspect of de Man's work for the critical community. To make unreliability proportionate to investigative rigor is to put into question the foundation and political justification of literary criticism. If the most disciplined and rigorous critical work is the one most likely to delude itself – even when it asserts as a mark of its superiority the knowledge of that delusion – criticial authority can no longer be a function of disciplinary obedience. When one reads this suspension improperly, which is to say according to the laws of objective truth which it suspends, it seems a negative, indeed nihilistic, assertion of infinite meaninglessness. For those critics of de Man who are unable to read his gesture otherwise, it necessarily implies the loss of all values based on authority, such as truth, the self, shared knowledge, and even historical fact.

Read in the light of its own premises and logic, however, de Man's work reasserts, expands, and even insures the power of such categories, albeit in what one might call an ironic mode. By acknowledging the paradoxical slippage in notions like "the truth" and constantly reasserting the excess of meaning with regard to any simple concept, one can guarantee that the truth will never be abused through unquestioned subordination to a single intention or identification with a single structure. De Man's apparent nihilism is a weapon against interpretive expropriation: it undoes the proprietary claims of the institution – and those whose power is vested in the institution – by showing that the act with which we would control meaning is itself out of control. In this sense nihilism is a *positive* force of disruption not unlike Barthes' paradoxical reading.

At the same time, however, de Man's ironic reading depends, like any irony, on the existence of its converse. It acknowledges the necessity of a "literal" meaning or truth claim within the ironic gesture itself and thereby reinstates the need for a positive gesture of certainty that Barthes disavows. Like Fish, de Man believes; but he does not believe in his belief. He thus avoids the fall into historical passivity that menaces Fish's reader. For the ironic reader belief is always accompanied by the belief that what one believes cannot be the full story: there is always something further, something more, to be understood in understanding.

This does *not* mean that de Man's writing smugly situates itself beyond self-delusion. De Man rejects simple categories like meaning as intention (rhetoric as persuasion, truth as metaphoric combination and totalization, understanding as symbol and symbolization) to the degree that he also sees such notions as their converse (rhetoric as structure of tropes, metaphoric totalization as metonymic aggregate, understanding as allegory and allegoresis) and vice versa. But he is not duped by the lucidity of his own gesture. The power of his writing lies in its refusal to read such reversals and duplicities as closures or recuperations invulnerable to further deconstruction *and* in its recognition that it has already failed to carry out such a refusal. In other words, de Man shuns both the positive certainty that Fish's dialectic offers, and the negative power that Barthes claims. His writing charts the impossibility of controlling our historical predicament (cf. Fish) in the same breath that it rejects that impossibility (cf. Barthes) and recognizes the failure of that rejection.

The infinite regress such irony entails can be abstractly stated, but it is cursedly difficult to chronicle. Because the putting-into-question of one's own conclusions can become a self-reinforcing pattern that increases exponentially with accumulated knowledge, de Man's writings attain a density that eludes mere paraphrase. And because that putting-into-question occurs positively – that is, as the result of further intentions and categories beneath one's current understanding – de Man's work cannot be grasped by any single conceptual system. In spite of his loyalty to the metalanguage of rhetoric, he draws on a variety of philosophical schools, from Pascal to speech act theory.

His consistency is to be found in his ironic attitude, not in his terminology.

Yet one can discern an itinerary of sorts, running from the now classic "Rhetoric of Temporality"[1] through *Blindness and Insight*[2] and *Allegories of Reading*.[3] Three moments in this progression seem particularly relevant to our study: an early preoccupation with the temporality of meaning as representation and intention, a later shift to the theme of rhetoric as both tropological system and act of persuasion, and a more recent fascination with the performative or positional force of language as grammar.

The Temporality of Rhetoric

Since de Man's early work was strongly influenced by phenomenology, it comes as no surprise that his first observations on the complexity of meaning center on intentionality and its objects. In a particularly straightforward essay on New Criticism, he describes the relationship between structure (here, "form") and the act of understanding in terms that should now be familiar: "literary 'form' is the result of the dialectic interplay between the prefigurative structure of the [interpreter's] foreknowledge and the intent at totality of the interpretive process. . . . form is never anything but a process on the way to its completion" (*Blindness*, p. 31).

Just as analogous conclusions lead Holland, in *5 Readers Reading*, or Fish, in "Interpreting the *Variorum*" to a quasi-autobiographical notion of reading, so too de Man stresses that "we can only understand that which is in a sense already given to us and already known, albeit in a fragmentary, inauthentic way that cannot be called unconscious" (*Blindness*, pp. 29–30). This "fragmentary" knowledge also correlates with Ingarden's theory of aspects.

But where other critics, and particularly Holland, dash off in pursuit of the reading subject's biography as the ultimate critical closure, de Man from the outset recognizes the limitation of such a project. This is because the structuration of the self that subjective criticism aims for is, like the totalization of the text the critic desires, a time-bound process:

hermeneutic understanding is always, by its very nature, lagging behind: to understand something is to realize that one had always known it, but at the same time, to face the mystery of this hidden knowledge. . . . The act of understanding is a temporal act that has its own history, but this history forever eludes totalization. (*Blindness*, p. 32)

This disjunction between the history of understanding and the understanding of history characterizes Stanley Fish's belief-bound subject. But Fish closes the question through an act of faith that gives up on historical closure, while de Man accentuates his predicament by readdressing it in the totalizing logic of rhetorical classification. In "The Rhetoric of Temporality," the lag or discontinuity between semantic experience and conceptual totalization finds rhetorical embodiment in the notion of *allegory*, which de Man opposes to the traditionally dominant category of the symbol, "conceived as an expression of unity between the representative and the semantic function of language" ("Rhetoric," p. 175). And just as de Man concludes that "the most original and profound moments in the works, when an authentic voice becomes audible" ("Rhetoric," p. 188), are those which portray the self "in its authentically temporal predicament" ("Rhetoric," p. 189) and therefore display "allegorizing tendencies" ("Rhetoric," p. 188), so too does he conclude that the most complete critical understanding will be that which acknowledges its lag and thereby integrates the notion of its own shortfall into its conclusion.

The authentic literary work, through allegory, "designates . . . a distance in relation to its own origin, and, renouncing the nostalgia and the desire to coincide, it establishes its language in the void of this temporal difference" ("Rhetoric," p. 189); the poet acknowledges, through a rhetorical figure, that his experience of meaning can never coincide with the totality it represents. The critic attains a similar sort of privilege by putting into question his critical closure: "understanding can be called complete only when it becomes aware of its own temporal predicament and realizes that the horizon within which the totalization can take place is time itself" (*Blindness*, p. 32). Such a "complete" understanding is ironic to the extent that it foregrounds its "conclusion" against the horizon of its inconclusiveness, but it is allegorical to the extent that it designates, beyond its surface conclusion, its own inability to be complete. Transposed into the structural analog of textual meaning, this paradigm gives rise to the well-known Demanic insistence that every text is the allegory of its own misreading.

Far more important, though, is the way in which de Man's

postulation of a "complete" understanding opens the way for its own deconstruction: as a quasi-conclusion itself, it invites repudiation by history. In fact, de Man, unlike the other critics we have treated, never waits for history; he appropriates its privilege by putting his conclusions into question almost before they have been reached. Notice, for instance, that de Man does not himself call ironic understanding complete but merely indicates that it *can* be called complete.

More generally, we find a persistent dismantling or inversion of each formulation or concept that might otherwise stand as a "conclusion." For instance, recognizing that his theory implies a set of intentional operations "within" every conceptual structure *and vice versa*, he reconsiders various intentional acts in terms of the structure they imply and then scrutinizes those structures in terms of the (further) acts *they* imply. This procedure enacts in a deliberately propositional key the infolding/unfolding we encountered in Barthes. It forms the dynamic for much of de Man's writing and accounts for the difficulty many readers have in following him. Because he does not hesitate to read rhetorical gestures as conceptual structures and then translate those structures into a further (philosophical or exegetic) intention, his interpretations glide through propositional and figurative language indifferently and with no outward indication that each might warrant distinct treatment. A variation of the same procedure allows him to read figures of speech as vehicles of conceptual propositions and vice versa.

This process of displacement from the structural to the intentional and back underlies the standard deconstructive gesture of desimplification, which de Man performs in terms drawn from rhetoric. The assumption of the deconstructor is that beneath every apparently monadic, and therefore fundamental, category one can uncover previous recombinations, totalizations, or exchanges, such that no original moment or structure can be found that would ground truth: "a deconstruction always has for its target to reveal the existence of hidden articulations and fragmentations within assumedly monadic totalities" (*Allegories*, p. 249).

This is merely the obverse face of the critical inability to conclude. Even as it advances in time, the exegetic will to conclude pushes the critic backwards in history towards an original truth immune to breakdown into prior intentions or structure. By instigating that very breakdown and deconstructing each successive monadic concept into the prior (further) acts and relationships it conceals, critics like de Man aim to prove that *every* "simple" truth constitutes itself within the discrepancy of its identity – the gap between experience and its representation, act and fact, meaning as intentional event and meaning as grammatical structure. To succeed in such a project is to ensure a future for criticism.

It is characteristic of de Man's criticism to carry out this project in the metalanguage of rhetoric, which category itself becomes increasingly desimplified in the process. To illustrate the strategies alluded to above, while simultaneously providing an insight into de Man's notion of rhetoric, two of the essays from *Allegories of Reading* will suffice. The opening essay of the collection concisely illustrates how the logic of deconstruction functions at the most general level of rhetoric, conceived as both a system of tropes and an act of semantic recombination.

The Rhetorization of Grammar/The Grammatization of Rhetoric

For de Man, rhetoric has a tradition of doubled identity, pertaining historically both to eloquence or persuasion and to a system of tropes. In his essay "Semiology and Rhetoric," whose straightforward argument furnishes an especially convenient point of entry into his recent work, he seizes on semiology's valorization of the systematic side of rhetoric, its "reduction of figure to grammar" (*Allegories*, p. 7).

This reduction, which de Man associates with both semioticians and speech act theory, corresponds to the theoretical stance I outlined above in the section on structuralism. It would explain all verbal acts, and in particular literature, in terms of structures, or "grammars," thereby subsuming individual intention within shared system. De Man takes exception to this "grammatization of rhetoric" first by citing two theoreticians – Burke and Peirce – who postulate the necessary subversion (deflection, interpretation) of grammar whenever it is instantiated. Then, in a typically Demanic move, he subverts even the opposition between grammar and performance which these examples might suggest.

He presents a fictional scene presumed to underwrite the delimitation of sense into literal and figural meaning, but which he then shows to define rhetoric as an act of suspension beyond binary choice. When Archie Bunker answers one of his wife's queries with an exasperated "What's the difference?", de Man sees rhetoric emerging in all its complexity:

The same grammatical pattern engenders two meanings that are mutually exclusive: the literal meaning asks for the concept (difference) whose existence is denied by the figurative meaning ["I don't give a damn what the difference is"]. (*Allegories*, p. 9)

But it is not the simple option between two meanings that constitutes a rhetorical question for de Man. Rather it is the emergence, within one's question, of contradictory meanings *and* of the impossibility of choosing between them by linguistic means alone:

It is not so that there are simply two meanings, one literal and the other figural, and that we have to decide which one of these meanings is the right one in this particular situation. . . . The grammatical model of the question becomes rhetorical not when we have, on the one hand, a literal meaning and on the other hand a figural meaning, but when it is impossible to decide by grammatical or other linguistic devices which of the two meanings (that can be entirely incompatible) prevails. (*Allegories*, p. 10)

The initial and foregone conclusion that rhetoric cannot be monadic is thus doubled by the discovery that neither can its duplicity be grasped by a single system of figuration: that of conceptual, i.e., systematic or categorical, opposition. Rhetoric, in this sense, is no longer just a duplicitous concept or structure, but an event: "the grammatical model . . . *becomes* rhetorical . . . *when* it is impossible to decide" (my emphasis). The "when" in this formulation is the emblem of rhetoric itself as well as of de Man's reversal. It is that place and moment when structure (the system of tropes balancing two meanings against each other) reveals itself as constitutive of and constituted by an event (the intentional act of persuasion suspending choice).

However subversive the reading of structural relationships as intentional events may appear, it only realizes – that is, puts into practice for a specific case – the repressed theoretical paradox underlying all literary criticism: that a text's meaning, or literal grammatical structure, is somehow identical with its author's meaning, or act of figuration. Instead of shying away from the practice this traditional assumption would underwrite if taken seriously, de Man performs it – by losing control over the distinction regulating his own gesture.

This occurs almost immediately in the essay in question, when he hypostatizes the anguish of suspension into the literal meaning of Archie Bunker's frustration: "the very anger he [Archie] displays is indicative of more than impatience; it reveals his despair when confronted with a structure of linguistic meaning that he cannot control and that holds the discouraging prospect of an infinity of similar future confusions, all of them potentially catastrophic in their consequences" (*Allegories*, p. 10).

Here the very gesture that puts conceptual recuperation into question becomes itself a structure of recuperation: the episode is "about" its own rhetoricity and the despair that rhetoricity triggers. However, this second-level proposition cannot simply be read as a deluded interpretive closure. It is not just referential but also allegorical to the extent that the object it designates cannot be grasped in its actuality or presence, but only obliquely and nostalgically through the performance and structure of its antithesis. In other words, rhetoric is precisely *not* merely a structure or event, much less an emotive reaction, yet that is precisely how de Man must designate it.

One can, of course, "understand" this paradox dialectically, as a sequence of displacements, such that de Man's thematic statements represent the structural precipitates of corresponding interpretive moments in his reading: to every critical reading (act) corresponds a critical reading (structure). But it is important that no causality be assigned to this pattern, which is no more a simple structural principle than a sequential process. To grant rhetorical events a causal role with respect to conceptual structures, or vice versa, is to miss the point as surely as if one elects the essay's simple referential meaning ("rhetoric is meaning as suspension") over its figural meaning ("to say 'rhetoric is meaning as suspension' in the context that suspends such linguistic gestures between multiple, incompatible meanings is itself an unreadable gesture").

At moments like this in the Demanic text, the reader might well start to feel the titillation of *jouissance* as he flirts with the abyss of infinite regress. De Man, however, unlike Barthes, never pauses to savour his suspension. Instead, he typically extends to his reader the steady ground of a provisional conclusion and introduces new exegetic evidence to bolster his case. Needless to say, neither the conclusion nor the "evidence" are firm ground at all since they inevitably set up another demystification all the more troubling because it originates in a purportedly demystified moment.

In the essay at hand, the lure of solid ground and the ensuing demystification come in rapid succession and relatively painlessly. Having just demonstrated how rhetoric consists in a kind of undecidability that transcends the simple opposition between literal and figural, de Man deftly reintroduces that very distinction on a much more general level and, as it were, *en passant*:

Rhetoric suspends logic and opens up vertiginous possibilities of referential aberration. And although it would perhaps be somewhat more remote from common usage, I would not hesitate to equate the *rhetorical, figural* potentiality of language with literature itself. I could point to a great number of antecedents to this equation of literature with figure. (*Allegories*, p. 10, my italics)

This passage is very nearly the allegoreme of its own warning: the referential aberrations it discusses could scarcely outdo its own aberrant referentialization, namely that rhetorical = figural, and figural = literary. But sure enough, just when de Man seems about to reinforce this comforting equation through a reading of Yeats' "Among School Children," the ground begins to shift. Having elaborated two completely opposed readings on the basis of the famous line "How can we know the dancer from the dance?" (another rhetorical question), de Man demonstrates how in this case the literal meaning ("how can we possibly make the distinction that would shelter us from the error of identifying what cannot be identified?") "leads to a greater complication of theme and statement" than the figural reading ("sign and referent are so exquisitely fitted to each other that all difference between them is blotted out") (*Allegories*, p. 11). He concludes that neither has precedence over the other, nor can they be separated, since each depends on the contrastive horizon of the other for its effect. The figural meaning is constituted by the very distinction it denies: we could not identify it as figural were there no literal horizon against which to distinguish it. Rhetoric in this sense emerges not from the opposition of two categories, but from meaning's difference from itself:

Neither can we say, as was already the case in the first example [of Archie's question], that the poem simply has two meanings that exist side by side. The two readings have to engage each other in direct confrontation, for the one reading is precisely the error denounced by the other and has to be undone by it. Nor can we in any way make a valid decision as to which of the readings can be given priority over the other; none can exist in the other's absence.

There can be no dance without a dancer, no sign without a referent. (*Allegories*, p. 12)

If this is true, our equation of literature with figural meaning cannot stand – or at least figural meaning must be redefined to encompass the indecision between literal and figural that the definition presumed to exclude.

De Man performs reversals like these with such speed that it would be fruitless to try to paraphrase all of the turns in even his simplest essay (and this is probably the simplest essay in *Allegories*). Nevertheless it is worthwhile looking at the final opposition with which he leaves his reader in the essay, because it marks a recurrent conclusion in his work and foreshadows the problem his essays confront at what one might call the third "stage" of de Man's itinerary.

Following his reading of the Yeats' line, de Man turns to a passage from Proust in order to explore further the relationship between inner associations (here correlated with figural language, intention, and metaphor), and outer relationships, which he characterizes as grammatical, repetitive, and metonymic. By reading one of Proust's ostensible celebrations of inner, metaphoric representation in terms of its own use of tropes, de Man shows that "the assertion of mastery of metaphor over metonymy owes its persuasive power to the use of metonymic structure" (*Allegories*, p. 15). Consequently, "the Proust passage shows that precisely when the highest claims are being made for the unifying power of metaphor, these very images rely in fact on the deceptive use of semi-automatic grammatical patterns" (*Allegories*, p. 16).

While this conclusion would seem to echo earlier attempts to draw a neat line between grammatical structure and figural aberration, de Man is careful to point out that it was arrived at differently. Rather than working from syntax towards intention, as in the Archie Bunker episode, his reading of Proust moves from "the self-willed and autonomous inventiveness of a subject" (*Allegories*, p. 16) to the structure of that subject's intention: "our first examples dealing with the rhetorical questions were rhetorizations of grammar, figures generated by syntactical paradigms, whereas the Proust example could be better described as a grammatization of rhetoric" (*Allegories*, p. 15).

This distinction can be understood in the context of this study as the arbitrary serialization of the critical dialectic (an arbitrary decision as to which face of meaning "comes first"), and de Man initially proposes the distinction to explain an apparent advantage to the grammatization of rhetoric:

> There seems to be a difference, then, between what I called the rhetoriza-tion of grammar (as in the rhetorical question) and the grammatization of rhetoric, as in the reading of the type sketched out in the passage from Proust. The former ends up in indetermination, in a suspended uncertainty that was unable to choose between two modes of reading, whereas the latter seems to reach a truth, albeit by the negative road of exposing an error, a false pretense. After the rhetorical reading of the Proust passage, we can no longer believe the assertion made in this passage about the intrinsic, metaphysical superiority of metaphor over metonymy. We seem to end up in a mood of negative assurance that is highly productive of critical discourse. (*Allegories*, p. 16)

Needless to say, de Man will deconstruct this mystification as well, showing finally that "we end up . . . in the case of the rhetorical grammatization of semiology, just as in the grammatical rhetorization of illocutionary phrases, in the same state of suspended ignor-ance" (*Allegories*, p. 19). However, the delusive hope for assurance through demystification does seem to reappear, in passing, in most of de Man's work. More often than not, the deconstructive itinerary will work from presumed intention to tropological structure, and the necessary delusions it proposes itself will inevitably be reached "by the negative road of exposing an error." There is a very good reason for this, and it has to do with the recurrent tension between critical discipline and theory.

Because a critic's conclusions must correlate with specific texts and somehow enrich the particulars of those texts, they cannot be of a general theoretical nature, nor can they refuse to decide between readings. As we saw above, readings that move from specific gram-matical structures like rhetorical questions to the conclusion that such structures underwrite multiple meanings among which no decision is possible cannot themselves make any decision. Having taken the first step in the exegetic process, they find themselves at the end of their interpretive rope: they cannot continue with their reading without deciding in favor of one meaning or another, but they cannot make that decision without denying their thesis. By the same token they cannot referentialize any particular moment of a text, but if they refuse to do so, they fail the discipline's requirement that they illuminate the text in its particulars.

On the other hand, the exposure of an error can meet this

requirement by virtue of the very fact that it is negating something specific and making a positive exegetic decision in spite of itself. As it undoes the structures of authority, deconstruction leaves in their place the authority of its own structure:

The deconstruction of a system of relationships always reveals a more fragmented stage that can be called natural with regard to the system that is being undone. Because it also functions as the negative truth of the deconstructive process, the "natural" pattern authoritatively substitutes its relational system for the one it helped to dissolve. (*Allegories*, p. 249)

Thus, the grammatization of rhetoric appears to offer the deconstructive critic a means of reconciling his need to demystify with the discipline's demand for a critical stand. It does so at a certain price, however, since it risks reintroducing notions of priority and causality. Because negation is dependent on prior assertion, the critical reading cannot get started without a pre-existent, "self-evident" reading that it can dismantle. In the essay discussed above, for instance, de Man has to assume Proust's intent to celebrate metaphor, and he does so through simple fiat: "the figure here dramatized is that of metaphor, an inside/outside correspondence as represented by the act of reading" (*Allegories*, p. 13).

To insure deconstruction against reduction to one of the simple notions it claims to undo, de Man must be able to show that this initial "intention" belongs neither to the author, nor to the deconstructive critic, nor to any of his less averted predecessors. Having found a way to reiterate endlessly, but in specifics, that meaning has no end, the critic must yet demonstrate that it has no beginning either.

Language as Position and the Position of Performatives

One might rephrase the problem in these terms: having collapsed the simple opposition between grammar and figure, syntactic fact and subjective act, the deconstructive critic appears nonetheless to have retained a certain subjective privilege: the prerequisite for the interpretive act seems to be linked to subjective action; the figural patterns deconstructed are still assumed to be the product of an intention. The tension between subjective experience and cognitive discourse that informs "The Rhetoric of Temporality" and grants primacy to meaning as a function of the subject, seems yet to be with us, albeit in an attenuated form. We may not be able to control meaning but we seem to be able to *make* it; we can still *do* things with language, although we may not know what we do.

For de Man to undo this assumption requires that he demonstrate the fallacy of correlating action with the subject – that he show a performative side of language not dependent on the intervention of a meaning act. Success in this venture will also necessarily mark a "second-level" deconstruction that puts into question the truth value or elementarity of the structures resulting from the first-level "exposure of an error." If one can show the efficacy of linguistic performatives to be a function of their independence from acts of personal will, the "initiation" and the "conclusion" of the critical reading will no longer appear the result of an authorial intervention. Textuality, rather than a dialectic between meaning experience and cognitive structure, will assume responsibility for meaning – even figural meaning (that is, meaning as a series of substitutions or slippages, as in the reading of Proust).

As a first step in this direction, de Man extracts from Nietzsche's deconstruction of non-contradiction two distinct models of language's relation to reality. On the one hand, we can define language de-nominatively, as a constative event that "assumes the prior existence of an entity to be known and that predicates the ability of knowing by ways of properties" (*Allegories*, p. 121). Thus conceived, language "does not itself predicate these attributes, but receives them, so to speak, from the entity itself by merely allowing it to be what it is" (ibid.).

There is no question that such predication may involve a correlate verbal intervention, but, according to de Man, "since the predicate is nonpositional with regard to the properties, it cannot be called a speech *act*. We could call it a speech *fact*, or a fact that *can* be spoken and, consequently, known without necessarily introducing devia-tions" (*Allegories*, p. 122).

In contrast to this constative language, Nietzsche, as de Man reads him, postulates a *positional* linguistic force capable of grounding entities merely by positing them, by bringing them into being. This second function allows "for the radical possibility that all being, as the ground for entities, may be linguistically 'gesetzt,' a correlative of speech acts" (*Allegories*, p. 123). Because the knowledge that results from such "acts" is "not necessarily intentional but grounded in the structure of rhetorical tropes" (ibid.), one can say it is no longer the subject that acts, but language, as an absolutely non-subjective positional force.

It is only in de Man's more sustained readings of Rousseau that this notion of a non-intentional performative emerges in all its complexity. In his reading of the *Social Contract*, for example, de Man uncovers a relationship of non-identical being within the notions of property, national state, and statutory law, and he extends that relationship to textuality in general, conceived as the suspension between performative and constative. In each case, a central notion can be seen as partaking of two radically incompatible relational systems. The law, or legal text, for instance, is first and foremost characterized by its absolute generality, the fact that it is formulated without reference to a particular individual or instance. Only "this generality which ruthlessly rejects any particularization" (*Allegories*, p. 268) allows the legal text to come into being. At the same time, however, "no law is a law unless it also applies to particular individuals. It cannot be left hanging in the air, in the abstraction of its own generality. Only by thus referring it back to particular praxis can the *justice* of the law be tested" (*Allegories*, p. 269).

For de Man, this schizoid character of the law mirrors the status of the text in general, as both grammar and figure, system and instance. On the one hand, the text "ruthlessly rejects any particularization":

The system of relationships that generates the text and that functions indepedently of its referential meaning is its grammar. To the extent that a text is grammatical, it is a logical code or a machine.... just as no text is conceivable without grammar, no grammar is conceivable without the suspension of referential meaning. Just as no law can ever be written unless one suspends any consideration of applicability to a particular entity including, of course, oneself, grammatical logic can function only if its referential consequences are disregarded. (*Allegories*, pp. 268–9)

On the other hand, the text, like the law, must pass the test of particularity: "the *justesse* of any statement can only be tested by referential verifiability" (*Allegories*, p. 269). And it is the text's structure that assures this referentialization: "every text generates a referent that subverts the grammatical principle to which it owed its constitution" (ibid.). The act of subversion, which marks the "incompatibility between the formulation and the application of the law" (*Allegories*, p. 270) is thus associated with the definition of the text as grammar: it is the capacity of language to generate meaning grammatically, in the absence of any referentialization, that makes the text possible *and* guarantees its subversion in meaning. Any "reading" necessarily deceives, to the extent that it conceals or subverts the text's grammar, but a text can only put its grammar into action through such a deception:

> It seems that as soon as a text knows what it states, it can only act deceptively ... and if a text does not act, it cannot state what it knows. The distinction between a text as narrative and a text as theory also belongs to this field of tension. (*Allegories*, p. 270)

This passage underlines two important points. First, de Man has managed to retain his suspension of closure while at the same time suspending the "opening" of meaning. Because the ground of meaning has been shifted to grammar, the subversion of meaning, in the form of a dummy (or dumb) referential reading can be said always already to be "in" the text. Second, this shift can occur only because de Man has explicitly correlated the text's performative potential with its grammar. This can be made clearer through a final analogy with the law.

Blending his language with that of Rousseau, de Man recasts "the discrepancy within the contractual model [of the law]" in historical terms:

> Considered performatively, the speech act of the contractual text never refers to a situation that exists in the present, but signals toward a hypothetical future ... All laws are future-oriented and prospective; their illocutionary mode is that of the *promise*. On the other hand, every promise assumes a date at which the promise is made ... "when the Law speaks in the name of the people, it is in the name of the people of today and not of the past" ... The definition of this "people of today" is impossible, however, for the eternal present of the contract can never apply as such to any particular present. (*Allegories*, p. 273)

As grammatical law, the text can only mean (speak) in the name of today's readers, but the definition of these readers is impossible to the extent that the text's grammar cannot, as such, apply to any particular present reading. Any meaning a text has, then, is "in the name of" a refusal of particularity that can never be known as such and a referential subversion of that refusal that can never be found. The degree to which language has escaped from our control here becomes more apparent in the final essay in *Allegories of Reading*.

When he takes up the discussion of the "excuse" in Rousseau, de Man explicitly forestalls any temptation to reintroduce the subject into performatives by demonstrating that the efficacy of Rousseau's excuses depends precisely on the possibility of an "entirely gratuitous and irresponsible text," a fiction, in other words (*Allegories*, p. 296). Rousseau exploits such a notion to explain the emergence of lies in his own discourse: they are the product of a random fiction generated by the machine of language. Yet the power of such a machine is matched by the difficulty one has in understanding it. Pure performative eludes simple conceptual location, but it seems a logical necessity to explain the infinite plurality of meanings the text can generate:

> It seems to be impossible to locate the moment in which the fiction stands free of any signification; in the very moment at which it is posited, as well as in the context that it generates, it gets at once misinterpreted into a determination which is, *ipso facto*, overdetermined. Yet without this moment, never allowed to exist as such, no such thing as a text is conceivable. (*Allegories*, p. 293)

Here the constative function of language persists alongside its performative counterpart but it is consistently phrased as a secondary moment, which deprives the subject of its last vestiges of priority, even as regards cognition: "any speech act produces an excess of cognition, but it can never hope to know the process of its own production (the only thing worth knowing)" (*Allegories*, p. 300).

The consequences of this rephrasing are substantial. In the case of Rousseau, for example, de Man suggests that "far from seeing language as an instrument in the service of a psychic energy, the possibility now arises that the entire construction of drives, substitutions, repressions, and representations is the aberrant, metaphorical correlative of the absolute randomness of language, prior to any figuration or meaning" (*Allegories*, p. 299). In the case of de Man himself, this possibility redefines the central trope of the critical endeavor, irony. Rather than being confined to the continual grammatization of rhetoric, or the negative cognitions so useful for the critical discipline, the field of irony must be extended to put into question even the cognitive project of the deconstructive critic. This is imperative if ironic reading is to maintain its two-faced relationship with the institutions that empower it. We have seen how irony, like Barthes' model of paradox, exploits existing certainty as a springboard. But where paradoxical reading inaugurates subversion through historical displacement – by contradicting and thus relegating to the past its (now) former assumptions – de Man's approach generates history out of the tension between meaning's warring identities. In other words, Barthes grounds his meaning in the historical moment/structure he wants to dispell, and he assumes that his meaning too will become in time just such a *doxa*. De Man extracts *his story* from the permanent, omnipresent tension between meaning's incompatible, yet reciprocally constitutive identities, and he strives to prevent either of those identities from attaining the pre-eminence Barthes accepts as inevitable. Ironic reading can maintain its voice – and the authority of the narratives that voice articulates – only to the extent that its meaning resists reduction to the self-identity of literal truth.

It is by resisting the truth of its own meaning, then, that irony hopes to outpace the petrification of history Barthes finally sidesteps by means of hedonism. A subversion that takes its truth literally only reinforces the institution and pronounces its own canonization – at which point one is already a "believer" (in Fish's terms). De Man himself acknowledges this: "the deconstruction of tropological patterns of substitution (binary or ternary) can be included within discourses that leave the assumption of intelligibility not only unquestioned but that reinforce this assumption by making the mastering of the tropological displacement the very burden of understanding" (*Allegories*, p. 300).

We saw an example of such a discourse in the essay on semiology and rhetoric, covered above. True to course, that essay "engenders its own narrative, which can be called an allegory of figure" (ibid.). The introduction of a randomly performative model of language, however, puts into suspension both the logic of substitution underlying "grammatization" and the priority of subjective control in the generation of such substitutions. It thereby dislocates the truth of the ironic reading, disenfranchising the reader and suspending his narrative's truth claims before they can "take their place" in history. The irony of irony, then, is that it disqualifies the possibility of its own provocation; it sustains itself on the certainty that it cannot be sustained:

Irony is no longer a trope but the undoing of the deconstructive allegory of all tropological cognitions, the systematic undoing, in other word, of understanding. As such, far from closing off the tropological system, irony enforces the repetition of its aberration. (*Allegories*, p. 301)

Thus Demanic irony does more than smugly put into question the "naive objectivism" of its detractors. It undoes its own negative knowledge as well. If this be nihilism, it is a positive nihilism determined not to fall victim to the excesses of authority that institutions generate. By suspending its own truth claims at the very moment of their articulation, it hopes to insure itself of a continued voice, a future and past that will not always already be the image of the petrified self. It does not do away with the traditions of knowledge, it animates them − both through the precipitation of further "truths" that can always be taken as such by "believers," and by postulating a history beyond identification, an ongoing textuality both entirely "other" and completely personal, both incomprehensible and, because it is recognized as such, entirely conceivable. Stating the necessity of truth *and* its inadmissibility, ironic reading nurtures the tradition it subverts; it seeks to control history by relinquishing control.

We are now in a position to see to what degree this most intense form of dialectic reading exhibits more power than its predecessors. To the extent that de Man's writing constantly asserts and denies its own authority, it draws nearer to the kind of language it most admires, the fictional language of literature. If de Man goes to so much trouble to show that his readings are not "his" but the text's, it is at least in part to abolish the distinction between literature and exegesis. When he aligns the tension between performative and constative with the distinction "between a text as narrative and a text as theory," he also does away with that very traditional distinction and places his own work firmly within the field of all figural/ grammatical texts.

By its own logic, then, de Man's writing is really neither theory nor criticism, neither truth nor fiction: it is at all times both the theory of narration and the narration of a theory. And that is, in my opinon, one of deconstruction's strategic moves: by dissolving the distinction between poetry and proposition, it hopes to attain literature's edge over history (one can never disprove a literary text) and force the discipline to implicate its most revered category in any direct criticism. As de Man bluntly puts it, "poetic writing is the most advanced and refined mode of deconstruction; it may differ from critical or discursive writing in the economy of its articulation, but not in kind" (*Allegories*, p. 17).

If this is true, critical writing in the wake of deconstruction ought logically to exhibit the awareness of its new status. The examination of that likelihood and a consideration of the possible shapes criticism might take in the future will form the basis of my concluding chapter.

Conclusion

It would be an exercise in self-contradiction to argue the permanent truth of a dialectical model of meaning. To the extent that such a proof could succeed, it would deny its own thesis by reaffirming an immutable structure and the control over history that thesis questions. Thus if my account of meaning is correct, it must disqualify its own closure: analytic discourse is as self-differing, its truths as slippery, as any literary work. This is the obverse side of Barthes' dialectic of paradox: we can no more impose petrification than we can avoid it.

In that sense, my "demonstration" that the self-differing discourse of post-structuralism is already latent in its precursors means any number of different things. Indeed, it already means something other than it did, if only by virtue of its extension: in the introduction I valorized theoretical truth over historical causality, yet that distinction has dissolved in the course of the study. A historical filiation of sorts has surfaced within my theoretical analysis. This merging of theoretical truth and historical narration is inevitable in a gesture that reiterates the delusion of conceptual closure. As both story and theory, such a gesture can take itself on its own terms: neither just conceptual truth, nor trivial fiction, it presents a necessarily serious proposition that knows its triumph to be illusory – although no more so than its demystification.

To keep the spirit of this new discourse, we must reassess dialectical meaning's conceptual logic as an historical event. Taking as our point of departure the work of Stanley Fish, we can eliminate from the outset speculation on the success of post-structuralism: it has already succeeded in infiltrating our belief systems; if it had not, we could not understand it – I could not have written and you could not have read this book. That considerable controversy still surrounds post-structuralism proves only that its political implications make many people uncomfortable. The proliferation of complex theoretical writing, for instance, is frequently decried as a threat to the primacy of the literary classics. Presumably, we will all spend so much time reading de Man that we will never read Rousseau. Behind this accusation lies the assumption that the text's primacy is somehow better preserved by the traditions that post-structuralism seems to challenge. But as Fish convincingly argues, the "text's meaning" we are to revere can never be anything more than the institution that determines it.

Not surprisingly, those who decry dialectical criticism are scholars with vested interests in seeing the meaning *they* helped consolidate survive. They find post-structuralism so threatening not because it lays a claim to authority – claiming to know what the text means in a direct challenge to established understanding – but because it denies the fundamental convention of meaning as property. By disrupting that system, post-structuralism denies established authorities the possibility of ever regaining their lost investment.

In fact, *two* systems of authority have controlled meaning – and the discipline – for the past fifty years. On the one hand, and possibly in emulation of science, whose prestige has devalued literary study for most of this century, critics of a theoretical bent have attempted to isolate the structure and function of meaning from its incarnation in particular historical acts. We have seen how this tendency culminates in the structuralist attitude, but we have not stressed how it informs the politics of the discipline.

By imitating science and postulating their object of inquiry to be transcendent of any individual, yet available to all, the structuralists implicitly subscribe to what one might call, for want of a better term, a social notion of literature. Depriving individual persons of the right to "claim" a reading, they dispute – in principle, at least – the concept of meaning as personal possession. As they see it, any meaning one might come up with in an interpretation is as much the property of the collective that furnished the conventions of reading as of the individual that instantiated them. This challenges the metonymic association of tenant with property that underlies the authority of "established scholars" and "definitive" readings.

In direct proportion to its theoretical rigor, however, this "socialization" of meaning spawns an attendant bureaucracy that ultimately reinstates an authoritarian privilege. As an exponentially growing theoretical lexicon displaces the historical erudition of scholarship, a new class of technocrats takes control of the literary critical economy. Mastery of meaning turns out to hinge on the mastery of a recondite metalanguage most critics find beyond their grasp. So rapidly do the subcategories and refinements to the theoretical grammar proliferate that even the best-intentioned critic has difficulty maintaining fluency – and hence a share in the conventions he is supposed to subsidize.

Vying with theory for control of the discipline, historical scholarship underwrites a system of proprietary interest. By dint of long work and faithful tenancy, "recognized authorities" establish a claim to their particular bailiwick. Accumulated scholarly property, in the form of notes, references, bibliography, and the like, assures them of the respect of newcomers – and provides them an inheritance to pass along to their chosen heirs. Those heirs in turn will become the wardens of the domain, once they have cultivated it sufficiently. At that point they will have the right to determine what the authors under their jurisdiction mean, and the discipline will respect their opinions.

These two systems for controlling meaning are equally coercive, although they are to a large extent inevitable in a discipline informed by our larger social and cultural matrix. Yet it is precisely the need to choose between them that post-structuralism disputes. Functioning as a purge, dialectical practice uses the logic of each system of authority to demonstrate that system's shortcomings. Declaring meaning to be the property of no one and each one, it restores to the text its own authority as an endless system and event. Emancipated from canon, discipline, and even subjective consciousness, post-structuralist *textuality* shames by contrast the meager autonomy granted literary *texts* by the New Critics. No longer just the product and property of critics, textuality constitutes texts in the form of history. In this respect, asking whether it will carry the day just doesn't make any sense. It already has, according to Fish.

In one sense, then, Fish's version of dialectical meaning should bring comfort to those who fear the revolution: they have already missed it. To the extent that we can conceptualize, polemicize, and evaluate meaning as a dialectical self-difference, the historical period over which that belief system held sway must already be past. For its younger practitioners, deconstruction has become something they believe in, rather than the belief system underlying the faith. As

Barthes would point out, it has already become the *doxa* in more than one context and is therefore ripe for subversion.

Of the critics we have studied, de Man is most acutely aware of this moment, whose inevitability he tries to forestall through an ever renewed irony. Unfortunately, irony's dizzying spell has a certain allure, no doubt attributable to its structural similarity to the abyss of rapture Barthe foregrounds. And this allure spells its ultimate petrification: as ironic reading gains popularity and epigones proliferate, what commenced as revolutionary gesture becomes institutional norm. When deconstruction becomes the unexamined truth for a significant number of students, it will, true to its own paradigm, mean something entirely different – something predictable and shared. And predictable reversal is no reversal at all; it cannot provide the ungrounding of irony – much less rapture. The success of deconstruction spells its failure.

It is perhaps for this reason that critics like Barthes and Eco turn to a new mode of discourse that draws explicitly on the conflation of literature and criticism to which I alluded at the conclusion of the preceding chapter. By renouncing the axis of truth in favour of a discourse neither critical nor literary, yet in some respects both, such writers hope to subvert their reintegration into academic criticism. Through such works as his *Fragments d'un discours amoureux*,[1] which explores love through a series of first person dramatic fragments blending personal reminiscence, philosophical and literary citation, and theoretical speculation into a single elusive voice, Barthes hopes to sidestep the petrification into truth that awaits more propositional critics like de Man.

Whether or not this strategy can achieve its ends would seem to rest on its ability to resist subsumption within pre-existing generic classes. More traditional appropriations of literary voice, such as Umberto Eco's novel *The Name of the Rose*, would seem to succeed at the cost of any subversive potential.[2] To take refuge from the regress of criticism within the folds of literature – which presumably states its truth in a non-propositional mode that cannot be disproven – is to reinforce that most traditional distinction of the canon, namely the difference between original work and critical work. This in turn reauthorizes the discipline that thrives on that distinction and puts the subversive writer at the mercy of his interpreters: as *literature*, a text requires the mediation of criticism to state any truths or provoke any revolutions.

It may finally be the case that, to the extent it cannot inaugurate a radically new voice, the post-structural awareness of our historical predicament can reiterate and aggravate that predicament, but never solve it. Enclosed by the structure/event it seeks to enclose, the truth of dialectical criticism lies in its fallacy. One cannot get *out of* history: as process its petrification will always overtake the most vigorous subversion; as structure it is always there as the system of belief or truth that allows us to understand. Neither can one get *into* history: the systems we would claim as our grounding and sur-rounding matrix can never be the system grounding that claim; the moment of absolute self-identity and presence we call "the present" can never be attained. We can only know our selves as historical others; we can never penetrate the world we are in.

Still, once the awareness of this double bind has been institution-alized, one might expect a general realignment of literary studies towards historiography. When all one can know or say is already something else(where), the boundary between "present" intuition and past "event," or between "our" experience and the experience of "others," loses its edge: talking about "the past" becomes a perfectly "natural" way to talk about ourselves; exposing the belief systems of a former age becomes a reasonable strategy for examining our own. That this new discourse is already upon us is confirmed by the numerous theoretical/historical interpretations of deconstruction that have appeared recently. One such account that reinforces my thesis not just by presenting an instance of the type of discourse in question, but by furnishing a similar argument for the historical roots of deconstruction, is that of Jonathan Culler. In his two recent books, *In Pursuit of Signs* and *On Deconstruction*,[3] Culler locates the origins of deconstruction in the structuralist project's desire to locate meaning in grounding matrices. Providing an implicit ex-planation of his own failure to carry through with the development of a structuralist poetics, he describes, using metaphor as an ex-ample, why such taxonomy cannot succeed:

to account for the signification of . . . a metaphor is to show how the relationship between its form and its meaning is already virtually present in the systems of language and rhetoric. . . . Yet the value of the metaphor . . . lies in its innovatory inaugural force. Indeed, our whole notion of literature makes it not a transcription of preexisting thoughts but a series of radical and inaugural acts: acts of imposition which create meaning. The very conven-tions to which we appeal in explaining literary meanings are products:

products which, it would seem, must have acts as their source. (*Pursuit*, p. 39)

On the other hand, the critic's discovery that acts produce meaning only leads him back to the pre-eminence of structure:

acts of signification are necessary to create signifying differences. But this perspective gives rise to no discipline; it is not a position that can be maintained because if one tries to discuss acts of signification one immediately is led to describe the oppositions which enable an act to signify; one immediately finds oneself back in the semiotic perspective, describing a system. (*Pursuit*, p. 41)

Starting from a decidedly structuralist perspective, Culler arrives at the same recuperation I have proposed, namely, that the structure of meaning is such that it draws one into a dialectical regress:

the semiotics of literature thus gives rise to a "deconstructive movement" in which each pole of an opposition can be used to show that the other is in error but in which the undecidable dialectic gives rise to no synthesis because the antinomy is inherent in the very structure of our language, in the possibilities of our conceptual framework. (*Pursuit*, p. 39)

That Culler locates the "origin" of the dialectic in semiotics should not confuse us. We have seen in the early sections of this book that it is in fact "everywhere" and always has been – and indeed Culler does not insist on correlating the semiotic perspective with any particular historical school or period. What is important is that his writing, although ostensibly less "innovative" than Barthes' *Fragments*, nonetheless reconciles two traditionally incompatible modes of critical discourse – that of history and that of theory. In other words, Culler historicizes deconstruction in terms of the scientific project it displaces and blends his theoretical analysis with exegesis and narration. In so doing, he not only confirms the assimilation of the deconstructive endeavor but exemplifies the positive heritage it bequeaths the discipline.

Divested of their closure, the writing of history and the writing of theory can transcend the dispute over authority. In a "demystified" post-scientific age, the opposition of theory to history becomes less necessary; one need no longer pit system against narrative, permanent fact against temporal act. It is in this sense that the *institution* of dialectical meaning can merge history and theory into a single gesture rendered innocent by the loss of its truth claims. Accustomed to the everyday humdrum of infinite regress, yet awed by the proliferation of intertextuality to which the post-structuralist liberation of the text has given rise, future critics will recover, on the far side of irony's absolute freedom, the charm of simple historical (arti)fact. At this point our writing will regain its power through the loss of its privilege; history and theory will merge with interpretation in an eclectic form of literary study less obsessed with controlling truth than (perhaps) with its ability to provoke the pleasure of new ideas.

Bibliographical Note

Readers interested in pursuing the topics or authors covered in this study will find excellent topical bibliographies in the following works.

On Phenomenological and Reader-Response Criticism

Tompkins, Jane P., ed. *Reader-Response Criticism*. Baltimore: The Johns Hopkins University Press, 1980. Bibliography, pp. 233–72.

On Structuralism, Semiotics, and their Precursors

Culler, Jonathan. *Structuralist Poetics*. Ithaca: Cornell University Press, 1975. Bibliography, pp. 273–93.

On Structuralism and Post-Structuralism

Culler, Jonathan. *On Deconstruction*. Ithaca: Cornell University Press, 1982. Bibliography, pp. 281–302.
Harari, Josue V., ed. *Textual Strategies*. Ithaca: Cornell University Press, 1979. Bibliography, pp. 443–63.

Notes

Introduction

1 New Haven: Yale University Press, 1967, p. 4.

Chapter 1: Poulet, Sartre, and Blanchot

1 October 1969, pp. 53–68.
2 Paris: Gallimard, 1948. Citations are from the "Collection Idées" reprint of 1967. All translations are my own.
3 Paris: Gallimard, 1955. Citations are from the "Collection Idées" reprint of 1973. All translations are my own.
4 Georges Poulet, *Les Lettres Nouvelles*, 24 June 1959, p. 11.

Chapter 2: Sartre and Dufrenne

1 Paris: Les Editions Nagel, 1948.
2 Paris: Gallimard, 1940. Citations are from the "Collection Idées" reprint of 1975. All translations are my own.
3 *Le Livre à venir* (Paris: Gallimard, 1959). Citation is from the "Collection Idées" reprint of 1971, p. 18; my translation.
4 *New Literary History* (October 1969).
5 To avoid confusion with the many connotations of imagination, I shall employ the term "imaging" to refer to the process of constituting an image mentally, regardless of the status of that image.
6 *Critique littéraire (Situations*, I) (Paris: Gallimard, 1947). Citation is from the "Collection Idées" reprint of 1975, p. 43; my translation.
7 2 vols. (Paris: Presses Universitaires de France, 1953). All translations are my own.

Chapter 3: Ingarden and Iser

1 Originally published in Polish and then translated and revised by the

author for the German editions that appeared in 1960 as *Das Literarische Kunstwerk*, 2nd revised and expanded edition (Tübingen: Max Niemayer Verlag) and *Vom Erkennen des Literarischen Kunstwerks* (Tübingen: Max Niemayer), both works are now available in English: *The Literary Work of Art*, tr. George C. Grabowicz (Evanston: Northwestern University Press, 1973) and *The Cognition of the Literary Work of Art*, tr. Ruth Ann Crowley and Kenneth R. Olson (Evanston: Northwestern University Press, 1973). All citations are from these translations.

2 Baltimore: The Johns Hopkins University Press, 1978.
3 2 vols. (Paris: Presses Universitaires de France, 1953). All translations are my own.
4 Paris: Gallimard, 1940. Citations from "Collection Idées" reprint. All translations are my own.
5 *New Literary History* (October 1969).

Chapter 4: Ingarden, Iser, and the Geneva School

1 Tr. George C. Grabowicz (Evanston: Northwestern University Press, 1973).
2 *The Cognition of the Literary Work of Art*, tr. Ruth Ann Crowley and Kenneth R. Olson (Evanston: Northwestern University Press, 1973).
3 Baltimore: The Johns Hopkins University Press, 1974.

Chapter 5: Norman Holland

1 Oxford: Oxford University Press, 1968; all citations are from the 1975 Norton edition.
2 New Haven: Yale University Press, 1975.
3 Cf. *Fiction and the Unconscious* (Boston: Beacon Press, 1957).
4 *Criticism*, 13, No. 4 (Fall, 1976).
5 A fuller account of such a subjectivity-based notion of truth follows in the chapters on David Bleich and E. D. Hirsch.
6 "Gothic Possibilities," with Leona F. Sherman, *New Literary History*, 8, No. 2 (Winter, 1977), p. 280.
7 "UNITY IDENTITY TEXT SELF," *PLMA* [Publications of the Modern Language Association] 90, No. 5 (October 1975), p. 813.
8 New York: Norton, 1975.
9 David Bleich aptly notes the atavistic implications of Holland's model: "if the act of self-enlightenment is only an act of self-replication, the idea that consciousness is an organ of self-enhancement has to be discarded" (*Subjective Criticism* [Baltimore: The Johns Hopkins University Press, 1978], p. 121).

Chapter 6: David Bleich

1 Chicago: The University of Chicago Press, 1962.
2 Baltimore: The Johns Hopkins University Press, 1978.
3 Bleich defines at some length the origins of objectification in the development of the child as psychoanalysts see it. As one might expect, this account, and much of the rest of *Subjective Criticism*, abounds in "well-established facts" (p. 46) borrowed from psychological doctrine. Since I have already established, in the discussion of Holland, the degree to which such "proof" undercuts subjective logic, I shall omit similar arguments here and accept Bleich's obvious belief in the truth value of psychology as his adaptive response to needs beyond our surmise.
4 See, for instance, Bleich's discussion of ministers, experts, I. A. Richards, and Northrop Frye, pp. 33–6.
5 In fact, in his introduction to *Subjective Criticism* Bleich justifies his project on the basis of academic literary study's obvious economical and social importance (pp. 4ff.).

Chapter 7: E. D. Hirsch

1 New Haven: Yale University Press, 1967.
2 Chicago: University of Chicago Press, 1976.
3 The holistic logic of this continual reassessment closely approximates Iser's concept of continual gestalt formation. This is the closest Hirsch comes to acknowledging that meaning might have an evanescent, event-like quality as well as a structural identity.
4 For a more extensive and precise illustration of the many applications of these principles in making decisions about meanings, see *Validity*, pp. 181–95.
5 Declaring infoldings to be implications is, of course, a standard rhetorical device of theoreticians and critics alike, designed to attribute to the author – or the principle he elucidates – an idea or meaning first explicitly raised by the critic.
6 It is because we assume implications already to "be there" that they have a factual status not shared by our own integrations. This is why one conventionally declares his *apercus* to be "implicit" in a prior, accepted meaning, rather than a spur-of-the-moment revelation. Hirsch furnishes an excellent example of this technique in the retraction I cite above from *Aims*, p. 33, but I am certain my own text furnishes abundant examples as well.

Chapter 9: Jonathan Culler

1 Umberto Eco, *A Theory of Semiotics* (Bloomington, Indiana: Indiana UniversityPress, 1976), p. 61.
2 Jonathan Culler, *Ferdinand de Saussure* (New York: Penguin Books, 1977), pp. 76–7.
3 Ithaca: Cornell University Press, 1975.
4 *Cours de linguistique générale*, publié par Charles Bally et Albert Sechehaye (Paris: Payot, 1955), 5ᵉ édition, p. 30; my translation.
5 "Text, Theme, and Theory," *Yale Review*, 63 (1973–74), p. 441.
6 In fact, Culler never does put his theory into practice. As we shall see in the conclusion, his more recent work explicitly acknowledges the untenability of a purely taxonomic approach to meaning.

Chapter 10: Umberto Eco

1 Bloomington: Indiana University Press, 1976 and 1979 respectively.
2 I shall limit my discussion to the first and last chapters of the book, since the intervening sections consist of articles originally published elsewhere and in different contexts. Because these sections do not explicitly address my topic and in fact scarcely cohere into an argument, I feel their inclusion would overburden the current discussion.

Chapter 11: From Structuralism to Post-Structuralism

1 Because most of his work does not fall within the tradition of literary criticism that here concerns us, and because I could in any case scarcely do justice to the volume and complexity of his writing in an overview of this sort, I shall forego any in-depth analysis of Derrida's work and refer interested readers to the prefaces of his various translated works and the eminently accessible discussion by Jonathan Culler, in *On Deconstruction* (Ithaca: Cornell University Press, 1982).
2 "Signature Event Context" (*Glyph* I), p. 183. The original appears in *Marges de la philosophie* (Paris: Editions de Minuit, 1972), pp. 365–93.
3 Out of deference to the printers, I am using parentheses to allude to the suspended status of the beast in question. Derrida himself instituted the practice of crossing out words such as "concept" or "origin" whenever he used them to refer to *différance* – a practice known as writing "under erasure" (*sous rature*).
4 Publié par Charles Bally et Albert Sechehaye (Paris: Payot, 1955), 5ᵉ édition; my translation. Jonathan Culler provides an excellent discussion of the central role these principles play in Saussure's thought and structuralism, in his *Ferdinand de Saussure* (New York: Penguin Books, 1976).

5 Paris: Editions de Minuit, 1967. All citations are from this edition; the translations are my own.
6 In *Marges de la philosophie*; my translation.
7 The most obvious example of such a key term is that of *écriture*, or the *trace*, but others spring to mind: the *supplément* in his work on Rousseau, the *crypt* in his introduction to the work of Abraham and Torok ("Fors," preface to *Cryptonymie*, N. Abraham and M. Torok [Paris: Aubier-Flammarion, 1976], translated in *Georgia Review* 31, 1 [1977]), or *communication* and *iterability* in his treatment of Austin (cf. "Signature," or "Limited Inc" [*Glyph* II, pp. 162–254]).

Chapter 12: Stanley Fish

1 New York: Macmillan and Company, 1967.
2 Cambridge: Harvard University Press, 1980.
3 Berkeley: University of California Press, 1972.
4 *New Literary History*, 2 (Autumn 1970). This essay has been reprinted in *Self-Consuming Artifacts* as well as in *Is There a Text*.
5 *Critical Inquiry*, 2, No. 3 (Spring 1976), 465–85.
6 *New Literary History*, 5 (Autumn 1973).
7 "Facts and Fictions: A Reply to Ralph Rader," *Critical Inquiry*, 1, No. 4 (June 1975), pp. 888–9; italics added.
8 *Critical Inquiry*, 4, No. 4 (Summer 1978), pp. 625–44.
9 "Is There a Text in This Class?", in *Is There a Text in This Class?* (Cambridge: Harvard University Press, 1980).
10 "One More Time," *Critical Inquiry*, 6, No. 4 (Summer, 1980), pp. 749–51.
11 *Critical Inquiry*, 8, No. 4 (Summer, 1982).

Chapter 13: Roland Barthes

1 Paris: Editions du Seuil, 1953. All translations are my own.
2 Paris: Editions du Seuil, 1973. All translations are my own.
3 Paris: Editions du Seuil, 1975. All translations are my own.
4 "Collection Points" (Paris: Editions du Seuil, 1975). All translations are my own.
5 In the game in question, all players put their hands on top of a continually evolving pile of hands, the hand at the bottom moving up to the top.
6 The similarity of this notion to Bleich's idea of resymbolization should need no elaboration.
7 Cf. *S/Z*, "Collection Points" (Paris: Editions du Seuil, 1970), p. 19. All translations are my own.

8 There is no single translation for *jouissance*, which can mean simple enjoyment, the savouring of a sensual pleasure, or the rapture of orgasm. Like many post-structuralist terms, it encloses meanings at odds with one other and thus emblematizes Barthes' new notion of meaning within its own self-difference.

Chapter 14: Paul de Man

1 In *Interpretation: Theory and Practice*, ed. C. Singleton (Baltimore: The Johns Hopkins University Press, 1969), pp. 171–209.
2 New York: Oxford University Press, 1971.
3 New Haven: Yale University Press, 1979.

Conclusion

1 Paris: Editions du Seuil, 1977.
2 It is perhaps a mark of its complete assimilation that Eco's novel, recently translated and published in English (New York: Harcourt, Brace, Jovanovitch, 1983), appeared as a "Book of the Month Club" Selection and has been a best seller in several countries.
3 Ithaca: Cornell University Press, 1981 and 1982 respectively.

Index